D0934121

Capitalizing on Crisis

CAPITALIZING ON CRISIS

The Political Origins of the
Rise of Finance

GRETA R. KRIPPNER

Harvard University Press
Cambridge, Massachusetts, and London, England   2011

Library of Congress Cataloging-in-Publication Data

Krippner, Greta R.
Capitalizing on crisis : the political origins of the rise of finance /
Greta R. Krippner.
   p.   cm.
Includes bibliographical references and index.
ISBN 978-0-674-05084-6 (alk. paper)
1. Finance—United States.
2. Financial services industry—United States.
3. United States—Economic conditions—2001–2009.
4. Monetary policy— United States.   I. Title.
HG181.K725   2010
332.0973—dc22   2010004511

For Sandy

Contents

Figures

Acknowledgments

As a historical sociologist, I am especially cognizant that our efforts as scholars are both cumulative and collective. In tracing the financialization of the U.S. economy to a series of political, economic, and social dilemmas confronted by policymakers in the 1970s, I have relied on the writings of an earlier generation of scholars who described those dilemmas—and without whose work the ideas contained in this book would be unthinkable. While the contributions of these scholars to this book were unknowing, my task here is to acknowledge those who made contributions of a more deliberate sort. It is a great pleasure to finally be able to do so.

This work has had the long gestation typical of books that begin as dissertations, and as such I have generated a long list of debts, spanning several stages of my life, shifting constellations of mentors, colleagues, and friends, and three academic institutions. My first debt is to my dissertation advisors, Jane Collins and Erik Wright, who helped me to launch this project at the University of Wisconsin. Jane gave me my initial orientation to sociological research, and her model of following one's questions no matter where they lead was formative. Erik's analytical rigor is famous among his students, and honing my arguments to his objections provided excellent training over the years. Other members of the dissertation committee—Jamie Peck, Mark Suchman, and Stephen Bunker—served their function on the committee admirably. As a fellow traveler exploring a set of related questions about neoliberal states, I found Jamie's various contributions especially welcome. Mark proved that he is perhaps the most intellectually versatile person I know by providing me with a set of written comments following the defense that kept me busy for approximately two years. I would like to think that Stephen Bunker's free spirit (I can still see him leaning back, cowboy boots propped up on his desk) lives in these pages.

Two other remarkable scholars became involved with this project at the dissertation stage and continued to be involved in subsequent years. As I was preparing a prospectus, Giovanni Arrighi generously invited me to come to Baltimore to consult with him on the project. Those initial conversations provided intellectual sustenance that would carry me through first the dissertation and later the writing of this book. Giovanni urged me to think boldly about the questions I was asking and not to be constrained by narrow disciplinary debates. I have endeavored to follow this advice, even when it sometimes led me in a different direction than the one in which Giovanni himself was traveling. Fred Block has the unique distinction of being the one person who read both the prospectus and the final version of the manuscript—and nearly every piece of paper I produced in between those two documents. Over the years, Fred has provided me with perceptive, detailed comments that typically went beyond merely pointing out the problems in various formulations to offer very concrete and tractable solutions. At a more personal level, Fred is one of the most reliable, loyal, and kind people I know, and I'm delighted that what began as a series of exchanges over national income accounting has developed into an enduring friendship.

I began my postgraduate school career as an assistant professor at the University of California, Los Angeles, where a number of my colleagues provided helpful comments on earlier versions of this manuscript, including Bill Roy, Michael Mann, Rogers Brubaker, and Ruth Milkman. I am especially grateful to Ruth, not only for her contributions to the work, but also for being a grounding presence as I negotiated multiple transitions in my life. The University of Michigan, my current intellectual home, has provided a wonderfully conducive environment for finishing this book. I could not imagine a warmer or more embracing intellectual community, and I especially want to thank Mark Mizruchi, Gerald Davis, Margaret Somers, and the participants of Michigan's Economic Sociology Workshop for their perceptive comments on various chapters of this book. Elizabeth Bruch did not read chapters but nevertheless told me at a particularly difficult moment that I had a "wonderful book inside"— words for which I will always be grateful.

Outside of my own institution, many other scholars took time away from their own work to provide comments on mine. Although I have attempted to keep good records, this list will inevitably be incomplete, and

I apologize to anyone who has been omitted. For their comments, spanning many years, I thank Sarah Babb, Dean Baker, Eduardo Canedo, James Crotty, Gerald Epstein, Peter Evans, Neil Fligstein, Robert Pollin, Monica Prasad, and Engelbert Stockhammer. Nitsan Chorev deserves special mention as someone whom I have subjected to multiple drafts and who has dutifully complied with these requests, in the process developing into a key interlocutor and close friend.

Over the course of working on this book, I had the opportunity to present preliminary versions of chapters at invited talks at numerous institutions, including UCLA, the Johns Hopkins University, the University of Michigan, the University of California, Berkeley, Cornell University, Harvard University, York University, the University of British Columbia, Brown University, the Ohio State University, and the New School for Social Research. I am grateful to these audiences for their patience and their interest and for many excellent suggestions.

Funding for research for various components of this work has been provided by the Graduate School at the University of Wisconsin, the National Science Foundation, UCLA's Center for American Politics and Public Policy, and the Rackham Graduate School at the University of Michigan. Some of these funds enabled me to hire three excellent research assistants. Anthony Alvarez and Angela Jamison at UCLA helped me to compile a database of congressional hearings that formed the basis of the analysis in Chapter 3. At Michigan, Dan Hirschman's assistance in navigating the final manuscript revisions can only be described as heroic.

Research is only as good as the material at the researcher's disposition. In this regard, I am grateful to the interview subjects who shared with me their perspective on the events explored in this book: Stephen Axilrod, C. Fred Bergsten, Ron Blackwell, Alan Blinder, Douglass Cliggot, Jeffrey Frankel, Benjamin Friedman, David Huether, Donald Kohn, Roger Kubarych, William Niskanen, Martin Regalia, Alice Rivlin, Charles Schultze, Beryl Sprinkel, Albert Wojnilower, and Janet Yellen. Jane D'Arista not only agreed to be interviewed (and put me up at her lovely Connecticut home while we conducted the interview over the course of two days), but also continued to serve as an informal consultant on the project, sharing her vast knowledge of the workings of the international monetary system. I also benefited from the assistance of the excellent research staff at the Bureau of Economic Analysis and the Federal Reserve Bank of New York, who responded kindly, promptly, and competently to many research queries.

My editor at Harvard University Press, Michael Aronson, has offered excellent guidance through the process of revising this book. I am appreciative of his skills as an editor and his belief in the project from an early stage. I am also grateful to the five anonymous reviewers who provided insightful comments on the manuscript during two rounds of review.

Portions of Chapters 2 and 5 have appeared elsewhere. An early iteration of Chapter 2 was published in the *Socio-Economic Review* 3 (2005): 173–208; a different version of Chapter 5 appeared in *Theory and Society* 36 (2007): 477–513. I am grateful to Oxford University Press and Springer Science+Business Media, respectively, for allowing me to reprint this material.

Finally, I owe a debt of gratitude to my family. My two grandmothers, both formative influences, saw the beginning of this project but not its end. Helen Krippner was the first banker in the family, perhaps providing the original inspiration for my interest in some of the questions explored in this book. More likely, though, Grandmother Krippner's contribution lies elsewhere, as her drive and discipline and relentless pursuit of self-improvement have generally translated well into the academic environment. Luella Brandt was a master storyteller. Her love of narrative has, I believe, made its way into these pages, hopefully stripped of her tendency to embellish. My parents, Ray and Clarice Krippner, encouraged a love of learning but also maintained a healthy skepticism toward academic institutions. This orientation has enabled me to partake of the intellectual excitement of the academic life without getting too caught up (I hope) in its trappings. My sister, Leah Krippner, has distracted from the proceedings with her zany humor—and her wonderful family. Margot Canaday, my twin sister, has been my close intellectual companion for much of this journey. Our shared trajectory through graduate school and into professional academic careers has been a source of deep satisfaction and only occasional (contained) sibling rivalry. To those who wonder whether we feel the same pain, the answer is "no," but we did develop the same revision strategy for our books without discussing it. Finally, I owe a debt of gratitude to Margot's witty and gracious partner, Rachel Spector, who has tolerated not just one but two book projects in her personal life.

My deepest debt is to Sandy Levitsky, my partner, whose contributions to this book are impossible to enumerate. Almost ten years ago, Sandy helped me track down contact information for some of my more elusive interview subjects. A few nights ago, she helped me embed figures in the final manuscript. In the years in between, she has been involved in this project in every way imaginable, from spotting misplaced commas to seeing (before I did) the argument that connected the empirical chapters of the book. Sandy has helped me to strategize every aspect of the research and writing of this book, counseling me through various setbacks and keeping faith alive when I, frankly, had lost it. Everyone who has written a book knows the suffering and the joy in such an endeavor. How much more bearable the suffering and how much greater the joy when it is shared so completely with another person. For this, I dedicate this book to Sandy.

Capitalizing on Crisis

CHAPTER ONE

Introduction

I N 1967, the sociologist, cultural critic, and social forecaster Daniel Bell made a prediction about U.S. society in the year 2000. Observing the social and political turmoil of the late 1960s, Bell argued that the state would become embroiled in explosive social conflict as its role in managing economy and society became increasingly politicized. He wrote, "The only prediction about the future that one can make *with certainty* is that public authorities will face more problems than they have at any time in history" (1967: 7; emphasis added). But this prediction was not borne out. A second prediction, for which Bell is better known, was linked to the first and fared considerably better. Bell (1973) suggested that the trend already evident toward the dominance of services in the U.S. economy would continue, inaugurating a "post-industrial" society by century's end. This prediction that the dramatic ascent of services would define the contours of the economic structure of late twentieth-century society *was* realized, although with a slight twist: rather than the rise of services in a generic sense, the rise of a particular kind of service—*finance*—proved to be the dominant trend in subsequent decades.[1]

Bell was more prescient than is suggested by a superficial accounting of how well his two predictions performed, however. Indeed, Bell never intended his forecasts as "point-in-time" predictions, but rather as "speculative constructs" against which developments in later decades could be compared in order to tease out the forces shaping the changing structure of society (Bell 1973: lxxxvii).[2] Looking backward from the year 2000, it is possible to discern a different relationship between Bell's successful and unsuccessful prognostications than Bell himself posed looking forward to the millennium. Bell had assumed that the main driver of the growth of services would be the *public* sector as a "revolution of rising entitlements" led to ever-expanding demands for state provision. The resulting burden on the state would increase inflationary pressures, undermining the ability of policymakers to negotiate competing social demands and plunging the state into political conflicts over the allocation of scarce resources (Bell 1973, 1976). But, as we now know, the growth of the service economy in the post-1970s period was accompanied not by the expansion of state provision but by a dramatic turn to the market. In fact, this turn to the market—in particular, the turn to *financial* markets—was integrally related to the crisis that did not materialize for the state.

The central thesis of this book is that the turn to finance allowed the state to avoid a series of economic, social, and political dilemmas that confronted policymakers beginning in the late 1960s and 1970s, paradoxically preparing the ground for our own era of financial manias, panics, and crashes some three decades later. In the following pages, I develop this argument by introducing the notion of *financialization* as a more specific way of describing the underlying shift in the structure of the U.S. economy that Bell identified with the term "post-industrialism."[3] By financialization, I refer to a broad-based transformation in which financial activities (rather than services generally) have become increasingly dominant in the U.S. economy over the last several decades. Although changes in firm strategy, market structure, and the availability of new technologies all shaped financialization, the state was not merely passive in this transformation. Rather, as policymakers improvised solutions to the various difficulties that Bell and other observers writing in the late 1960s and 1970s believed would soon overwhelm the state,[4] they constructed a policy regime that deepened and extended the turn to finance in the U.S. economy. Thus financialization was not a deliberate outcome sought by policymakers but rather an inadvertent result of the state's attempts to solve other problems.

This element of inadvertency is worth underscoring. A starting point for many accounts of the rise of the market in the period since the 1970s is Karl Polanyi's (2001: 147) famous dictum that "laissez-faire was planned"—that is, that "freeing" the market has required the active hand of state intervention.[5] The account presented in this book is in fundamental agreement with the Polanyian view that state action was absolutely central in producing conditions conducive to financialization through the deregulation of financial markets and other related policy changes typically captured under the rubric of "neoliberalism."[6] But it takes a step away from overly voluntarist conceptions of this role by suggesting that the rise of the market resulted from a series of contingent discoveries on the part of policymakers. Laissez-faire may have been planned, but this planning process was an emergent one, subject to trial and error, and not nearly as seamless as it has sometimes been presented.

In emphasizing how the state's efforts to extricate itself from the crisis conditions of the late 1960s and 1970s sowed the seeds of the turn to finance in the U.S. economy, this book offers a rather different perspective on financialization than offered by existing accounts. The conventional way of understanding the rise of finance is to suggest that the U.S. economy has been caught in the grip of a speculative mania in recent years, pulling households and firms alike into the vortex created by spiraling asset values (Shiller 2000, 2008). A second, very different perspective on financialization points to the emergence of new conceptions of management, arguing that the notion of "shareholder value" has reoriented firms to financial markets, reorganizing the broader society in what sociologist Gerald Davis (2009) refers to as a "Copernican Revolution"[7] (cf. Fligstein 2001). A third approach associated with Marxist and world-systems theories interprets the turn to finance as rooted in the crisis of the 1970s, but views this as a structural pattern generated by deep-seated tendencies operating at the level of capitalist system as a whole (Arrighi 1994; Bellamy Foster and Magdoff 2009; Harvey 2003). Although all three perspectives have a great deal to offer to our understanding of recent developments in U.S. political economy, none provides a fully satisfactory account of the role of the state in shaping the turn to finance or, conversely, of the role of the turn to finance in shaping the state (but see Davis 2009: chap. 6).

The Rise of Finance

There is little question that the U.S. economy has experienced a remarkable turn toward financial activities in recent years. By the time the U.S. stock market was cresting in 2001, financial sector profits had rocketed up to represent more than 40 percent of total profits in the U.S. economy.[8] This figure, although striking, actually underestimates the importance of financial activities in the U.S. economy, as *nonfinancial* firms too have become increasingly dependent on financial revenues as supplement to—or at times *substitute for*—earnings from traditional productive activities. One careful study, for example, showed that the Ford Motor Company, the quintessential American manufacturing company, has in recent years generated its profits primarily by selling loans to purchase cars rather than through the sale of the cars themselves (Froud et al. 2006). Like Ford, General Motors, and General Electric, many U.S. nonfinancial firms own captive financial companies, and even for those firms that are not owners of financial services operations, managing financial investments has become a major focus of activity—and profits (see Davis 2009; Fligstein 2001). As one Morgan Stanley investment strategist observed, "Corporate America is rapidly becoming Bank America."[9]

In this book, I describe these trends with the term "financialization," which I use to refer to the tendency for profit making in the economy to occur increasingly through financial channels rather than through productive activities (cf. Arrighi 1994). Here "financial" references the provision (or transfer) of capital in expectation of future interest, dividends, or capital gains; by "productive," I refer to the range of activities involved in the production or trade of commodities. In offering this definition of financialization, I do not intend to mystify the distinction between "finance" and "production," nor to suggest that financial activities are necessarily *unproductive*.[10] Financial and productive activities are closely related to each other, and much financial activity supports production— although clearly not all of it does (Harvey 1999; Leyshon and Thrift 2007). It is nonetheless possible to draw a distinction between profits realized on the car loan and profits made on the sale of the car, even though the one facilitates the other. To suggest that the economy has become financialized is to claim that the balance between these two sets of activities has swung strongly toward finance, not that the financial economy has become entirely uncoupled from production.

Speculative Manias

The existing literature offers at least three distinct vantage points on this transformation, each emphasizing different (and sometimes incongruous) aspects of the rise of finance. The most prevalent view—especially in the wake of the recent financial crisis—treats the growing importance of financial activities in the economy as a consequence of a speculative mania that carried first equities and then real estate prices to unsustainable levels in the 1980s, 1990s, and 2000s (Shiller 2000, 2008). The popular notion that a financial bubble developed in the U.S. economy in recent years, shaping (or more aptly, distorting) patterns of economic activity, rests on a now venerable academic literature that contests the idea that financial markets are "efficient."[11] Arguments for market efficiency make the claim that assets traded on financial markets are always valued correctly, because if they were not, traders (or arbitrageurs) could profit by buying or selling mispriced assets—quickly eliminating any divergence from fundamental values. Economists from a variety of different approaches have cast doubt on the efficient markets hypothesis, suggesting that situations exist where the only reason that a financial asset is priced highly today is the expectation that its price will be still higher tomorrow (Stiglitz 1990). Once such expectations are unleashed, prices in financial markets can quickly become divorced from intrinsic values—the defining characteristic of a speculative mania.

The key to this perspective is the claim that the mechanisms that generate bubbles are endogenous to financial markets. In this respect, theories of speculative bubbles directly contradict the efficient markets hypothesis, which sees market processes as tending naturally toward equilibrium until interrupted by some unexpected, external event (Cooper 2008: 13). In contrast, bubble theories view processes internal to markets as inherently destabilizing rather than stabilizing. For theorists of speculative bubbles, an external event may precipitate a speculative mania, but this external shock is not the ultimate source of instability. For example, in economic historian Charles Kindleberger's (1978) well-known theory of financial manias—which draws on the ideas of heterodox economist Hyman Minsky (1975, 1982, 1986)—a speculative episode begins when some "displacing event" changes profit opportunities in the economy. The event that initiates a speculative mania may take a variety of forms— the introduction of a new technology, a bumper harvest or a crop failure, war or the cessation of war, or a policy mistake. But whatever the nature of the displacing event, it sets into motion social and psychological processes intrinsic to financial markets that quickly build into a speculative mania (cf. Shiller 2000).

In particular, the tendency of economic actors to become overconfident over the course of a business expansion creates a sense of euphoria among investors. In this context, the belief that asset prices will continue their upward trajectory becomes a self-fulfilling prophecy as investors acting on this belief propel markets higher. In addition, credit standards tend to deteriorate during periods of financial exuberance, allowing speculators to leverage their bets and further inflating asset prices. Paradoxically, this expansion of credit makes the economy vulnerable to a sudden reversal should optimism turn sour on the news of a bankruptcy, a financial scandal, or any other development that causes investors to revise their expectations—events that are increasingly likely as the economy comes to rest on a precarious foundation of debt-fueled growth. Once expectations turn negative, the same self-fulfilling prophecies that fueled the boom on the way up can quickly give way to panic on the way down. In this

manner, the economy cycles between boom and bust, as periods of prosperity engender excessive risk-taking and the accumulation of unsustainable levels of debt, eventually bringing the crash and starting the cycle
anew (Minsky 1982, 1986).

For Kindleberger and Minsky, the state has a critical role to play in
mitigating the depth and intensity of these cycles by acting as a lender of
last resort, providing liquidity to distressed financial institutions during
periods of panic. Of course, this role is a tricky one: if financial institutions know that they will be bailed out, they are encouraged to speculate
with abandon, making the crash more severe when it finally comes (see
especially Minsky 1982, 1986). But these theorists ultimately remain confident that, with some trial and error, policymakers are capable of reining
in excesses and containing the credit expansion that drives the boom.
Minsky (1986: 11) notes, "Incoherence need not be fully realized because
institutions and policy can contain the thrust to instability. We can, so to
speak, stabilize instability." To the extent that the state fails to do this, the
failure is typically conceptualized as an intellectual one—policymakers
simply do not understand that the boom rests on unsustainable asset
price movements, often because they have fallen under the sway of the
efficient markets hypothesis (e.g., Cooper 2008; Shiller 2008). In this regard, policy imperfections can be addressed by providing policymakers
with a correct model of financial market behavior.

There is little doubt that asset price bubbles—typically in the stock
market, but also in real estate markets—have played a significant role in
propelling the rise of finance in the U.S. economy in recent years. But there
are also some important limitations associated with a perspective that
understands financialization solely in terms of speculative dynamics in
financial markets. The most important is that in focusing on intrinsic
properties of financial markets, this approach treats the state and politics
as exogenous to the analysis. In other words, although state actions may
provide the trigger that sparks a speculative mania, and although the state
may also attempt to contain the mania once it is under way, these actions
are *outside the frame* of what is to be explained. This in part accounts for
the overly sanguine view of the state's role in managing financial manias
in this literature—a corollary of the position that instability is generated
by processes internal to financial markets is a rather benign view of the
state as a source of stability. More broadly, the emphasis on processes internal to financial markets also means that this approach cannot explain
why certain historical periods seem more prone to episodes of financial
exuberance than others. To understand why the decades since the 1970s
have been characterized by serial asset price bubbles, for example, we can-

not simply point to the tendency of investors to become overconfident following a period of sustained prosperity (because this tendency is not unique to the post-1970s period).[12] Rather, it is necessary to put speculative manias on a wider analytical canvas by investigating the social and political conditions that provided fertile ground for the turn to finance in the U.S. economy over the past several decades. Such an analysis suggests that financialization represents a broader transformation of the economy, with deeper historical roots, than is indicated by a focus on speculative manias.

Shareholder Value

The sociological literature on the emergence of "shareholder value," developed primarily by organizational theorists, offers a second perspective on the rise of finance in the U.S. economy. This literature broadens the analysis from processes internal to financial markets to examine the relationship between nonfinancial firms, financial sector actors, and the state in creating and enforcing a new paradigm for management. The concerns of this literature are somewhat orthogonal to the literature on speculative manias, as the objective is not to explain how speculative bubbles emerge and develop, but rather to examine the growing orientation of nonfinancial firms to financial markets (Davis 2009). Although these are ostensibly quite different problems, both are relevant for the more general problem of understanding why finance and financial activities have assumed greater salience in the economy in recent years.

The literature on shareholder value contains multiple strands, but it is possible to distill from various contributions a more or less unified account of the basic transformations driving the turn to finance in the U.S. economy in recent decades (e.g., Davis 2009; Davis, Diekmann, and Tinsley 1994; Davis and Stout 1992; Davis and Thompson 1994; Dobbin and Zorn 2005; Fligstein 2001, 2005; Lazonick and O'Sullivan 2000; Useem 1996; Zorn et al. 2004). The notion of "shareholder value" refers to the idea that the sole purpose of the firm is to return value—in the form of an appreciating share price—to the owners of the company. The central question raised by this literature is how shareholder value became the privileged metric for assessing corporate success (or failure) in the 1980s and 1990s[13]—with attendant changes in corporate governance that have drawn nonfinancial firms increasingly into the orbit of financial markets. Rather than viewing this development simply as an "efficient" solution to problems posed by the separation of ownership and control of corporations,[14] sociologists offer a nuanced historical account

that sees the emergence of shareholder value as the outcome of a fundamental reconceptualization of the nature of the firm (Davis 2009; Davis,
Diekmann, and Tinsley 1994; Espeland and Hirsch 1990; Fligstein 2001).

According to this account, the shareholder value revolution rested on
an earlier transformation in which firms came to be viewed as "bundles
of assets" rather than as bounded entities with discrete organizational
identities centered on a product or industry (Davis 2009; Espeland and
Hirsch 1990; Fligstein 1990, 2001). This "portfolio theory of the firm"
was associated with the construction of large conglomerates in the 1950s
and 1960s in which risk diversification was achieved by combining firms
in unrelated industries, much as a mutual fund attempts to diversify risk
by spreading capital across unrelated investments. The creation of these
sprawling enterprises was encouraged by the passage of a law in 1950
restricting horizontal and vertical mergers, with the result that in order
to grow, firms had to combine businesses in unrelated lines. The conglomerate strategy was also promoted by finance executives, whose own
power inside firms rose with the growing size of corporate behemoths as
these executives had unique technical expertise to evaluate the performance of subunits in different industries (Fligstein 1990; cf. Zorn 2004).
Paradoxically, because the portfolio view of the firm treated "businesses . . .
[as] mere commodities for trading in the marketplace as casually as a
sack of sugar or a suburban house" (Sloan 1985: 134), finance executives
were also best equipped to oversee the dismantling of conglomerate enterprises when competitive conditions in the economy changed beginning
in the 1970s (Davis, Diekmann, and Tinsley 1994; Fligstein 2001).

Once the firm was conceptualized as a stream of cash flows to be shuf-
fled and reshuffled in whatever configuration would produce the highest
return (Espeland and Hirsch 1990), a number of transformations occurring in the institutional environment of firms gave this conception the
more specific imprint of shareholder value. The first and arguably most
important of these changes was the emergence of a corporate takeover
market in the early 1980s—a result of deteriorating macro-economic conditions, changes in state policy, and a series of financial innovations occurring in this period (Davis and Stout 1992; Davis and Thompson 1994;
Dobbin and Zorn 2005; Lazonick and O'Sullivan 2000; Stearns and Allan 1996). In particular, the inflation of the 1970s had the contradictory
effect of inflating the value of corporate assets (plant and equipment)
while depressing stock prices, with the result that the book value of many
firms exceeded their market value. In this context, there was money to be
made by buying firms at depressed prices and selling the assets at a profit
(Fligstein 2001). These profit opportunities were merely theoretical, how-

ever, until the Reagan administration relaxed anti-trust restrictions on intra-industry mergers in 1982. This more permissive regulatory environment, together with the creation of new financial instruments such as the junk bond, unleashed a hostile takeover wave that reconfigured the economic landscape. The resulting reorganization of the American economy broke up large conglomerates in favor of leaner, more focused firms and fixed executive attention relentlessly on the stock price (because a low valuation in the stock market invited takeover attempts).

A second major transformation—the emergence of institutional investors as powerful new intermediaries in financial markets (Useem 1996)[15]—reinforced executives' newfound obsession with the stock market (Dobbin and Zorn 2005; Lazonick and O'Sullivan 2000). Institutional investors exerted pressure on firms in a number of ways, but one of the most pernicious was their insistence that executives receive compensation in the form of stock options. Stock options are warrants that allow the holder to purchase the company's stock at the current price for some specified period of time into the future. Thus, if the price of the company's stock increases between the time the option is issued and the time it is exercised, the holder can effectively buy stock at below the market price and then turn around and sell the shares for a tidy (and riskless) profit. Taken together, these changes had a profound effect on the behavior of firms, with the threat of takeover acting as stick and stock options as carrot to fulfill the imperatives of financial markets, whether through selling off unprofitable divisions (Davis, Diekmann, and Tinsley 1994), laying off workers (Fligstein and Shin 2007; Lazonick and O'Sullivan 2000), or engaging in financial engineering that allowed firms to meet analysts' quarterly earnings projections (Dobbin and Zorn 2005). As sociologist Gerald Davis (2009: 5) argues, "From a social system orbiting around corporations and their imperatives, we have moved to a market centered system in which corporations themselves—along with households and governments—are guided by the gravitational pull of financial markets."

The literature on shareholder value offers a very compelling account of the broad shifts in the U.S. economy that have been associated with the growing dominance of finance in recent decades—one that provides a wider lens than the literature on speculative manias by integrating the actions of nonfinancial firms, financial sector institutions, and the state in reshaping the contours of the American economic landscape. The emphasis on state policy is particularly notable, as organizational theory has more typically left the actions of the state outside the analysis, focusing instead on internal political coalitions inside the firm or eclipsing politics altogether by invoking ecological metaphors of evolutionary change.[16] In this context, the attention to legal and regulatory changes that allowed or disallowed various forms of corporate structure is especially welcome, but here we should also note a limitation of this literature that is shared in common with theories of speculative bubbles. Although state policy is understood in the shareholder value literature to be an important parameter influencing strategic action by firms, state action is treated as an exogenous constraint on firms rather than itself something to be explained (e.g., Fligstein 2001). We learn from this literature, for example, that changes in anti-trust enforcement created opportunities for actors inside and outside firms to press a new vision of the firm into service, with significant consequences for the growing salience of financial activities in the economy. We do not learn what motivated officials in the Reagan administration to adopt this policy change, or what those officials believed would be the likely result of this shift for the structure of the U.S. economy. More broadly, the same point extends to the state's promotion of a macro-economic environment conducive to the turn to finance. We learn from the shareholder value literature that changes in the macro-economic environment were critical for orienting firms to the imperatives of financial markets, but we do not learn why state officials promoted policies that contributed to these changes. In short, in focusing on the strategic action of firms but failing to provide an account of state action on its own terms, the shareholder value literature offers a one-sided political economy of the turn to finance (cf. Clemens 2005; Mizruchi and Kimeldorf 2005).

Marxist and World-Systems Theories

A final perspective on financialization is represented by Marxist and world-systems perspectives that consider the turn to finance in more epochal terms, understanding it as a phase of capitalist development akin to the globalization of capital. This literature is arguably more successful than either of the first two literatures in capturing the interplay of state actions and firm strategic behavior in shaping the turn to finance, but it does so by developing its analysis at such a high level of abstraction that some of the mechanisms present in the other approaches considered here fall from view. Marxist and world-systems perspectives are internally quite diverse,[17] explaining financialization as a response to the stagnationist tendencies of mature capitalism (Bellamy Foster and Magdoff 2009; Magdoff and Sweezy 1987), the resurgence of the class power of "finance capital" (Dumenil and Levy 2004; Epstein and Jayadev 2005), or a phase in a cycle marking the end of U.S. hegemony (Arrighi 1994, 2007; Harvey

2003). Rather than attempting to fully trace all of these threads, I will concentrate my discussion here on what these various contributions have in common—an insistence that there is something deeply systemic in the recent flourishing of financial activities—focusing primarily on Giovanni Arrighi's (1994, 2007) work as an illustration.

Like all of the contributors to this literature, Arrighi locates the origins of the turn to finance in the response of governmental and business organizations to the crisis of the 1970s. For Arrighi this is not an unprecedented event, but a regular feature of the capitalist world system, reoccurring since the origins of capitalism in the Italian city-states to the current day. More specifically, Arrighi sees capitalist development occurring through the alteration of two phases—a phase of "material expansion," in which profits accrue through the normal channels of trade and commodity production, followed by a phase of "financial expansion," in which profit making shifts from trade and commodity production to financial channels. The phase of material expansion coincides with the emergence of a new hegemonic power, the ascension of which to the commanding heights of the world capitalist system rests in part on some organizational innovation that creates expanded opportunities for enterprise. Initially, this innovation is associated with "positive sum" competition among capitalists in different national economies, as the expansion in the productive capacity of the economy far outstrips the claims of competing capitalists for a share of the profits. As the material expansion proceeds, however, competition intensifies and eventually becomes "zero-sum" in nature, driving down returns from productive investment and precipitating a shift into financial activities as firms search for refuge in an increasingly adverse economic environment. The transition from material to financial expansion is accelerated by state actions, as governments confronting declining revenues compete aggressively for capital in international financial markets, ballooning state debts and creating profits for the capitalist organizations that finance these obligations. In general, financialization defers the impending crisis, at least until such time as a new organizational innovation under the auspices of a rising hegemonic power prepares the ground for another round of material expansion in the world economy, restarting the cycle.[18]

Although Arrighi's theory of "systemic cycles of accumulation"— his term for the full arc traveled from material expansion to financial expansion—describes a general pattern present in all world hegemonies, its more specific objective is to account for the transition from the "Golden Age" of U.S.-led prosperity in the 1950s and 1960s to the "Leaden Age" slump beginning in the 1970s (Arrighi 1994; cf. Pollin 1996). Seen from this perspective, the emergence of the United States as a hegemonic power following World War II was associated with the creation of the vertically integrated, multinational corporation—an innovation that gave U.S. corporations a strong advantage competing for profits in an expanding world economy. But this advantage eroded as other national economies—led by Germany and Japan—recovered from the devastation of war and emulated U.S. forms of business organization (cf. Brenner 2006). Beginning in the late 1960s and 1970s, the competitive challenge from abroad precipitated a crisis of profitability for U.S. firms, encouraging capitalists to withdraw from productive investment and instead channel capital toward financial markets. The Reagan administration's enormous buildup of debt absorbed much of this capital, providing easy profits for the financial sector and fueling a strong upward surge in the stock market that would continue into the next decade. But a new "belle époque" of finance could not provide any answer to the underlying difficulties facing the U.S. economy, and while Americans were living high, the baton of leadership over the world economy was being passed to Asia (Arrighi 2004, 2007).

In this specific account of U.S.-led financialization in the period since the 1970s, Arrighi's theory converges in certain aspects with the competing perspective outlined by Marxist economists Paul Sweezy and Harry Magdoff in a series of contributions to the *Monthly Review* (cf. Bellamy Foster and Magdoff 2009). Like Arrighi, Magdoff and Sweezy (1987) suggest that the turn to finance is a response to the lack of profitable investment opportunities in the economy in the context of stagnation beginning in the late 1960s and 1970s. Unlike Arrighi, Magdoff and Sweezy locate the cause of stagnation in the growing monopolization of the economy rather than in intensified competition (Orhangazi 2008). Advanced industrial capitalism tends toward stagnation because the productive capacity of large, oligopolistic firms far outstrips demand for their products, especially in the absence of mechanisms to redistribute wealth to the working classes. Thus, for Magdoff and Sweezy, stagnation rather than dynamism is the natural state of mature capitalism, and the emergence of financialization as a response to stagnation therefore represents a secular shift rather than a cyclical one.

This raises the question of *how,* precisely, financialization is a response to stagnation. In other words, where do financial profits come from if the underlying condition of the economy is stagnation (cf. Pollin 1996)? Magdoff and Sweezy are more explicit on this point than Arrighi is (but see Arrighi and Moore 2001), arguing that as nonfinancial firms with few outlets for productive investment channel capital into financial markets, the price of financial assets becomes inflated. This sets in motion "a speculative psychology which comes to pervade the financial community and provides its own justification" (Magdoff and Sweezy 1987: 104). This would seem to bring us full circle, back to theories of speculative bubbles, except that for Magdoff and Sweezy (and for Arrighi) financialization is not an end-of-boom phenomenon in which speculative euphoria feeds on an accelerating expansion; instead, it is a much longer-term and more durable shift in the structure of the economy (Magdoff and Sweezy 1987: 143). Indeed, Magdoff and Sweezy (1987: 104) were prescient in arguing in the early 1980s that the coexistence of stagnation in the productive economy and high profits in the financial sector could go on "for a long time" before precipitating a crisis (cf. Crotty 2005).

There is much to learn from Marxist and world-systems scholars in understanding the nature of the current turn to finance. These scholars place financialization on a firm historical foundation, and the state is no longer treated as exogenous, but as fully internal to the analysis. However, there are some important limitations of an analysis that conceptualizes financialization as a response to crisis at the level of the capitalist system as a whole. Without taking issue with the *theoretical* argument that financialization is a property of the world capitalist system, not an isolated occurrence in any given subunit of that system (Arrighi 1994; Arrighi and Moore 2001), we may still object to the *analytical* consequences of operating at such a high level (cf. Tilly 1984). Two such consequences are particularly troublesome. The first is that, although this analysis does integrate state actions and firm behavior into a unified account, it is difficult to make out these entities as discrete social actors from so lofty a height. This tends to result in formulations that either treat the "system" itself as an actor or impose too much coherence on the state by assuming a seamless alliance between government officials and business elites. Thus, in Arrighi's (1994) analysis, we have an otherwise unspecified "bloc" of governmental and business agencies; in Peter Gowan's (1999) work, we are given the "Dollar–Wall Street Regime," while Gerard Dumenil and Dominique Levy (2004) simply refer to "finance capital" to reference the merger of state officials and elite strata of the financial sector. In short, there is a kind of instrumentalism lurking in some of these accounts that supplants the interest of the financial sector for the interests of the state or simply assumes these interests to be identical.

A second problem is closely related and similarly derives from the level at which Marxist and world-systems theorists tend to cast their arguments. The notion that financialization offered a "solution" to the crisis of the 1970s is an intriguing idea—and one that directly informs my own analysis—but given the vast macro-historical sweep of many of these accounts, we do not really learn precisely how this is the case.[19] It is clear enough that firms gained a reprieve from declining returns on productive investment by directing capital into financial markets, as Magdoff and Sweezy (1987) suggest, and Beverly Silver (2003) has usefully elaborated on how the "financial fix" also resolved conflicts at the point of production in favor of capital (cf. Harvey 2003; Watson 1999). But the claim in the literature is much broader than this: financialization is presumed to have resolved not only the profits crisis faced by firms, but also the wider social and political crisis in which this economic crisis was embedded (Arrighi and Moore 2001: 74–75; cf. Arrighi and Silver 1999). Here, the literature has offered only hints, and indeed the notion of the "financial fix" retains a somewhat vague, even mystical flavor. To give this idea more structure and specificity, it is necessary to break apart the presumed unity of "finance capital" to examine, in a more fine-grained way, how the emergent responses of state officials to the crisis of the late 1960s and 1970s contributed to the turn to finance and made this resolution to the crisis sustainable, at least for a time.

An Emerging Agenda

The approaches to financialization surveyed here offer a number of useful insights. Without suggesting that these three approaches fit together seamlessly—although all ostensibly deal with the rise of finance, they concern somewhat different objects of analysis—we can nevertheless work across them to define the agenda of the present work. The literature on speculative bubbles usefully describes intrinsic properties of financial markets that, once set into motion, draw economic activity inexorably toward finance. But by operating on a narrow canvas—one that excludes the state, other than as an external stabilizing force—this approach fails to provide a historical account that could help us to understand why our current era is so prone to such speculative manias. The sociological literature on shareholder value broadens the canvas, providing a valuable account of the growing orientation of nonfinancial firms to financial markets. But in similarly treating the state as exogenous to the analysis, this approach offers only a partial view of the transformations associated with the rise of finance. Finally, Marxist and world-systems theorists integrate state action into their account more fully, but here the canvas is arguably too broad. From the dizzying heights of world historical analysis, we lose sight of the concrete mechanisms and institutional details that the first two perspectives provide.

The approach adopted here is to retain the question (implicitly) raised by the third perspective—how did the turn to finance offer a "solution" to the crisis of the 1970s, particularly from the perspective of the state?— but to scale back the analysis to more manageable proportions where precise mechanisms and specific social actors are more visible. This compromise is imperfect, of course, and presents limitations of its own. In offering a close empirical analysis of the role of the state in creating conditions conducive to financialization, I will necessarily omit attention to many issues considered central in the existing literature. Most egregiously, while I have faulted organizational theorists examining the emergence of shareholder value for developing a "one-sided" political economy of the turn to finance, the account here will be equally one-sided—although dealing with the side that is less well-known to researchers (i.e., state action). Needless to say, my intention is not to supplant existing accounts, but to provide a broader foundation for them.

Even on the terrain of the state, the account presented in the following pages is a highly selective one. I do not offer a comprehensive or exhaustive account of state policies that contributed to the financialization of the U.S. economy—such an endeavor would require a vastly longer book or a more superficial analysis. Instead, I limit my study by examining three interrelated policy shifts that created a macro-economic environment conducive to the turn to finance in the U.S. economy: (1) the deregulation of U.S. financial markets, which occurred incrementally over the course of the 1970s, culminating in landmark legislation passed in 1980; (2) the growing dependence of the U.S. economy on foreign capital inflows to finance deficits beginning in the early 1980s; and (3) the radical change of course in U.S. monetary policy initiated with the so-called Volcker Shock of October 1979.[20]

Taken together, these three policy changes transformed the macro-economic environment by increasing interest rates to extraordinary levels in the 1980s and by dramatically expanding credit in the U.S. economy in the 1980s and subsequent decades. Both higher and more volatile interest rates and a rapid pace of credit expansion created conditions that were conducive to the turn to finance (as I elaborate in Chapter 2). Most critically, increased credit flows cycling through financial markets generated profits for the financial sector actors managing these flows, as well as making the economy as a whole prone to asset price bubbles (Bank for International Settlements 2001; Borrio and Lowe 2002). In addition, high and volatile interest rates—with short-term rates rising as high as 20 percent in the wake of financial deregulation and the Federal Reserve's shift to a "tight money" policy—created considerable uncertainty for nonfinancial firms, reinforcing the speculative behavior associated with the shareholder value revolution (cf. Espeland and Hirsh 1990). As the cost of borrowed funds soared, corporate treasurers weighed long-term investments in plant and equipment against purely financial maneuvers that would bring higher and more immediate returns, such as buying and selling other firms. As the American Business Conference informed Congress in 1983, "The majority of companies in the United States face such a high cost of capital compared to returns that, for many of them, the *only* economically viable investment is to acquire other companies."[21] Responses to this uncertainty—the development of new financial instruments such as interest rate swaps and other forms of derivative contracts—inoculated firms to some degree from interest rate risk, but did so by creating an entirely new financial industry, further engorging the financial sector (Steinherr 1998).

In short, this policy regime reinforced changes in financial markets and inside nonfinancial firms that were, through other channels, propelling the rise of finance in the U.S. economy. But if state actions contributed to the creation of a macro-economic environment conducive to the turn to finance, this was not a deliberate outcome sought by policymakers. What, then, were policymakers seeking to achieve in implementing this policy regime? To answer this question, we must return to the crisis confronted by the state in the late 1960s and the 1970s.

The Crisis of the State (That Wasn't)

In the most general terms, the difficulties that confronted policymakers beginning in the late 1960s and 1970s reflected the growing strains on the state as it struggled to meet expanded commitments with increasingly limited resources. Over the course of the postwar period, the state had assumed responsibility both for providing direction to the economy and for managing the social consequences of growth (Bell 1976). These tasks became increasingly challenging as economic conditions deteriorated in the 1970s, marking a turning point from the broadly shared prosperity of the early postwar decades to a period of slower growth and higher un-employment on average in the neoliberal era (see Burnham 1999; Campbell and Pedersen 2001; Carruthers, Halliday, and Babb 2001).[22] These conditions presented three sets of challenges for policymakers, which I distinguish as *social crisis, fiscal crisis,* and *legitimation crisis,* following contemporary observers of the period (Bell 1976; Habermas 1973; O'Connor 1973; Offe 1984). These aspects of the crisis of the state were not fully separable from each other; rather than conceptualize each as analytically distinct, it is more accurate to imagine we are looking through a prism in which the same elements are refracted differently depending on the angle of vision. I nevertheless treat these three crises as distinct for purposes of constructing a narrative in the chapters that follow, but this should be understood as an organizational device rather than a theoretical claim about the internal logic of each crisis.

The social crisis reflected heightened distributional conflict as economic growth slowed, requiring various social groups to scale back their claims to resources that were necessarily more limited in a post-affluent society.[23] The difficulty was that there was no viable social mechanism for negotiating these reductions: technically, this was the domain of the market, but over the course of postwar development, the state had increasingly guaranteed the claims of various social groups. As a result, questions of allocation had migrated from the economic realm to what Bell referred to as the "political market," with troubling implications for the emergence of divisive social conflict. As Bell (1976: 226; emphasis added) warily observed, "The economic constraint on private wants is the amount of money that a man has, or the credit he is able to establish. *But what are the constraints on political demands?*" The answer, familiar to the theorists of "democratic overload," was that there were no such constraints: each group pressed its demands on the polity without limit (Brittan 1976). The predictable result—evident in most advanced industrial economies by the mid-1970s—was roaring inflation.[24] In Albert Hirschman's (1980: 195) apt description, inflation represented a "curious social game" in which each group attempts to advance its position knowing that this advance will be voided by the next "move" in an endless series of plays. If capitalists attempt to increase their profits by raising prices, for example, workers who experience a reduction in their real income as a result will demand higher wages, cutting into profits and provoking capitalists to ratchet up prices again (Gough 1981: 87).

The irony was that as long as the various social actors were fully engaged in this game of leapfrog, inflation could serve as a solvent for social conflict, avoiding more direct forms of confrontation between social groups and also making it difficult to determine who was ahead and who was behind at any given point in time (Crouch 1978; Goldthorpe 1987: 373). State actors used this ambiguity to their advantage, as inflation was a surreptitious way for the state to say "no" when it could not do so openly (Hirschman 1980: 202): social expenditures could increase in nominal terms while rising prices eroded the real value of these claims. In general, the distributional effects of inflation tended to be somewhat veiled as price changes occurred unevenly across sectors of the economy, with different social groups more or less exposed to the effects of price changes on income. But if these effects were indirect, they nevertheless became increasingly visible as inflation accelerated. In this sense, although inflation avoided conflict for a time, it became the focal point of acute social tensions once individuals realized the distributional outcomes involved (Hirschman 1980).

The fiscal crisis similarly reflected the movement of questions of growth and distribution into the "political market" as increased pressure on the state to provide services that supported economic growth (or failing this, compensated for declining incomes) far outstripped its capacity to generate revenues (Bell 1976: 227). Scholars introduced the notion of a "fiscal crisis" to refer to a structural gap between state expenditures and the tax revenues needed to pay for those expenditures (Block 1981; O'Connor 1973). For theorists of the fiscal crisis, the sources of intensified fiscal pressures on the state were twofold. First, as the complexity of the economy grew in the postwar decades, the state was increasingly responsible for supplying inputs to production to support the profits of industry (Gough 1981; O'Connor 1973; Offe 1984). These expenditures—running the gamut from investments in the physical infrastructure of the economy (e.g., roads, electricity grids, telecommunications), to social programs that "reproduced" the labor force (e.g., support of education and job training), to expenditures associated with supplying a market for the products of industry (such as the use of military contractors)— were increasingly a prerequisite of successful accumulation in the private sphere (Gough 1981; O'Connor 1973). However, they contained a basic contradiction: although private industry was the ultimate beneficiary of state spending, capitalists were not willing to pay for these expenditures through increased taxation.[25] In addition, as the size of the state sector absorbed an ever greater share of economic activity, the lower productivity of state (service) sector workers acted as a drag on the economy as a whole, eroding growth and therefore the tax revenues that the state could claim (Bell 1976; cf. Gough 1981).[26]

These pressures were exacerbated by a second source of strain on the state budget: growing demands for social spending to ensure social harmony in a period in which economic prosperity was no longer as widely shared as it had been in the immediate postwar decades. This spending was especially problematic from the perspective of the state: unlike the first type of spending, these expenditures did not contribute (even indirectly) to profits but rather were a net drain on private accumulation. As such, capitalists were likely to show especially vigorous resistance to taxation associated with increased social expenditures, with the result that the state relied increasingly on deficit financing, adding to inflation and further exacerbating the strain on the state budget. There was some debate about the ultimate cause of rising social expenditures, with Marxists such as O'Connor pointing to the tendency of monopoly capitalism to slough off workers, while social conservatives such as Bell and Huntington emphasized the unrealistic expectations of a generation nursed on Keynesian economic policies. But no matter the cause, the outcome was the same as the state struggled to meet proliferating demands with increasingly limited revenues.

To the extent the state failed to deliver on these social commitments, the fiscal crisis could quickly evolve into a crisis of legitimacy (Block 1981: 22; Habermas 1973). The only way to break the cycle of deteriorating budgets and increasing inflation was to impose a program of austerity, but in doing so policymakers risked a dramatic erosion in public confidence in the ability of the state to sustain economic growth and support social objectives. By the late 1960s and 1970s, this loss of confidence in the state—the defining feature of the legitimation crisis—was clearly evident in U.S. society. One widely circulated poll reported that, in 1970, 69 percent of those surveyed indicated that they believed government officials "did not know what they were doing," as compared to only 27 percent of respondents in 1964 (Miller 1974, cited in Wolfe 1977). Such findings were grist for political scientists, who began to discuss the problem of the "governability" of advanced capitalist nations, noting paradoxically that the hallmark of modern government seemed to be that the state was doing *more* but achieving *less* as a result (Brittan 1976; Crozier, Huntington, and Watanuki 1975; King 1975; cf. Wolfe 1977).

Like other facets of the crisis of the state, the ultimate cause of the legitimation crisis was a source of some controversy among contemporary observers. For Marxist theorists, the legitimation crisis reflected the capitalist nature of the state, which required that the state conceal its role in supporting capitalist accumulation by engaging in various forms of social spending that would deflect attention from policymakers' more fundamental objective (Habermas 1973; Offe 1974). For non-Marxists, such as Bell (1976), the legitimation crisis was better conceptualized not as a problem of the capitalist state but rather of the democratic polity. All democracies faced the problem of maintaining public support while making decisions about how to balance spending that favored economic growth against spending that supported social consumption. The difficulty for the state in the late 1960s and 1970s was that the state's deteriorating finances drew policymakers more deeply into questions of allocation,

politicizing the state's management of the economy by focusing the public's attention increasingly on this role.

Theorists exploring the intersection of these various problems were
not optimistic about the prospects for the state. Marxist, liberal, and
conservative thinkers alike saw ever-increasing demands on policymakers, as expectations for state provision were continually ratcheted up
(and apparently could not be ratcheted down). In this context, two possible roads lay ahead for the state. Marxists predicted the collapse of
the capitalist state under the weight of its accumulating burdens, with
the realization of socialism offering the only way to dissolve the growing
gulf between the socialization of production and the private appropria-
tion of profits (O'Connor 1973; Offe 1974, 1984).[27] Liberal and conservative thinkers, in contrast, saw the solution to the state's difficulties occurring on the more ethereal terrain of values. A new ethos of restraint
would contain the untrammeled passions of Western consumer culture,
as individuals assumed more realistic expectations for the level of material wealth they could achieve. Although some thinkers saw this adjustment of expectations occurring through restrictions on democratic participation (e.g., Huntington 1975), a somewhat less pessimistic view argued
for developing a public consensus about how scarce resources should be
allocated in society (e.g., Bell 1976; Brittan 1976; Janowitz 1976; Thurow 1980). The state's role as planner and allocator would be continued,
even enhanced, but bolstered by a new public philosophy that provided
explicit justification for this role. Bell (1976) used the evocative term "the
public household"[28] to describe the creation of a social compact that
would guide allocation decisions.

Notably, Bell's public household was not the outcome of the crisis of
the state in the 1970s; neither, of course, did the capitalist system collapse altogether. Instead, something like the inversion of Bell's vision was
realized: rather than decisions about allocation moving into the strong
light of public debate and discussion where a new social consensus could
be forged, these decisions drifted ever further into the shadowy realms of
the market. That neither contemporary social and political theorists[29]—
nor, for that matter, policymakers themselves—foresaw this outcome is
striking, given that it followed directly from the most prevalent diagnosis
of the difficulties confronting the state during this period. Put simply, if
these difficulties stemmed from the fact that the "political market" lacked
a genuine mechanism for disciplining private wants, why not reimpose
market discipline?

One problem was that it was not at all clear that it would be possible
for the state to extricate itself from its responsibility for guiding eco-

nomic outcomes simply by asserting market rule. As Offe (1974, 1984) astutely observed, a paradoxical result of the steady expansion of the state's role in managing the economy over the postwar period was that economic events were redefined as the product of state actions rather than the blind operation of the market. Where the government defined price stability as a policy objective, for example, inflation appeared as the result of a failed state policy rather than an exogenous "shock" to the economy. Where there was an employment policy in place, similarly, unemployment was no longer interpreted as an unavoidable result of the business cycle, but as an outcome for which policymakers were fully culpable. In this context, observers at the time wondered whether the expansion of state activities in regulating the economy was perhaps irreversible. "The most that can be hoped for," noted political scientist Anthony King (1975: 296), "is a marginal reduction in . . . some of the more routine elements of public administration." If these efforts could be made while meekly reminding the public that government does not control *everything*, King suggested, some pressure on policymakers might be alleviated.

At a more fundamental level, even if economic outcomes *could* be depoliticized, how would individuals disadvantaged by market processes come to accept the outcomes generated by the market as legitimate? Only ideologues assumed that the market provided its own moral justification and that actors in a market society would accept the hand dealt them without contest (Goldthorpe 1987; Hirsch 1978). Moreover, it was one thing for the market to govern in an era of abundance and quite another for the market to be the master in an era of permanent scarcity. In such an environment, as Bell (1976) pointed out, markets could not resolve the divisive distributional issues that continually presented themselves. These problems were inherently political; and, without political resolution, leaving them to the market would only provide an opportunity for the underlying social tensions to fester and grow.

But in fact, scarcity did *not* represent the hard, immutable reality that observers at the time perceived, and the stark contrast that theorists of "democratic overload" drew between the political market and the economic market was misleading. According to these theorists, in the political market there were no constraints on the demands of competing social groups for resources or on the state's efforts to meet those demands. By contrast, in the economic market, the unforgiving logic of the price mechanism imposed the discipline that more superfluous considerations had banished from the political realm: just as households lived within their means, so too would the state, without appeal to any higher principle such as equity or justice (Bell 1976). Instead, as policymakers discovered, reliance on market mechanisms transformed the resource constraints of the 1970s into a new era of abundant capital. This occurred, first, as changes in the structure of domestic financial markets allowed credit to flow freely across sectors (Chapter 3), and second, as foreign capital inflows entered the U.S. economy in unprecedented volumes, providing an unexpected source of financing for U.S. deficits (Chapter 4). The resulting expansion of credit in the economy threatened to unleash inflationary pressures—revisiting distributional dilemmas on policymakers at the precise moment when they appeared to have escaped such problems—but policymakers' imposition of a high-interest-rate regime behind the veil of "market forces" avoided this outcome (Chapter 5). Taken together, these developments allowed policymakers to avoid politically difficult decisions about how to allocate limited resources between competing social priorities. "Capitalizing on crisis" refers to these efforts on the part of state officials to tap into domestic and global capital markets to resolve domestic political dilemmas.

Although the loose-credit, high-interest-rate regime of the early 1980s offered an appealing resolution to a number of difficulties confronted by policymakers beginning in the late 1960s and 1970s, it proved a volatile mix for the economy more generally, setting in motion a number of transformations that would reinforce the turn to finance in the U.S. economy in subsequent years. To reiterate the central argument in this book, policymakers did not pursue this policy regime with the intention of producing financialization; rather, the turn to finance was an unintended consequence of policymakers' attempts to extricate themselves from the problems they confronted in the guise of social crisis, fiscal crisis, and the legitimation crisis of the state. But if financialization offered a resolution to the crises of the late 1960s and 1970s, this resolution was necessarily a partial and temporary one (cf. Arrighi 1994). In this sense, the turn to finance did not so much remove the resource scarcities of the late 1960s and 1970s as suspend them, while at the same time introducing a number of fragilities into the economy that have periodically threatened to revisit previous dilemmas on policymakers. As of this writing, with the economy balanced on a precipice between a weak recovery and a deepening financial collapse, it appears more likely than ever that financialization has now traveled its full arc (see Chapter 6). If this assessment is correct, it means that policymakers will once again face many of the difficult choices that they have managed to avoid for nearly three decades.

One important caveat to the argument should be noted before proceeding. In discussing the "state" and "policymakers" here and below,

I compress what in reality are multiple state agencies and polyvalent state actors into what appears to be an undifferentiated whole. This compression is necessary in an abbreviated presentation of a complex historical reality, but it should be emphasized that no such unified whole is presumed to exist. Rather, I understand the state to be made up of multiple agencies and actors, with distinct and often (as we will see) conflicting objectives. But while these policymakers are not presumed to share the same objectives, what they hold in common—and what unifies a multi-stranded narrative—is the set of problems to which they were responding. As a general matter, state actors sought to avoid the social and political conflicts engendered by the emergence of new limits as postwar prosperity turned to stagnation beginning in the late 1960s and 1970s. The narrative in the following chapters tells the story of how policymakers learned to tap into first domestic and then global financial markets in order to evade these limits, setting the stage for the financialization of the U.S. economy.

The Plan of the Book

This book analyzes how the state's ad hoc responses to crisis conditions beginning in the late 1960s and 1970s have reinforced the broader turn to finance in the U.S. economy over the past several decades. Before undertaking such an analysis, an important preliminary task is to establish financialization as an appropriate way of characterizing developments in the U.S. economy in recent decades. This is important because—much as occurred in the early waves of the globalization literature—enthusiasm for the concept of financialization has run far ahead of serious attempts to establish evidence for this phenomenon. Accordingly, Chapter 2 examines the data supporting the thesis that the U.S. economy has undergone a process of financialization. Evidence for long-term shifts in the structure of the economy typically relies on changes in employment or in the mix of products and services produced. But these are not appropriate places to look for the rise of the financial sector, which is not employment intensive and the "products" of which do not show up in transparent ways in national economic statistics. As such, I investigate where profits are generated in the U.S. economy, both by examining the growth of the financial sector and the increasing reliance of nonfinancial firms on financial sources of revenue. My analysis provides strong evidence for the financialization of the U.S. economy in the period since the 1970s.

The next three chapters present the main argument of the book. Each of three historical chapters links policymakers' responses to social crisis, fiscal crisis, and legitimation crisis, respectively, to the policy regime undergirding the financialization of the U.S. economy. As such, each chapter is organized topically, but because the main action around each policy shift corresponds to a different time period, the chapters follow a rough chronological order as well. I begin my story of financialization in the mid-1960s and close in 2001. The end point is determined to some extent by data limitations (see the appendixes for a discussion of sources used in constructing my analysis), as well as the historical sociologist's natural reluctance to bring the analysis too close to the present, where there is the allure of timeliness but the inability to clearly make out patterns. In addition, the stock market sell-off of 2001 appears to represent a significant change in phase (if not a definitive end) in the process of financialization that characterized the period of the 1980s and 1990s (see Fligstein 2005). For these reasons, it marks our stopping point, and I leave it to subsequent research to unpack the developments associated with the real estate boom and bust of the 2000s.

Chapter 3 offers an analysis of the domestic deregulation of financial markets in the 1970s, arguing that in removing controls on credit flows in the U.S. economy, policymakers significantly eased the social crisis associated with the eruption of inflation in the 1970s. In the context of a regulated financial system, inflation continually presented policymakers with the necessity of choosing which sector to favor in allocating credit between uses—industry or housing, large corporations or small businesses, urban areas or farmers. This choice became an increasingly difficult one as a middle-class movement of homeowners politicized access to credit, demanding that the burden of credit restraint be more equitably shared across social groups. In removing regulations on financial markets, policymakers effectively opened the taps on credit expansion, with the result that the market, rather than regulators, would determine access to credit. The consequences were twofold. On the one hand, credit became more expensive as users were now unconstrained in bidding up the price of credit, contributing to an environment in which financial activities were favored over productive investment. On the other hand, (more expensive) credit also flowed more freely across the economy, alleviating social conflict while fueling a credit expansion that provided further impetus to financialization.

Chapter 4 examines the Reagan administration's response to the fiscal crisis of the state. The narrative in the chapter centers on a collision between the Reagan administration's fiscal policies and the Volcker Federal Reserve—a collision that resulted in a transition from a low to a high interest rate regime in the U.S. economy, creating punishing conditions for productive investment and drawing economic activity toward financial markets. Critically, high interest rates in the U.S. economy also pulled foreign capital into the U.S. economy in unprecedented amounts, allowing the Reagan administration to escape the tight fiscal constraints that had bound previous administrations while avoiding calamity in the financial markets. This result was unanticipated both by Reagan officials and by Federal Reserve policymakers: in the early 1980s, the liberalization of international financial markets was a recent phenomenon (and still a work in progress), and policymakers were not yet accustomed to thinking of the world in terms of a sea of open capital flows. But once it became clear that foreign investors could fund U.S. deficits, the Reagan administration began to pursue these sources of financing as a conscious policy objective, even though this meant embracing a policy regime that contributed to the financialization of the U.S. economy.

Chapter 5 examines changes in the implementation of monetary policy over the period from the late 1970s to 2001 in the context of the legitimation crisis confronted by the state. As domestic and international financial markets were deregulated over the course of the 1970s—freeing flows of credit from institutional constraints—monetary policy assumed special importance as the one remaining lever policymakers could use to exert restraint on the economy. Given the distributional outcomes associated with high interest rates, policymakers preferred to exercise this restraint discreetly, balancing the need to regulate the economy and at the same time avoid blame for unfavorable economic outcomes (cf. Carruthers, Halliday, and Babb 2001). The Federal Reserve's adoption in the late 1970s of *monetarism*—the policy of targeting the money supply rather than directly setting interest rates in order to control the rate of growth in the economy—represented an attempt to negotiate these contradictory imperatives by relying on covert methods of policy implementation. Yet, for a variety of reasons, monetarism was not a sustainable policy regime. This chapter follows policymakers' attempts to experiment with new methods of policy implementation that avoided state officials taking direct responsibility for unfavorable economic outcomes after monetarism was abandoned in 1982. As policymakers seeking to depoliticize monetary policy gradually learned to "follow the market" in implementing policy (cf. Burnham 2001), the Federal Reserve abdicated control over the pace of credit expansion to the market. Here, as in the other policy contexts examined in this book, the market proved to be a rather lax master, contributing to a dramatic expansion in the supply of credit that fueled the turn to finance in the U.S. economy.

Chapter 6 returns to the questions raised in the opening pages of this introduction. The chapters in this book chronicle how state officials managed over several decades to avoid difficult political choices by turning to financial markets, but critically, these strategies deferred rather than resolved the underlying social and political tensions that gave rise to them. Now that financialization appears to be failing as a model of economic development, these tensions appear to be coming to the fore once again. In particular, in the context of the current financial crisis, questions regarding the allocation of scarce resources are now unavoidable in U.S. society. Yet the experience of financialization has not prepared us particularly well to answer these questions. For several decades, financialization has largely eclipsed concerns with distribution, eroding collective capacities to confront issues of economic justice (cf. Bell 1976). In exploring the historical antecedents of the turn to finance in the U.S. economy in the post-1970s period, this book attempts to make a modest contribution toward remedying this deficiency.

CHAPTER TWO

What Is Financialization?

IN THIS BOOK, I argue that the policy regime that has supported the financialization of the U.S. economy over the past several decades was an inadvertent result of policymakers' attempts to extricate themselves from a series of political dilemmas beginning in the late 1960s and 1970s. Before making this argument, a preliminary task is to establish that a process of financialization has in fact occurred in the U.S. economy in recent decades. Observing financial news on the front pages of newspapers day after day, many readers will not need much convincing. It is nevertheless important to examine the data behind the claim that the U.S. economy has become financialized in a careful and systematic manner. It is all too frequent in social science to declare the advent of some new era or social process without clearly delineating the phenomenon or establishing evidence for it (Merton 1959).

In this chapter, and throughout this book, I use the term "financialization" to refer to the growing importance of financial activities as a source of profits in the economy (see Chapter 1). Other definitions of financialization are possible and have been used by scholars studying closely related developments.[1] As discussed in Chapter 1, some scholars use the concept of financialization to refer to the ascendancy of "shareholder value" as a mode of corporate governance (Froud et al. 2000, 2006; Lazonick and O'Sullivan 2000; Williams 2000). Another use of the term— harkening back to the beginning of the twentieth century (Hilferding 1981; Hobson 1971; Lenin 1939)—refers to the increasing political and economic power of a *rentier* class (Dumenil and Levy 2004; Epstein and Jayadev 2005). Finally, the term is sometimes used to describe the explosion of financial trading associated with the proliferation of new financial instruments (Phillips 1994).

These various definitions are not necessarily mutually exclusive. One advantage of the definition of financialization I adopt is that it is consistent with a variety of causal accounts (if by the same token also somewhat indeterminate) and therefore is capable of encompassing alternative usages of the term. In other words, in an economy in which systems of corporate governance reflect the imperatives of financial markets, we would expect profits to accrue increasingly through financial channels. Similarly, we would expect the growing power of social actors occupying strategic positions vis-à-vis financial markets to be parlayed into outsized economic rewards. Finally, we would expect increased financial flows and a rapid pace of financial innovation to generate profit opportunities in the financial sector of the economy. As I suggested in the previous chapter, my objective in this book is not to adjudicate between these various accounts, but rather to ground them all in an analysis of state actions—an objective for which the broadest possible definition of the phenomenon under study is most adequate.

In the following pages, I show that the financial sector has become increasingly important as a source of profits in the U.S. economy over the last several decades, providing strong evidence for the claim that the economy has undergone a process of financialization. In the 1950s and 1960s, financial sector profits ranged between approximately 10 and 15 percent of total profits in the U.S. economy. In the period since the mid-1980s, financial sector profits have accounted for approximately 30 percent of total profits in the U.S. economy, with this figure rocketing up to exceed 40 percent as the business cycle peaked in 2001.[2] Although the growth of financial sector profits suggests a dramatic transformation in the structure of the U.S. economy, this measure by itself represents a conservative estimate of financialization because it does not account for excess compensation occurring in the financial sector. Outsized compensation packages in the financial sector mean that reported profits (which are net of the payment of wages and salaries) are artificially low relative to what they would be were wages and salaries in this sector comparable to wages and salaries in other sectors.

Another, arguably even more important reason that the growth of financial sector profits represents a conservative estimate of financialization is that *nonfinancial* firms have themselves become increasingly dependent on financial activities as sources of revenue in recent years. We know this phenomenon primarily through the examples of several corporations that have received attention in the business press, such as General

Electric (GE), Sears, General Motors, and Ford. These firms all created captive finance units that were originally intended to support consumer purchases of their products by offering installment financing but which eventually became financial behemoths that overshadowed the manufacturing or retailing activities of the parent firm (Covert and McWilliams 2006; Froud et al. 2006; Hakim 2004; Henry 2005). The trajectories of these various companies are quite diverse, with the automotive finance units generally staying closer to their original purpose of subsidizing the firm's core business through automobile leasing operations, while the activities of GE Capital and Sears Financial have to a large extent become decoupled from the businesses of their parent companies. Indeed, GE Capital represents the quintessential industrial firm-turned-bank, offering a variety of consumer and commercial financial services, issuing private-label credit cards, managing trade receivables, financing leveraged buyouts, and most recently selling mortgage insurance (Froud et al. 2006). In the case of GE, we know that such activities have provided approximately half of total firm earnings in recent years (Eisinger 2004),[3] but what such examples do not tell us is how widespread these patterns are among nonfinancial firms more broadly (including those that have not established captive finance units). For this reason, in the following analysis I take a step back from firm-level case studies, attempting to gauge nonfinancial firms' growing reliance on financial sources of revenue across the economy.

Accordingly, in this chapter I construct two aggregate measures of financialization by examining both the growth of financial sector profits and the growing reliance of nonfinancial firms on financial activities to subsidize profits generated through more traditional productive activities. The data for this analysis is drawn from the Internal Revenue Service *Corporation Income Tax Statistics,* the Federal Reserve *Flow of Funds,* and the Bureau of Economic Analysis (BEA) *National Income and Product Accounts.*[4] I also consider two possible objections to the claim that the patterns observed indicate a process of financialization—namely, that these patterns can be attributed to forms of corporate reorganization or to the globalization of production. Although the primary objective of the chapter is to present descriptive evidence for financialization rather than to provide a causal analysis, I conclude the chapter by sketching some of the mechanisms that connect the historical analysis presented in the remainder of the book to the broad shift in the structure of the U.S. economy outlined here. The analysis covers the full postwar period, beginning in 1950 and ending in 2001. The end point is to some degree determined by data limitations,[5] although there is also a substantive argument to be made for ending the analysis with the stock market sell-off of 2001, which certainly represented a change in phase if not the definitive end of financialization (cf. Fligstein 2005).

Two Views of Economic Change

The examination of structural change in the U.S. economy undertaken in this book requires a different "lens" than that typically used by scholars examining such shifts. Although most characterizations of long-term change in the underlying structure of the economy rely for evidence on changes in employment or in the mix of goods and services produced (e.g., Bell 1973; Castells 1996; Clark 1940), these are not appropriate places to look for the rise of finance. The financial sector is not employment-intensive and its "products" do not show up in transparent ways in national economic statistics (Block 1987). Thus, in contrast to the standard perspective on long-term economic change, which is concerned with the tasks performed or with what is produced in an economy, this chapter engages another vantage point on economic change by examining *where profits are generated* in the U.S. economy. My objective in this section is simply to motivate the analysis presented in the following pages by showing how dramatically these two views of structural change in the U.S. economy diverge from each other. While the standard view of economic change points to the rise of the service sector or post-industrialism as the defining feature of recent economic development (see Bell 1973; Clark 1940), a focus on changing patterns of profitability suggests that financialization is the key development in the U.S. economy in recent decades.

I proceed through a simple comparison of the picture of structural change in the economy that emerges from employment, gross domestic product (GDP), and profit data—each reflecting a different vantage point on economic change.[6] Employment data[7] are the type of evidence most commonly marshaled in debates about how to characterize the nature of contemporary economic change (e.g., Bell 1973; Castells 1996; Clark 1940). Because just three industries—manufacturing, FIRE,[8] and services[9]—account for most of the change in the sectoral composition of the economy over the last fifty years, I report only these three industries here. Figure 1 shows relative industry shares of total employment between 1950 and 2001. The steep decline of manufacturing is evident in this figure. Also evident is the stratospheric ascent of employment in services. But note that viewed through the lens of employment, finance is not particularly significant. FIRE is neither very large relative to other industries, nor does it register significant growth over the period. Thus this evidence is

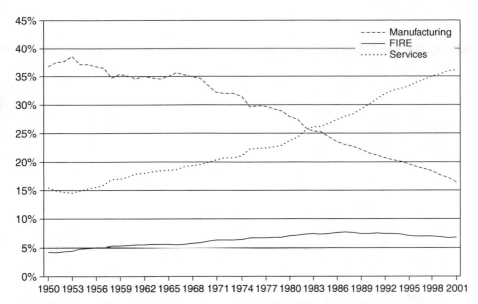

Figure 1.   Relative industry shares of employment in U.S. economy, 1950–
2001. (Data on full-time equivalent employees from *National Income and
Product Accounts*, table 6.5.)

consistent with an interpretation of recent developments in the economy
as reflecting the rise of the service sector or post-industrialism. These data
do *not* point to financialization as an apt way of understanding economic
change in recent decades.

Another kind of evidence—less common than employment data—
mobilized in debates about how to characterize the evolution of the
economy in recent decades relies on shifts in the contribution of different
sectors to GDP (e.g., Bell 1973: 17). GDP is both a measure of what is
produced and a measure of national income. In theory, the two concepts
are equivalent: the market value of goods and services produced should
equal the income earned in producing those goods and services. As such,
the BEA estimates GDP using two independent methods—the first is
based on adding the value of output produced, and the second is based
on adding incomes, including profits.[10] For purposes of this chapter, then,
GDP is a hybrid measure, reflecting both what is produced and where
profits are generated in the economy.

Figure 2 shows relative industry shares of current-dollar GDP between
1950 and 2001. I again report data for only those three industries that
account for most of the change in the sectoral composition of the economy. Like Figure 1, Figure 2 shows the decline in manufacturing over the

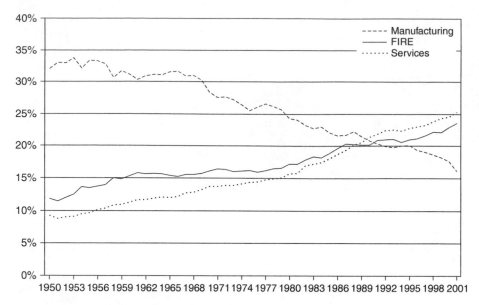

Figure 2.   Relative industry shares of current-dollar GDP in U.S. economy, 1950–2001. (Data on industry contributions to current-dollar GDP from BEA's *Gross Product Originating* series.)

postwar period. Similarly, the figure shows the dramatic growth of services, the largest industry in the economy on this measure. But now FIRE also appears as an industry in which significant growth has taken place over the postwar period. These data could be interpreted as providing evidence for both the post-industrial thesis *and* for financialization.

A third type of evidence for structural change in the economy is presented in Figure 3, which shows data on relative industry shares of corporate profits between 1950 and 2001 for manufacturing, FIRE, and services.[11] Profit data are considerably more volatile than employment data. Nevertheless, the picture of structural change in the economy that emerges is nearly the mirror image of the data presented in Figure 1, with the relative position of services and FIRE inverted. Again, the decline of manufacturing is dramatic in this figure, but now FIRE is the dominant sector of the economy, with services accounting for a relatively small share of total profits. This result is not in itself inconsistent with standard characterizations of economic change—finance is, after all, a service. But from this perspective, the rise of finance is so central to characterizations of economic change that merely subsuming finance under a broader category of service industries is, in fact, misleading (cf. Sassen 2001). Rather

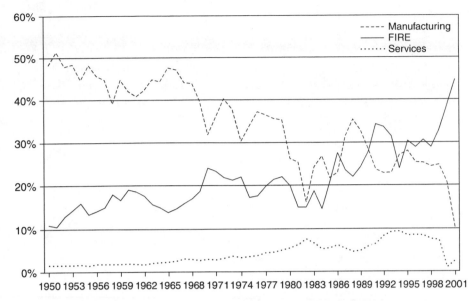

Figure 3.   Relative industry shares of corporate profits in U.S. economy, 1950–2001. (Data on corporate profits by industry from BEA's *Gross Product Originating* series.)

than post-industrialism, it is financialization that comes sharply into view when profit data rather than employment or GDP are the focus of analysis.[12]

Evidence for Financialization

Having contrasted two ways of "seeing" long-term structural change in the economy, I now turn to a more systematic evaluation of the evidence for the financialization of the U.S. economy. I use two discrete measures of financialization in this chapter. First, I examine sources of revenue for nonfinancial firms, demonstrating the growing importance of "portfolio income" (comprising income from interest payments, dividends, and capital gains on investments) relative to revenue generated by more traditional productive activities.[13] Second, turning to a sectoral analysis of the economy, I examine the growing importance of the financial sector as a source of profits, comparing financial to nonfinancial profits. These are not the only measures of financialization that could be devised, and indeed other scholars have relied on a broad range of data in examining the growing salience of finance in the economy (e.g., Crotty 2005; Dumenil

and Levy 2004; Orhangazi 2008). I have settled on these indicators because the data issues involved in constructing these measures are manageable and because they capture in a very intuitive way what it would
mean for an economy to become more oriented to financial activities. It
should also be noted that each of these measures has its own limitations,
but taken together they provide persuasive evidence of the financialization of the U.S. economy.

Portfolio Income

One indication of financialization is the extent to which nonfinancial
firms derive revenues from financial investments as opposed to more traditional productive activities. In the following analysis, I gauge the significance of financial revenues for nonfinancial firms by constructing a
ratio comparing portfolio income to corporate cash flow. *Portfolio income*
measures the total earnings accruing to nonfinancial firms from interest,
dividends, and realized capital gains on investments. *Corporate cash flow*
consists of profits plus depreciation allowances.[14] Thus the ratio of portfolio income to corporate cash flow reflects the relationship, for nonfinancial firms, between the return generated from financial versus productive activities.[15]

There are two reasons for comparing portfolio income to corporate
cash flow rather than simply using profit data as the denominator of this
measure. The first is that the liberalization of depreciation allowances over
the postwar period presents difficulties for the interpretation of profit
data.[16] The concept of depreciation is used to represent the continual using up of capital in the process of production. For example, if a manufacturing firm uses a given piece of machinery for ten years, then each year
some of the value represented by the machine is depleted. To encourage
investment, the government compensates firms for the value of the capital used in production by allowing firms to subtract a depreciation allowance from their total earnings in order to calculate taxable profits. Although capital depreciates continually over the lifetime of capital, firms
do not "pay" the cost of depreciation continually, but only as capital is retired and replaced—in this example, at the end of ten years. Thus, in any
given year, the total capital available to the firm consists of profits subject
to tax *plus* depreciation allowances (which can be thought of as profits
not subject to tax).

Critically, in recent decades, Congress has repeatedly mandated that
the Internal Revenue Service (IRS) shorten the length of time over which

capital is assumed to wear out, allowing firms to depreciate investments more quickly and hence take larger deductions from earnings in order to calculate taxable profits. The result is that, relative to the immediate postwar period, profits in recent years are significantly understated in national economic data as a result of changes in depreciation allowances rather than actual changes in patterns of capital use. Thus, to eliminate the possibility that an increasing ratio of portfolio income to profits could be an artifact of changes in the tax treatment of depreciation, it is necessary to add depreciation allowances into profits to calculate corporate cash flow.[17]

The second reason for using corporate cash flow rather than profit data to calculate this measure is that portfolio income is a pure revenue stream, whereas profits are reported *net-of-cost*, making a strict comparison between the two somewhat misleading. Ideally, portfolio income would be reported after the costs associated with managing financial transactions (office space, salaries, etc.) had been subtracted from the measure. However, it is impossible to allocate costs of production between financial and productive activities in order to construct a portfolio income measure net of the expenses associated with generating financial income streams (Crotty 2005). As such, rather than corporate profits, the appropriate comparison to portfolio income is a measure of the total capital available to the firm, which is arguably what cash flow data capture.[18]

Figure 4 shows the ratio of portfolio income to corporate cash flow among nonfinancial firms between 1950 and 2001. A five-year moving average is shown with the annual data. An increasing trend indicates a higher share of revenues coming from financial relative to nonfinancial sources of income and hence is consistent with a greater degree of financialization. The ratio is remarkably stable in the 1950s and 1960s, but begins to climb upward in the 1970s and then increases sharply over the course of the 1980s. In the late 1980s, the ratio peaks at a level that is approximately *five times* the levels typical of the immediate postwar decades. The ratio retreats somewhat from the high levels obtained during the 1980s in the first half of the 1990s before recovering in the second half of the 1990s. Although there is considerable volatility in the measure, what is most striking about the graph is the dramatic divergence in the structure of the economy between the immediate postwar period and the period beginning in the 1970s.

Figure 5 presents these data disaggregated by manufacturing and nonmanufacturing sectors of the economy. For purposes of comparison, the

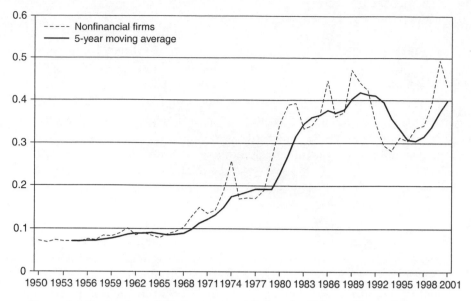

Figure 4. Ratio of portfolio income to cash flow for U.S. nonfinancial firms, 1950–2001. (Data on portfolio income from IRS, Statistics of Income, *Corporation Income Tax Returns.* Data on corporate profits from *National Income and Product Accounts,* table 6.16. Data on depreciation allowances from *National Income and Product Accounts,* table 6.22.)

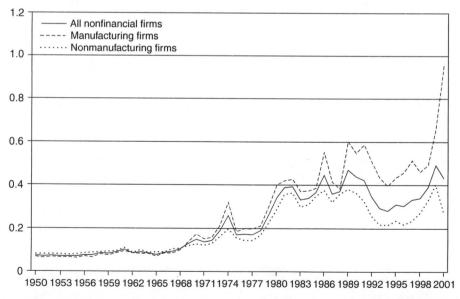

Figure 5. Ratio of portfolio income to cash flow for U.S. manufacturing and nonmanufacturing industries, 1950–2001. (Data on portfolio income from IRS, Statistics of Income, *Corporation Income Tax Returns.* Data on corporate profits from *National Income and Product Accounts,* table 6.16. Data on depreciation allowances from *National Income and Product Accounts,* table 6.22.)

data for all nonfinancial firms are also reported in Figure 5. The graph indicates that, beginning in the 1970s, manufacturing leads the trend in this measure for the nonfinancial economy as a whole. This pattern likely reflects the fact that manufacturing firms confronting large capital expenditures for plant and equipment were affected especially severely by uncertainty in the macro-economic environment, whether in the form of inflation in the 1970s or soaring interest rates in the 1980s. As I elaborate below, responses to this uncertainty were varied, but generally took the form of nonfinancial firms withdrawing capital from long-term investments in plant and equipment and diverting resources into financial investments. The manufacturing sector continues to lead the trend in the portfolio income measure through 2001, which is possibly a reflection of the extent to which firms in highly cyclical manufacturing industries increasingly depend on financial revenues to subsidize profits from productive enterprise.[19]

Figure 6 breaks out the components of portfolio income, reporting the share of the total accounted for by each. It reveals that the upward surge in portfolio income in the last three decades was largely accounted for by increases in the interest component, rather than by capital gains, which merely held steady over the period, or dividends, which lost share relative to the other two components. Critically, this result cautions against reducing financialization to developments in the stock market. As reflected by this measure, the increase in portfolio income was more a product of interest income swelling firm coffers as higher interest rates became embedded in the economy than it was a result of the soaring stock market of the 1980s and 1990s (see also Bryan and Rafferty 2006: 32).[20] Although there clearly is a relationship between financialization and the booming stock market of the 1980s and 1990s, this relationship is likely a more indirect one than is typically presumed, operating more through changing incentives for managers rather than contributing to firm revenues through capital gains (see Chapter 1).

One question these data do not answer is whether increases in portfolio income over the period reflect the increased acquisition of financial assets or higher returns on an existing portfolio of assets. Certainly, the growing contribution of interest income to portfolio income in the 1990s—a period in which interest rates were *declining* from their levels in the previous decade—suggests that the former process was in operation, although this outcome could also reflect the changing composition of financial assets rather than an absolute increase in total financial assets. Is there more direct evidence to allow us to examine the claim that nonfinancial firms were acquiring financial assets at an increased rate during

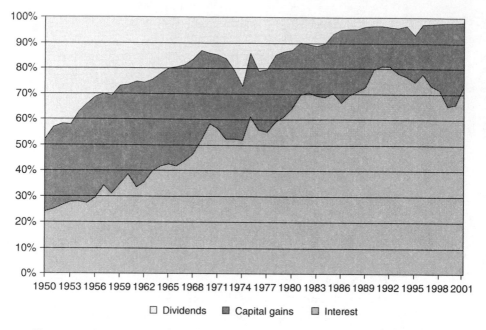

100%

90%

80%

70%

60%

50%

40%

30%

20%

10%

0%

1950 1953 1956 1959 1962 1965 1968 1971 1974 1977 1980 1983 1986 1989 1992 1995 1998 2001

☐ Dividends   ▨ Capital gains   ☐ Interest

Figure 6.   Components of portfolio income for U.S. nonfinancial firms, 1950–2001. (Data on portfolio income from IRS, Statistics of Income, *Corporation Income Tax Returns*. Data on corporate profits from *National Income and Product Accounts,* table 6.16. Data on depreciation allowances from *National Income and Product Accounts,* table 6.22.)

this period? Unfortunately, the data necessary to evaluate this claim are flawed, making any estimate of the acquisition of financial assets somewhat tenuous. Figure 7 presents a ratio of the net acquisition of financial assets relative to tangible assets in the U.S. economy from the early 1950s through 2001. The figure shows a dramatic acceleration over the period, indicating that capital was being diverted from productive to financial investment. However, these data are constructed from an incomplete (and by contemporary standards, rather staid) inventory of classes of financial assets, with a residual category labeled "other assets" accounting for a disproportionate share of the increase. We do not know exactly what kinds of assets constitute the "other" category or even whether these assets should properly be considered as "financial." Researchers examining these data carefully have speculated that corporate "goodwill"[21] constitutes a large portion of this category, as well as the stock market investments of nonfinancial corporations (see Crotty 2005; Orhangazi

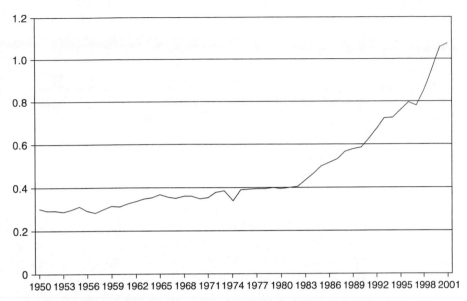

Figure 7.   Ratio of net acquisition of financial assets to tangible assets for U.S. nonfinancial firms, 1950–2001. (Data on the net acquisition of financial and tangible assets from Federal Reserve *Flow of Funds,* table B.102.)

2008). The bottom line here is that we have some evidence of increased acquisition of financial assets by nonfinancial firms in recent decades—an impression that is amply supported by reporting in the business press—but we do not know by precisely how much investment in financial assets increased over the period.

Financial and Nonfinancial Profits

A second source of evidence for financialization is sectoral in nature, comparing the profits generated in financial and nonfinancial sectors of the economy. In addition to the increasing weight of financial activities in generating revenue streams for nonfinancial firms, the financial sector itself has become an increasingly privileged site of accumulation in the economy. I previewed the sectoral composition of profits earlier in the chapter for purposes of comparing the view of economic change elaborated in this book with more conventional interpretations,[22] but here it is necessary to be more careful in how measures of profitability are constructed. In particular, it is necessary to take account of some of the difficulties associated with the liberalization of depreciation allowances already discussed in conjunction with the portfolio income measure. In the following analysis, I report ratios of both financial to nonfinancial sector profits and financial to nonfinancial sector cash flow to avoid these problems.

More specifically, as I explained above, the liberalization of depreciation allowances in recent decades results in profit figures that are artificially low relative to figures from the 1950s and 1960s. Even more problematic in this context, depreciation allowances are not evenly distributed across firms, but will be highest for firms in capital-intensive industries, such as manufacturing. Thus use of profit data will bias a comparison of the relative size of financial and nonfinancial sectors, overstating the growth of financial relative to nonfinancial profits, especially in recent years. Using cash flow data instead of profit data partially corrects for these problems. By adding depreciation allowances back into profit figures, such a measure eliminates the risk that financial profits appear high relative to nonfinancial profits solely as an artifact of the differential tax treatment of financial and nonfinancial firms. But in this context, corporate cash flow data suffer from the opposite bias as that of corporate profit data. In particular, although liberalized depreciation allowances overstate true depreciation, *true depreciation is not zero,* and it represents a cost borne by firms against profits. As before, this cost is not evenly distributed across firms, but will be highest in capital-intensive industries. Thus reliance on corporate cash flow data produces an inflated estimate of profits in industries such as manufacturing, understating financial profits relative to nonfinancial profits.

Because the flaws of these two measures are symmetrical and offsetting, we can be confident that the true, unobserved ratio of financial to nonfinancial profits lies somewhere in between the two measures. In Figure 8, I report both corporate profits and corporate cash flow as upper and lower bounds for financialization, respectively. A five-year moving average is shown with the annual data; an upward trend in the ratio is consistent with greater degrees of financialization. On either measure, the ratio is relatively stable in the 1950s and 1960s but becomes more volatile beginning in the 1970s. The ratio increases gradually in the 1970s, followed by a sharp upward surge during the 1980s. The ratio then retreats somewhat in the first half of the 1990s, but subsequently supersedes even the soaring levels of the previous decade by the end of the 1990s. At its highest point at the end of the period, the ratio varies (depending on which measure one follows) from approximately *three to five times* the levels typical of the 1950s and 1960s.

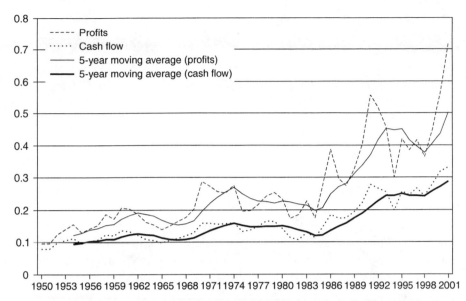

Figure 8.   Ratio of financial to nonfinancial profits and cash flow in U.S. economy, 1950–2001. (Data on corporate profits and depreciation allowances from BEA's *Gross Product Originating* series.)

Financialization and the Reorganization of Corporate Activity

Although the data presented in this chapter provide strong evidence of the financialization of the U.S. economy, several objections to this interpretation of the data should be examined. A general problem for scholars attempting to characterize recent changes in capitalism is the difficulty of distinguishing changes in the organization of economic activity from changes in the substance of those activities. There are two discrete developments to consider here, both of which potentially threaten the interpretation of the U.S. economy as currently undergoing a process of financialization. The first issue is the growing trend among firms toward outsourcing certain activities previously performed "in-house." Should the practice of contracting out financial functions once executed in the finance departments of manufacturing corporations, for example, be counted as evidence for financialization (or, for that matter, for post-industrialism)? In this case, it is not the activity per se that is new, but simply its sectoral location vis-à-vis shifting firm boundaries—and, consequently, where it is visible in the economic data. A second, related threat to the interpretation of the data as reflecting the financialization of the U.S. economy revolves around the increasing prevalence of subsidiary ownership among large industrial corporations (Boies and Prechel 2002). Here we must consider the possibility that changing ownership structures—and not financialization per se—have generated the results presented earlier in this chapter.

Outsourcing

Regarding outsourcing, the objection is that what appears in the data as "financialization" may in reality be an artifact of the reorganization of firms, such that financial activities that once took place inside nonfinancial firms now take place outside of them. If this were the case, then the presence of a "larger" financial sector would not necessarily indicate the expansion of financial activities in the economy as a whole. It is therefore important to consider to what extent outsourcing may compromise the results presented in this chapter. Although it is not possible to fully discount outsourcing as contributing to the trends observed in the data, I have constructed the evidence for financialization in a way that minimizes the risk that the results presented in the previous section are merely an artifact of corporate reorganization. I explain this using a concrete example.

The management of trade receivables represents a financial function that was formerly carried out within nonfinancial firms but is now commonly outsourced to specialized financial firms. Trade receivables are short-term credits extended between a firm and its suppliers to facilitate interfirm trade. For example, Firm A purchases machinery from Firm B. Rather than accepting payment for the machinery immediately, Firm B extends credit to Firm A for the amount of the sale. To make good on this debt, Firm A pays interest—and, eventually, the principal on the loan—to Firm B. In the early postwar decades, trade receivables were very often carried on the books of nonfinancial firms. In more recent years, nonfinancial firms commonly sell their receivables to financial firms that specialize in managing the risks associated with collecting on these debts. This development exerts a downward bias on the first measure—portfolio income—by depriving nonfinancial firms of a source of interest income. At the same time, the growth of a segment of the financial industry specializing in managing trade receivables generates profits in the financial sector, exerting an upward bias on the second measure of financialization, the ratio of financial to nonfinancial profits.

This very concrete example makes a general point: outsourcing affects the two measures of financialization in opposite directions. Thus the fact that both measures show the same trend in spite of these opposite biases increases confidence that outsourcing does not account for the patterns observed in the data.

Subsidiary Formation

Another threat to the results presented in the previous section relates to a second form of corporate reorganization—that of subsidiary formation. Subsidiary formation resembles the practice of outsourcing, but here the key relationship between firms is not contractual but one of ownership. A subsidiary is formed when a multidivisional firm sells one of its divisions, creating a separate legal entity in which the parent company holds a controlling interest by maintaining majority ownership of the subsidiary firm's stock. Subsidiaries may also be acquired when a company purchases a majority stake in another firm (i.e., not previously organized as a division of the parent). Evidence suggests that subsidiary ownership is far from a trivial phenomenon in the U.S. economy. Indeed, John Boies and Harland Prechel (2002) argue that the "multi-layered subsidiary firm" has replaced the multidivisional firm as the most prevalent organizational form among contemporary American corporations. As such, the implications of this development warrant careful consideration. There are two separate issues here: first, the possibility that changing ownership patterns might artificially inflate dividends and thereby distort estimates of portfolio income; and second, the potential for the nonfinancial ownership of financial subsidiaries to blur the lines between sectors of the economy.

The practice of "spinning off" divisions into subsidiaries directly affects the interpretation of the portfolio income data: as the majority stock owner, the parent company receives dividends paid out by the subsidiary corporation. Because dividend income is a component of portfolio income, part of the upward trend in that measure in the last two decades could simply reflect this form of corporate reorganization rather than the growing orientation of nonfinancial firms to financial markets. However, the timing of subsidiary formation does not correspond closely to the trend in portfolio income observed in Figure 4, suggesting that if subsidiary formation has contributed to these results, it does not determine them. More specifically, Boies and Prechel (2002: 302) note that although the largest 100 industrial corporations created 703 new subsidiaries between 1981 and 1987, the rate of subsidiary formation more than doubled between 1987 and 1993, with 1,796 new subsidiaries formed. Comparing these figures to the data on portfolio income reported in Figure 4, we note that portfolio income surged upward during the first half of the 1980s, but then slowed just as subsidiary formation was itself accelerating dramatically in the late 1980s and early 1990s. In addition, the data presented in Figure 6 weakens the plausibility of this alternative explanation for the upward trend in the portfolio income measure: dividends account for a decreasing share of total portfolio income over the postwar period.[23] Finally, whatever the role of subsidiary formation in contributing to portfolio income, this phenomenon does not affect the second measure of financialization—the ratio of financial to nonfinancial profits—as dividends are *not* included in the profit data used in this analysis.[24]

A related problem to consider is how nonfinancial ownership of financial subsidiaries might affect estimates of financialization by blurring the lines between financial and nonfinancial sectors of the economy. As with the issue of dividends, the implications of this problem diverge for our two measures of financialization. The divergence, in this case, results from the way in which economic units are assigned an industry classification for purposes of incorporation into national economic data. Industrial classifications may be determined on an *establishment* or on a *company* basis. An establishment is an economic unit at a single physical location. A company comprises one or more establishments owned by the same legal entity, regardless of physical location. Establishments are assigned an industrial classification on the basis of their principal product. Although companies may own establishments in many different industries, companies are assigned to an industrial classification on the basis of the activity that generates the largest revenue in *all* establishments. Thus, where data are reported on a company basis, individual establishments may be misallocated to whatever industry dominates revenues for the entire company.

The data used in constructing the portfolio income measure are reported on a company basis; the ratio of financial to nonfinancial profits is on an establishment basis. Thus the latter measure is *not* affected by the problem of subsidiary ownership. Unless the nonfinancial parent and financial subsidiary literally occupy the same physical space—a prospect that is unlikely in most cases—subsidiary ownership will have no bearing on the results reported. Portfolio income data, in contrast, *are* affected by patterns of subsidiary ownership. In cases in which nonfinancial parents acquire financial subsidiaries, the revenues of these financial subsidiaries may be incorrectly attributed to nonfinancial parents, potentially inflating the estimate of financialization reported in Figure 4. Thus, to the extent that such acquisitions have accelerated in recent years, it is possible that the upward trend in portfolio income reflects changing forms of ownership rather than a truly novel pattern of accumulation. However, because this particular measure is intended to show the dependence of nonfinancial corporations on financial sources of revenue, I would argue that, in this case, changing forms of ownership *do* reflect a novel pattern of accumulation (Froud et al. 2002). In short, although the portfolio income measure is reported on a company basis primarily because this is how data are reported, including the investment income of financial subsidiaries owned by nonfinancial corporations in portfolio income seems appropriate, given what the measure seeks to capture.

Financialization and the Globalization of Production

Another objection to the claim that financialization is occurring in the U.S. economy is that what appears as "financialization" is in fact a result of the spatial restructuring of economic activity where production increasingly occurs offshore but financial functions continue to be located in the domestic economy. It is important to note that both of the measures developed in this chapter, which rely exclusively on domestic data, are vulnerable to such an objection. In the case of portfolio income, the sharp upward trend in the measure could be a reflection not of a genuine increase of financial relative to productive sources of income, but rather the *relocation* of manufacturing activities (and associated income flows) outside the boundaries of the U.S. economy. In the case of the sectoral analysis of profits, the growing weight of financial relative to nonfinancial profits might similarly be generated by the increasing importance of U.S. nonfinancial profits earned abroad (which are *not* included in the reported measure). If such scenarios accounted for the trends observed in this chapter, we might still refer to the U.S. economy as having been "financialized," but the term would not then signal a new way of characterizing current developments in the U.S. economy. Rather, it could be subsumed into already existing literatures on deindustrialization and the changing international division of labor (Bluestone and Harrison 1982; Frobel, Heinrichs, and Kreye 1980).

There are, however, reasons to be skeptical of the claim that the findings reported here are better understood in terms of processes associated with the globalization of production. With regard to portfolio income, there is no reason to assume a priori that the movement of production offshore (and associated income flows) has outpaced revenues generated by increased investment in foreign financial instruments. Similarly, with regard to the sectoral analysis of profits, there is also no a priori reason to expect that nonfinancial profits dominate financial sector profits earned abroad. We know that with the development of the Eurodollar market in the 1960s, banking activities followed manufacturing offshore (Helleiner 1994); the internationalization of U.S. financial capital has continued apace in more recent years (Sassen 2001). With respect to both measures, more fundamentally, the U.S. economy is more inwardly focused than the popular rhetoric of "globalization" suggests (Hirst and Thompson 1999). Nevertheless it is important to examine the data on this question.

A note on terminology is necessary. In the analysis that follows, I use "domestic" portfolio income or profits to refer to the portfolio income or profits generated by economic activity undertaken inside the territorial United States. I use "foreign-source" portfolio income or "U.S. profits earned abroad" to refer to portfolio income or profits earned by U.S. corporations outside of the territorial United States. I use "global" portfolio income or profits to refer to portfolio income or profits earned in the territorial United States *plus* foreign-source portfolio income or profits earned abroad by U.S. corporations (i.e., global portfolio income = domestic portfolio income + foreign-source portfolio income; global profits = domestic profits + U.S. profits earned abroad). The same conventions apply to the labels used to describe Figures 9 through 12.

Global Portfolio Income of U.S. Nonfinancial Corporations

Beginning with the portfolio income measure, a first cut at the problem involves recalculating the measure by incorporating foreign-source income from financial and productive activities into the numerator and denominator of the ratio, respectively. There are significant data limitations involved in such a calculation: the appropriate data must be drawn from three different sources and are available at the correct level of industry disaggregation for only a handful of years: 1978, 1980, 1982, 1984, 1986, 1990, and 1992–1999.[25] In spite of the relatively limited number of data points, the period covered is a critical one in terms of the crisis of manufacturing, which precipitated a significant movement of production offshore (e.g., Brenner 2006). Thus these data should be sufficient to evaluate the hypothesis that what is driving financialization is not a substantive change in the nature of the economy but rather the spatial reorganization of economic activity associated with globalization.

Figure 9 presents the portfolio income measure recalculated to reflect

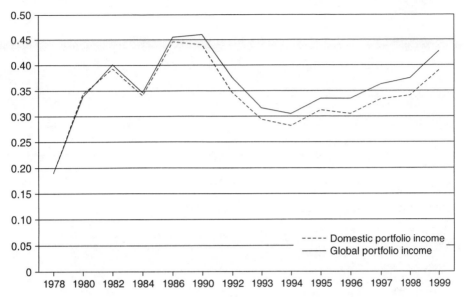

Figure 9. Ratio of global portfolio income to cash flow for U.S. nonfinancial firms, 1978–1999. (Data on dividends paid to U.S. corporations by foreign corporations from *Corporation Income Tax Statistics.* Data on interest earned on foreign investments, depreciation allowances claimed against foreign income taxes, and foreign taxes paid by U.S. corporations from *Foreign Tax Credit* data. Data on U.S. profits earned abroad for 1982 to 1999 from *Balance of Payments,* table 16. Data for 1977–1981 from *U.S. Direct Investment Abroad: Balance of Payments and Direct Investment Position Estimates, 1977–81,* table 10.)

the global economic activities of U.S. nonfinancial corporations—that is, incorporating both domestic *and* foreign sources of income. For purposes of comparison, I also plot the same data points using the original domestic measure. An examination of Figure 9 shows that the domestic and global portfolio income measures track each other very closely. This reflects the large size of the domestic economy relative to international activity: the results for the domestic economy dominate the trend for the global measure.

This being the case, it is informative to examine the foreign-source data separately. An examination of the ratio of foreign-source portfolio income to cash flow generated abroad (i.e., calculated so as to exclude domestic economic activity), shown in Figure 10, reveals a striking fact: financialization is even more strongly in evidence in the offshore activities of U.S. nonfinancial corporations than is the case for the domestic

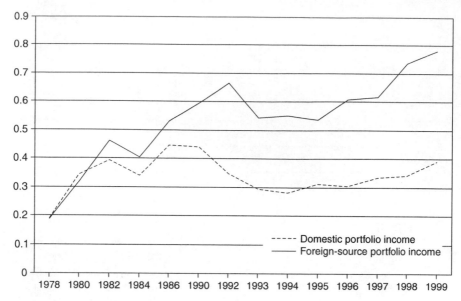

Figure 10.   Ratio of foreign-source portfolio income to cash flow for U.S. nonfinancial firms, 1978–1999. (Data on dividends paid to U.S. corporations by foreign corporations from *Corporation Income Tax Statistics*. Data on interest earned on foreign investments, depreciation allowances claimed against foreign income taxes, and foreign taxes paid by U.S. corporations from *Foreign Tax Credit* data. Data on U.S. profits earned abroad for 1982 to 1999 from *Balance of Payments*, table 16. Data for 1977–1981 from *U.S. Direct Investment Abroad: Balance of Payments and Direct Investment Position Estimates, 1977–81*, table 10.)

economy considered in isolation. Although some care is required in interpreting these data, given the relatively restricted number of years for which data are available, these results are not consistent with the claim that financialization in the domestic economy is simply an artifact of the movement of production offshore.

Global Financial and Nonfinancial Profits of U.S. Corporations

An analysis that is similar to the sectoral analysis of profits can be performed by recalculating the ratio of financial versus nonfinancial profits and including U.S. profits earned abroad in the measure. For this analysis of the global profits of U.S. corporations, data are available appropriately disaggregated by industry for all years between 1977 and 1999. Given the restricted number of years for which data are available, some caution should be used in comparing these results to those reported on the basis of domestic data alone. However, data from a twenty-two-year period beginning in the late 1970s should be sufficient to evaluate the hypothesis that what appears in the United States as "financialization" reflects the spatial reorganization of production when viewed globally.

Figure 11 presents the results of this analysis, which closely track the results obtained when examining domestic profits alone, also reported here for purposes of comparison. Based on the data, it does not appear that including profits earned abroad into the measure significantly attenuates the observed trend toward the increasing weight of the financial sector in the economy.

As was also the case with the analysis of portfolio income, this result in part reflects the fact that U.S. profits earned abroad are dwarfed by profits earned in the domestic economy. Independently of the magnitudes involved, however, we still might be interested in analyzing the ratio of

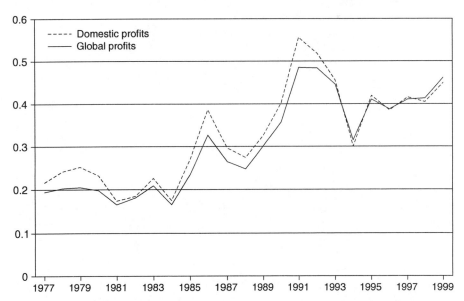

Figure 11. Ratio of financial to nonfinancial global profits earned by U.S. firms, 1977–1999. (Data on U.S. profits earned abroad for 1982 to 1999 from *Balance of Payments*, table 16. Data for 1977–1981 from *U.S. Direct Investment Abroad: Balance of Payments and Direct Investment Position Estimates, 1977–81*, table 10. Data on foreign income taxes paid by U.S. firms operating abroad from IRS *Corporate Foreign Tax Credit* and from *Corporation Income Tax Returns*.)

financial to nonfinancial profits for firms operating abroad. Figure 12 shows the ratio of financial to nonfinancial profits earned abroad by U.S. corporations. I again report the domestic data for comparison. Although the ratio of financial to nonfinancial profits earned abroad starts from a lower level relative to the domestic ratio, the measure climbs sharply, overtaking the domestic ratio by the end of the 1990s. Here, too, financialization is evident.

Reprise and Looking Forward

My purpose in this chapter has been to examine the evidence for the financialization of the U.S. economy. This exercise has required substituting the standard view, which characterizes economic change in terms of the tasks performed or what is produced in an economy for a *profit-centered* view of the economy. Shifting the "lens" in this way shows that financialization—rather than the rise of the service sector or post-

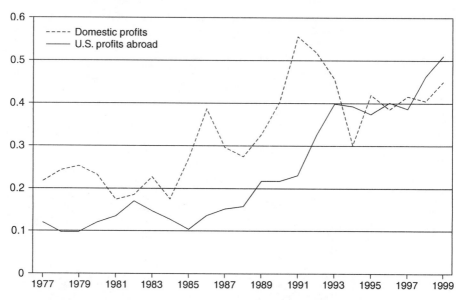

Figure 12. Ratio of financial to nonfinancial profits earned abroad by U.S. firms, 1977–1999. (Data on U.S. profits earned abroad for 1982 to 1999 from *Balance of Payments*, table 16. Data for 1977–1981 from *U.S. Direct Investment Abroad: Balance of Payments and Direct Investment Position Estimates, 1977–81*, table 10. Data on foreign income taxes paid by U.S. firms operating abroad from IRS *Corporate Foreign Tax Credit* and from *Corporation Income Tax Returns.*)

industrialism—emerges as the most important "fact" about the U.S. economy in recent decades. In suggesting that the trajectory of the U.S. economy is aptly characterized in terms of a process of financialization, my central empirical claim is that profit making in recent years has occurred increasingly through financial channels. During the 1980s and 1990s, the ratio of portfolio income to corporate cash flow ranges between approximately *three and five times* the levels characteristic of the 1950s and 1960s. The ratio of financial to nonfinancial profits (and cash flow) behaves similarly. For both measures, the first half of the 1990s represents something of a retreat from the dramatic turn to finance in the 1980s. But by the end of the 1990s, both measures regain levels typical of the 1980s, and, even during the first half of the 1990s, what is most striking about the data is the divergence from the immediate postwar decades. Although important differences exist between the two measures (for example, the behavior of the 1970s differs across Figures 4 and 8), the fact that both measures share the same basic trend enhances confidence that the fundamental patterns discussed here are robust in spite of the specific limitations of each individual measure.

Nevertheless, two caveats are in order. First, it is necessary to be explicit about what I am *not* asserting: specifically, that financialization represents an entirely novel phase of capitalist development. The data presented in this chapter relate only to *postwar* economic development; they do not allow us to form a judgment as to the role of finance in earlier periods. Certainly, the writings of Rudolf Hilferding (1981), John Hobson (1971), Vladimir Lenin (1939), and—more recently—Giovanni Arrighi (1994) and Fernand Braudel (1982) would tend to suggest that financialization is a recurrent phase in the evolution of capitalist economies. Fully exploring the historical precedents for the current turn to finance is a rich exercise (Arrighi and Silver 1999; Hirst and Thompson 1999), but one that lies considerably beyond the scope of this book. Similarly, just as this chapter does not suggest that financialization is a "new" phase of capitalism, neither do these data allow us to draw any conclusions regarding the permanency of the trends documented here. This chapter makes no attempt to forecast for how long or under what circumstances financialization will sustain itself—or reverse course, as appears increasingly likely in the wake of the financial crisis that began with the collapse of the mortgage market in the summer of 2007.

A second caveat is that the data presented here are purely descriptive and therefore are consistent with a variety of causal accounts. Providing a full causal analysis of the turn to finance is well beyond the scope of the current book, and indeed a phenomenon as complex as financialization is likely to have many drivers, as the discussion in Chapter 1 indicated. My more modest purpose here is to situate the various alternative accounts in the literature within a political context by understanding the role of the state in creating a macro-economic environment conducive to financialization. In contrast to the approach taken by prevailing accounts, the analysis presented in the following chapters suggests that state actions shaping the turn to finance should not be understood merely as "exogenous" factors influencing the behavior of economic actors from the outside. Rather than treating some factors as "inside" and others as "outside" the analysis, I examine how state actions and market responses evolved in tandem, analyzing the turn to finance in terms of broader patterns of historical development.

One final task here is to suggest how the macro-economic policy regime put in place in the 1980s and 1990s (and described in the remaining chapters of this book) provided fertile ground for the turn to finance in the U.S. economy. The historical narrative presented in the following chapters highlights a number of key elements of the policy regime constructed in response to the economic crisis of the 1970s. First, domestic financial markets were deregulated over the course of the 1970s, resulting in a dramatic expansion of credit as institutional restraints on the flow of credit in the economy were removed. Second, monetary policymakers imposed dramatically higher interest rates on the economy beginning in the early 1980s in response to both deregulation (without institutional constraints on the *supply* of credit, it was necessary to increase the *price* of credit much more sharply to restrain the economy) and to the Reagan administration's loose fiscal policy. Third, higher interest rates in turn drew unprecedented foreign capital inflows into the U.S. economy, contributing to the expansion of credit in domestic financial markets. Finally, as monetary policy became the privileged site for managing the various social dislocations associated with this policy regime, Federal Reserve officials increasingly relied on market mechanisms to implement policy, further expanding credit while increasing volatility in interest rates in the U.S. economy. In sum, a series of interrelated policy shifts in the 1970s and 1980s was associated with a dramatically expanded supply of credit in the U.S. economy and increased uncertainty in the cost of credit in the form of high and volatile interest rates (Figures 13 and 14).

How did this transformed macro-economic environment create conditions conducive to the financialization of the U.S. economy? Two mechanisms emerge as central in the analysis presented in the following chapters. The first, and more straightforward, mechanism was the role of expanded credit in increasing financial sector profits in the post-1970s period.

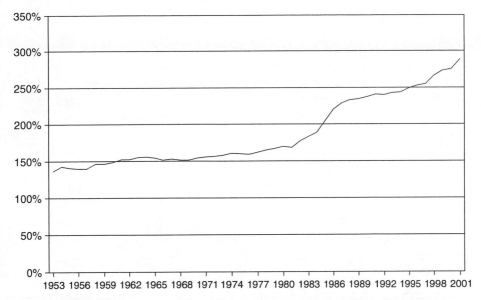

Figure 13. U.S. credit market debt as a percentage of GDP, 1953–2001. (Data on outstanding credit in the U.S. economy from *Flow of Funds,* table L.1. Data on GDP from *National Income and Product Accounts,* table 1.1.5., line 1.)

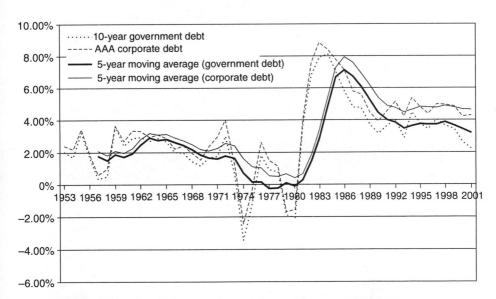

Figure 14. Real interest rates, 1953–2001. (Data on nominal interest rates from *Economic Report of the President,* table B.73. Inflation rate is the CPI-U, reported on a year-to-year basis in *Economic Report of the President,* table B.64.)

Although the circulation of credit through an economy increases corporate profits generally—by allowing investment and consumption expenditures beyond what would occur were firms and households restricted by their earned income (Cooper 2008)—*financial* profits are especially likely to ride the wave of credit expansion. As a general matter, financial institutions act as intermediaries for credit flows, and thus an increased pace of loan expansion generates revenues for the economic agents that manage these transactions. In addition, an increased pace of credit expansion creates propitious conditions for asset price bubbles, generating windfall profits for the financial sector (Bank for International Settlements 2001; Borrio and Lowe 2002; Evans 2003).[26] As noted in Chapter 1, the literature on speculative manias has emphasized psychological mechanisms in explaining this association: easy credit fuels the "euphoria" that is at the heart of a speculative mania (Kindleberger 1978; Minsky 1986; Shiller 2000). But as Cooper (2008) astutely observes, the relationship between a rapid pace of credit expansion and asset price bubbles need not imply irrational behavior (cf. Adrian and Shin 2009; Geanakoplos 2009). Rather, the wider availability of credit enables investors to purchase assets with borrowed funds, pushing the price of assets higher and thereby validating the original asset purchase in a self-reinforcing cycle. When the asset serves as collateral, this self-reinforcing dynamic is magnified: as the price of the asset increases, so does the value of the investor's collateral, enabling greater leverage, which feeds back into higher asset prices.[27] This process does not require overconfidence on the part of investors (although clearly the effect of increased leverage on asset prices would be amplified by such cognitive distortions); rather it is hardwired into an economy in which credit is not subject to *any* external control (Cooper 2008: 101).

The second mechanism through which transformations in the macroeconomic environment contributed to the rise of finance involved the role of high and volatile interest rates in reinforcing the growing orientation of managers to financial markets. More specifically, in the context of greater uncertainty about the cost of capital in a deregulated economic environment, nonfinancial firms increasingly diverted capital from productive to financial investment (Crotty 2005; Eatwell and Taylor 2000; Grabel 1997; Orhangazi 2008; Stockhammer 2004; Walter 1993).[28] The standard calculus that firms apply to making decisions about long-term investment in plant and equipment requires managers to weigh the cost of obtaining financing (including both debt and equity) against the projected return from the investment. To the extent that either the cost of financing or the projected return is uncertain, firms will be dissuaded

from making long-term commitments in which they sacrifice the flexibility of holding capital in a more liquid form.[29] To use the language of
economics, uncertainty in the economic environment causes firms to impose a higher "hurdle rate"—the required return in excess of the cost of
capital—on investment decisions. As interest rates climbed in the early
1980s, hurdle rates were revised steadily upward, with the result that potential investment projects were increasingly shelved as managers opted
instead to channel capital into financial markets.[30]

This shift was embedded in—and contributed to—the larger shift in
the conception of the corporation underpinning the financial revolution
in American business life (Davis 2009; Fligstein 1990, 2001). As Wendy
Nelson Espeland and Paul Hirsch (1990: 79) observe, "Older investment
decisions, which had centered on cutting costs, developing new products
or expanding market shares, were now pitted against plans to invest the
same resources in an endless variety of alternative assets." As corporations came to be seen as "bundles of assets" (Fligstein 1990), to be shuf-
fled and reshuffled according to the whims of the market, investment
plans took on an increasingly speculative character, unconstrained by any
coherent identity of the firm as the maker of a given product or a member of a specific industry (Davis 2009; Espeland and Hirsch 1990). "The
old view," *Business Week* informed its readers in 1986, "is that if you're
in the bolt business, you take risks in the bolt business. You don't take
risks with the cash."[31] Now, as corporate treasurers experimented with
an array of new financial instruments—money market mutual funds,[32]
"stripped" treasuries,[33] Euromarket and Caribbean offshore dollar markets,[34] foreign currency instruments,[35] and portfolios composed of options and futures contracts[36]—risk migrated from the core business to
the till.

Such experimentation was not entirely novel to the 1980s, as the experience of inflation in the previous decade had already sensitized managers
to the imperatives of "cash management."[37] But the extraordinarily high
interest rates of the early 1980s meant these were now not merely defen-
sive but increasingly opportunistic maneuvers.[38] As one large retailer reported, "A lot of companies are making more on cash investments than
on their capital plans." [39] As the cost of capital soared, firms found it difficult to justify new borrowing for plant and equipment expenditures,
especially because capital placed in a liquid money market account could
earn a very lucrative return, with little or no risk to the investor.[40] "It is
easy to understand," one anguished paper industry executive told Congress, "the recent moves by many older and some very modern manufacturing companies, including our own, into the financial services field."[41]

Echoing this view, President Reagan's Commission on Industrial Competitiveness sought to explain the eroding competitive position of American firms internationally by pointing to the fact that, beginning in the 1980s, returns on financial investments surpassed those available from manufacturing investment.[42] As the commission's 1983 report stated: "In the 1960s, the real rates of return earned by manufacturing assets were substantially above those available on financial assets. Today, the situation is reversed. Passive investment in financial assets has pre-tax returns higher than the rate of return on manufacturing assets. As a result the relative attractiveness of investing in our vital manufacturing core has been compromised."[43]

Critically, as higher interest rates proved an enduring feature of a deregulated economic environment and not merely a temporary aberration (Kaufman 1986), investment in financial assets became more than merely "passive." In a high interest rate environment, firms not only demanded a higher return on investment, but also wanted these investments to pay off in shorter time periods. By the mid-1980s, a 25 percent return and a *two-year* payback period was becoming normative for industry,[44] with mergers and acquisitions one of the few financial strategies that could meet these stringent criteria.[45] Paradoxically, the result of these new investment strategies was to increasingly inoculate the economy from interest rate changes: if a firm was contemplating making interest payments for a period of two years rather than for ten or fifteen years, the interest rate at which the loan was taken out became much less critical.[46] In addition, a variety of new financial innovations in the 1970s and 1980s, such as variable rate financing on loans, the securitization of assets, the use of interest rate swaps and other derivative instruments—all developed in response to greater volatility in the economic environment—allowed firms to increasingly protect themselves against interest rate risk (Kaufman 1986).[47] As individual firms protected themselves from risk, the economy as a whole became much more volatile, because freedom from the threat of catastrophe only encouraged more daring financial plays.[48] Ironically, such plays became more prevalent as interest rates gradually fell back to Earth from their 1980s peaks, and firms that were deprived of the narcotic of interest income moved on to even stronger addictions.[49] Although the extraordinary interest rate shock delivered to the economy in the 1980s has not persisted to the present,[50] the broader shift in the orientation of nonfinancial firms that it helped to bring about has proven a durable feature of a transformed economic environment.

It is important to note that the two mechanisms elaborated here—the role of expanded credit in inflating financial sector profits and the role of high and volatile interest rates in reorienting nonfinancial firms toward financial sources of income—hardly exhaust the channels through which state policies shaped the turn to finance in the U.S. economy. Given the preliminary state of research in this area, I have chosen to elaborate on two mechanisms that I think are most important rather than provide an exhaustive discussion. It should also be noted that the two mechanisms identified here did not operate in isolation from one another. That is, the same strategies and innovations that inoculated firms from interest rate risk also meant that borrowers were less likely to be deterred by rising rates, weakening a traditional source of constraint on the expansion of credit (Wojnilower 1980). This expansion of credit in turn contributed to increased interest rate volatility, further engorging the financial sector institutions that peddled interest rate swaps, derivatives, and securitized transactions.[51] In short, under financialization, the endless expansion of credit, increased volatility in the economy, and the growth of financial activities became locked in a tight embrace. Why were state policies that encouraged this dizzying embrace put in place in the 1970s and 1980s and extended in the 1990s? That is the subject of the remaining chapters of this book.

CHAPTER THREE

The Social Politics of U.S. Financial Deregulation

HE PREVIOUS CHAPTER provided evidence for financialization and described the basic contours of this process in the U.S. economy over the last several decades. The remaining empirical chapters of the book provide a historical account of the origins of the policy regime that created conditions conducive to the turn to finance. Critically, the creation of a macro-economic environment conducive to financialization was not a deliberate outcome sought by policymakers; rather, it was an unplanned result of policymakers' attempts to respond to a unique constellation of difficulties that confronted the state beginning in the late 1960s and 1970s. In this chapter I examine a key element of the policy regime supporting financialization by exploring how the deregulation of domestic financial markets emerged as a response to the social crisis associated with the eruption of inflation in U.S. society.

Efforts to deregulate U.S. financial markets spanned the period from the mid-1960s to the late 1990s and occurred on a number of fronts, encompassing changes in securities markets, the banking sector, and the relationship between them. But the aspect of deregulation that is most relevant to this book's account of financialization was the removal in 1980 of controls that limited the rate of interest that could be paid on consumer savings deposits. This seemingly arcane change in the structure of the U.S. financial system was associated with two developments that shaped the subsequent financialization of the economy. First, credit became significantly more expensive following interest rate deregulation as users were unconstrained in bidding up the price of credit. As elaborated in Chapter 2, higher and more volatile interest rates contributed to a

macro-economic environment that favored financial activities over productive investment (Crotty 2005; Eatwell and Taylor 2000; Grabel 1997;
Walter 1993). Second, interest rate deregulation removed built-in restraints on the extension of credit that had traditionally operated as "speed
limits" for the economy (Kaufman 1986; Wojnilower 1980). In a deregulated environment, credit flowed freely across the economy, fueling a
credit expansion that increased financial sector profits and provided further impetus to financialization.

At the time, policymakers did not anticipate these results of financial
deregulation. In the 1960s and 1970s, policymakers operated under the
assumption that they lived, and would always live, in a credit-short and
capital-starved world. Given this, policymakers saw their role as facilitating the rational distribution of scarce capital between sectors; they did
not contemplate the possibility that deregulation might produce an environment in which credit could increase without limit. The assumption
that capital was an inherently scarce resource guided policymakers' pursuit of deregulation—not as prelude to financialization, but rather as a
response to distributional conflict associated with the inflation crisis. In
the context of a regulated financial system, inflation distorted the flow of
credit across the economy, providing ample credit to business but draining capital from the cities and from suburban homeowners. In the wake
of urban riots in the rotting core of inner cities and growing middle-class
frustration with credit shortages, this situation appeared increasingly
untenable to policymakers.

As policymakers sought to redirect capital to social priorities, however,
they faced a dilemma. In a world in which capital was scarce, every attempt to allocate credit to one use required denying it for another. Under
the existing system of interest rate controls, inflation continually presented policymakers with the necessity of choosing which sector to favor
in allocating credit—industry or housing, large corporations or small
businesses, municipal finance or agriculture. Deregulation offered a way
to avoid this problem: removing controls meant that the *market,* rather
than state officials, could do the choosing in distributing capital between
competing sectors. Rather than directly allocating credit through regulatory controls, rationing could be accomplished indirectly through the
price mechanism. But, to the surprise of policymakers, prices did *not* ration very effectively, and in the context of institutional innovations in financial markets, the taps on credit were turned wide open. Free flowing—
and expensive—credit reconfigured the political terrain, disorganizing a
potentially broad-based coalition of middle-class homeowners and urban
advocates that demanded that the burdens of inflation be more equitably

shared. In this context, financial deregulation functioned both to allevi-
ate festering social tensions and to set the stage for the financialization of
the U.S. economy in subsequent decades.

The New Deal Financial System

The financial sector as we know it today was formed in the aftermath of
the financial crisis of the 1930s. The failure of financial markets to recover
following the 1929 stock market crash, along with an ever-mounting
number of bank collapses as the depression progressed, resulted in a
searching examination of the structure of the country's financial system.
There was no shortage of explanations for the onset of the depression
and its elusive recovery: the lack of deposit insurance, a weakly developed system of branch banks, excessive competition between financial
institutions leading to imprudent risk taking, and a lethargic response on
the part of government officials to the crisis, particularly in the domain
of monetary policy. But of all the proposed ills, perhaps none garnered
as much attention—among an outraged public, as well as among policymakers—as the alleged abuses stemming from the combination of commercial and investment banking activities. These abuses were the subject
of a congressional probe that produced such startling revelations of bank
malfeasance that the associated hearings are widely regarded as the key
event in securing the passage of controversial financial reform legislation
(Carosso 1970; Chernow 1990; Krus 1994).

The New Deal financial legislation comprised several distinct bills that
would remake the modern financial system and therefore shape the contours of deregulation efforts in subsequent decades. The most significant
legislation was perhaps the Banking Act of 1933, which created a national system of deposit insurance administered by the Federal Deposit
Insurance Corporation, liberalized bank branching rights, made it illegal
to pay interest on demand deposits, imposed ceilings on the interest that
could be paid on time and savings deposits (Regulation Q), and divorced
commercial banking and investment banking functions (the Glass-
Steagall Act).[1] Other New Deal financial legislation included the Securities Act of 1933, which established guidelines for appropriate disclosure
of information to investors and created the Securities and Exchange
Commission to enforce these guidelines, and the Securities Act of 1934,
which allowed the Federal Reserve to regulate the extension of bank
credit for securities purchases (so-called margin loans, widely held to
be responsible for the dizzying run up in the stock market in the 1920s).
The Banking Act of 1935 centralized control over monetary policy in the

Federal Reserve Board, diminishing the influence of the privately controlled regional Federal Reserve Banks.

The result of this legislation was a highly compartmentalized system in which distinct institutions serving discrete functions were protected from direct competition with one another. Investment banks underwrote and distributed new issues of corporate debt and equity,[2] commercial banks provided loans to corporate customers, savings and loan associations (also known as "thrifts") and mutual savings banks supplied mortgage finance, and finance companies and credit unions engaged in consumer lending. In some cases, compartmentalization between these various institutions was a novel product of these reforms; in other cases, the new regulations served to harden divisions that were already present but fluid in the prereform era.[3] In either case, the effect of New Deal legislation was to fragment the financial sector into diverse industry groups that found it difficult to cohere around a unified political agenda. The splitting apart of the newly chastened House of Morgan into Morgan Stanley (an investment bank) and Morgan Guaranty (a commercial bank) served as a particularly potent symbol of the manner in which financial reform reconfigured the political landscape in the post-New Deal era (Chernow 1990).

In addition to reorganizing interest group politics (Dumenil and Levy 2004; Ferguson 1990), New Deal banking reforms also established a system of financial regulation that would prove critical to the state's pursuit of stable economic growth. Financial regulation created a Rube Goldberg structure of levers and pulleys, in which restrictions on the activities of functionally differentiated institutions ensured that flows of capital would remain approximately balanced between competing social priorities. Regulation Q, which imposed interest rate ceilings on time and savings deposits held at depository institutions, was at the very heart of this system. Regulation Q drew a bright line between a tightly controlled credit market, which was subject to strict limits on what financial institutions could pay for funds, and an uncontrolled capital market, in which rates of return reflected the unbridled forces of supply and demand (Knodell 1994). At the time banking legislation was passed, the manifest reason for interest rate ceilings was to keep the cost of funds to depository institutions low so as to avoid tempting lenders into reckless lending—a common explanation for the rash of bank failures in the early 1930s. In later decades, Regulation Q was applied as a tool—an imperfect one, to be sure—to shield housing from the brunt of market competition.

Aside from these explicit functions, Regulation Q also provided a convenient lever for stabilization policy over much of the postwar period.

When a healthy economic expansion turned to excess and inflationary pressures stirred in the economy, market interest rates offered on Treasury bills and corporate debt instruments rose above Regulation Q ceilings, prompting the withdrawal of funds from depository institutions as investors sought instruments carrying a competitive rate of return. In such circumstances, rising market rates could cause a sudden outflow of deposits from commercial banks and thrifts.[4] These episodes of "disintermediation"—so called because they disrupted the typical function of savings institutions, which was to intermediate between suppliers and users of funds—contracted the capital available for new lending, affecting long-term mortgage loans especially severely.[5] An acute recession in the construction and housing industries quickly dampened activity in other sectors, restraining the broader economy. As the economy slowed and market interest rates fell, the mechanism quickly went into reverse: market interest rates below regulated ceilings drew capital back into depository institutions, which began lending anew, restarting economic expansion.

One could question the equity of this mechanism—the burden of restraint fell heavily on the housing sector—but not its effectiveness. These "stop-valves in the plumbing of finance," as journalist William Greider (1987: 177) referred to the Regulation Q ceilings, pumped with hydraulic efficiency. During periods in which market rates rose above regulated ceilings, the flow of credit to the economy was quite literally shut off. Unlike what occurs in a deregulated economic environment, in which credit becomes more expensive during periods of economic expansion, it was simply unavailable in the era before deregulation. The experience of Vivian Cates, who wrote to Congressman Wright Patman in the aftermath of a credit crunch in the summer of 1973, was typical.[6] Mrs. Cates's husband had been transferred to Crockett, Texas; as Mrs. Cates explained to the congressman, "Same job, same salary, different state." The Cates were homeowners and had managed to sell their attractive three-bedroom home with living room, family room, and carport the day after they put it up for sale. But by the time the Cates family arrived in Texas, market interest rates had risen above Regulation Q ceilings. With reputable employment in hand, and a down payment equivalent to 25 percent of the purchase price of a suitable home in Crockett, the Cates were denied a loan. "Because of the unsettled financial situation, the local savings and loan *made no loans of any kind to anybody* during part of July and August," Mrs. Cates wrote. There were no houses on the market during those months, and even the rental market had slowed to a trickle. She implored Patman, "I can feed my family meatless meals and more rice and beans, we can buy less clothing, wash it more often, and wear it longer, but we cannot postpone having a place to live."

However irrational such a system might appear to the contemporary financial consumer, Regulation Q ceilings had the significant advantage of imposing restraint at relatively low interest rates (Greider 1987: 177): interest rates only had to edge above the ceilings and the economy came to a grinding halt. As such, the typical postwar recession was mild and mercifully brief (Wojnilower 1980). In addition, using housing as the "balance wheel" of the economy required no direct action on the part of policymakers.[7] The levers and pulleys of Regulation Q turned first in one direction and then the other, starting and stopping the economy. That housing bore the brunt of every economic downturn generated some resistance from the building industry and from organized labor, but housing's special role as a countercyclical weight to the expansion and contraction of the economy was more or less accepted as sound economic management.

The social tensions embedded in this mechanism would become increasingly pronounced, however, as inflation became a persistent feature of the postwar economy. With inflation not just a cyclical occurrence but a permanent condition in the 1970s, Regulation Q's role in stabilizing the economy began to malfunction. In such an environment, market interest rates would remain continuously above Regulation Q ceilings, with the result that the depository institutions supporting housing experienced not a temporary outflow of funds but a hemorrhage. In addition to the routine angst of builders and mortgage lenders suddenly short on funds, policymakers now faced a much broader, and deeper, anger from individuals who found carrying out the mundane tasks of living without access to credit an unbearable hardship. As policymakers discovered, in an inflationary environment the task of balancing competing social priorities would become infinitely more complex.

Inflation and the Era of the Credit Crunch

As numerous commentators have observed, inflation is not exclusively, or even primarily, an economic problem, but rather a political one. Albert Wojnilower (1980: 325–326) perceptively writes that inflation is "the standard historical response for societies forced to reduce their economic aspirations—and is useful up to a point in averting divisive internal strife about how those burdens are to be distributed." Albert Hirschman (1980: 202) adds that for political authorities lacking the will or the ability to directly deny resources to particular groups in society, inflation is an indirect means of "saying no": by eroding purchasing power and the value of accumulated assets, inflation lowers living standards among social groups in society without requiring any explicit agreement that it is appropriate to do so. Of course, by the same token, the lack of an explicit social compact regarding redistribution means that, when exposed, inflation can itself become the focus of rather intense social conflict rather than a salve to ease such tensions. In short, inflation is historically a mutable phenomenon—a fact that is reflected in the controversy as to whether inflation is best considered cause or consequence of social conflict (Hirsch and Goldthorpe 1978).

Inflationary pressures first emerged in the U.S. economy in the mid-1960s, marking the transition from a period of easy abundance to an era defined by increasingly severe limits on the nation's prosperity. The existence of such limits required first and foremost that priorities be set and resources marshaled carefully to meet them. President Lyndon Johnson's failure to face up to this reality by choosing between financing the war in Vietnam or the Great Society's anti-poverty programs was widely blamed for unleashing the inflation demon as the nation struggled to meet its financial commitments. Only a few years later, President Richard Nixon reflected the new sobriety in policymaking, creating a National Goals Research Staff that was charged with defining a social agenda that could be achieved with strictly limited means (Collins 2000: 146).

Financial regulators were especially cognizant of this imperative; capital appeared to be among the most scarce of national resources—and the most vital to the nation's future well-being. As such, policymakers saw themselves as overseeing the rational distribution of credit between competing social priorities.[8] Through most of the postwar period, New Deal financial regulations had been an aid in accomplishing precisely this goal, but in the mid-1960s the system began to exhibit perverse effects. It was not only a matter of disintermediation occurring too frequently as cyclical tool became inflation pathology. In addition, a series of institutional innovations, in part a response to disintermediation, were restructuring the way the financial system worked, loosening the grip of regulations on some social actors while tightening the vise on others. Such inequities had always been part of macro-economic management—they were built into the strategy of leaning on housing to restrain the broader economy—but in the context of chronic inflation, these inequities began to assume unacceptable dimensions. As inflation accelerated, policymakers found themselves standing at the center of an increasingly bitter distributional struggle that pitted large corporations against urban residents, suburban homeowners, and proprietors of small business.

From the perspective of regulators, the key development in this emerging drama was the invention in the early 1960s of the negotiable certificate of deposit. A certificate of deposit (CD) is simply a form of time deposit—an account in which the depositor agrees to allow the lending institution access to funds for a specified period of time in exchange for a specific rate of interest. These instruments had been used since before the turn of the century and, in a formal, legal sense, had always been negotiable or marketable (Lindsay 1963: 620). But there was a glitch: certificates of deposit, typically issued in denominations of a million dollars or more, did not enjoy an active secondary market in which the certificates could be traded. This lack of an active secondary market meant that banks were essentially passive recipients of corporate funds (Cleveland and Huertas 1985).

That such passivity represented a possible problem became clear to banks in 1959—the first significant episode of disintermediation in the postwar period. As the business cycle peaked in 1959, Treasury bill rates rose above the regulated ceiling on time deposits, prompting corporations to withdraw funds from banks to purchase government securities (Knodell 1994: 127). This sudden loss of capital was startling to the large New York City banks who were principally affected by the 1959 disintermediation, and it hastened the efforts by one of these banks, National City Bank (the forerunner of today's Citicorp), to create a secondary market for certificates of deposit. In 1961, National City Bank arranged a relationship with a securities firm that agreed to buy and sell large-denomination CDs for its own account. In the following year, several other large money market banks joined National City Bank in offering negotiable certificates of deposit, and the market was open for business. The implication, recognized by many commentators at the time, was that banks could effectively bid for money, securing continual access to credit at a price (Wojnilower 1980: 285). Thus the liquidity of the new certificates, supported by a national market, gave banks a measure of flexibility in raising funds that they had not previously enjoyed.

In addition, regulators tended to accommodate banks' needs for funds, recognizing that heavy bank reliance on certificates of deposit introduced a new element of vulnerability into the financial system. During periods of rising interest rates, corporate treasurers would seek a higher yield on surplus funds, with the consequence that the banks would have difficulty "rolling over" maturing certificates. The prospect of a mass exodus of funds from the banking system as certificates of a given maturity fell due was as unwelcome to regulators as it was to the banks themselves. As a result, whenever market interest rates began to pinch against Regulation

Q ceilings, Federal Reserve officials responded by raising the ceiling on time deposits to avoid a sudden outflow of capital from the banks. By the time congressional hearings were held to consider the effect of negotiable certificates of deposit on the U.S. financial system in May and June 1966, this scenario had already played out not once or twice but on *four* separate occasions, the most recent in December 1965 when the Federal Reserve had raised the ceiling a full percentage point to 5.5 percent as the certificates came due.[9]

The problem was that, in protecting the banks, regulators shifted the burden of restraint elsewhere in the financial system. In particular, higher ceilings on certificates of deposit helped commercial banks to retain corporate funds, but also had the effect of pulling deposit money out of the thrifts, contracting funds available for mortgage lending.[10] This development was exacerbated by the banks' recent discovery of the household sector as an untapped source of capital (Cleveland and Huertas 1985). In the mid-1960s, banks introduced certificates of deposit in smaller denominations, directly competing for the thrifts' core constituency of household savers. Even more galling, the banks were advertising these so-called savings bonds—something that was unheard of at the time and considered not only unfair but also in poor taste. "I am haunted by the [memory] of walking down the street in Milwaukee," Senator William Proxmire reported, "and [seeing] these ads for CDs, very appealing ads for the saver, saying you can buy a certificate of deposit in fairly small denominations and get a yield that was better than the yield that you would get from savings and loan associations."[11] Proxmire's alarm was not entirely misplaced: the advertisements were garnering a strong response from consumers. "There is no way that our institutions can avoid losing money to commercial banks when ads like this appear in the *Chicago Tribune*," the president of the United States Savings and Loan League complained about an advertisement for a certificate paying a 9 percent return offered by the South Central Bank and Trust Company of Chicago. "This ad has been running in the *Tribune* for almost two weeks. . . . I understand they could have papered the walls in their offices with copies of this ad brought in from their own customers."[12]

These aggressive tactics were not only draining money from the thrifts, depriving the housing sector of financing, but also fueling inflationary dynamics in the economy. Inflation was set in motion when liquidity in markets outstripped the actual productive potential of the economy—as the monetarists crudely put it, it was a case of "too much money chasing too few goods." The result was that individuals bearing paper claims to wealth would inevitably come into conflict in the marketplace, bidding up the prices of a limited quantity of goods. These higher prices meant that a given quantity of money purchased a smaller amount of any commodity, leaving everything unchanged in real terms after prices had adjusted—everything, that is, except *expectations*. As individuals tried to stay one step ahead of inflation, a perverse psychology set in: if prices were certain to increase, then one was better off making a purchase today because it would cost more later. One was even better off if it was necessary to borrow to make the purchase as inflation would erode the value of the debt, with the result that the debt could be paid back in dollars that were worth less than the dollars originally borrowed. The end result was that inflation tended to accelerate, as business and consumers alike stepped up investment and consumption expenditures, pushing prices ever higher.[13]

Once inflationary expectations had been unleashed, regulators' only hope was to use pressure points to break the cycle. This was the impor tance of Regulation Q: a simple quantitative restraint denied credit to those who would otherwise add their demands to an overheating economy. If there simply was not money available to borrow to purchase a home or a new car, credit-constrained individuals would be rationed out of the market, slowing the inexorable spiral. But banks were increasingly finding ways to avoid the grip of Regulation Q ceilings. It was not only a matter of banks' increasing reliance on CDs to fund their lending activities. Other institutional innovations, such as the development of commercial paper and the emergence of the Eurodollar market were similarly loosening credit restraints on banks—and therefore on the business borrowers primarily served by banks. The Eurodollar market was an especially egregious case. This overseas market was outside of the regulatory controls of the United States government—or, for that matter, *any* government—with the result that money center banks[14] could avoid Regulation Q ceilings by borrowing dollars in the Euromarket through their foreign branches and then repatriating the dollars (Hawley 1984; Helleiner 1994). To be sure, the Eurodollar market was expensive—with prevailing rates in the market sometimes several points over regulated domestic credit markets—but banks could easily pass on the additional cost to borrowers.[15] Businesses in turn passed on higher interest costs to the final consumers of their products, leading some legislators to the paradoxical view that higher interest rates *caused* inflation.[16] The diagnosis was not entirely incorrect. The result of free-flowing, yet expensive credit in the Eurodollar market was that business could continue borrowing while inflation roared.

In this context, the Federal Reserve enjoined the banks to exercise restraint, curtailing unnecessary loans to business borrowers. Such moral suasion did not seem to have much effect, however, and banks failed to moderate lending activity even as inflationary pressures mounted. Thus policymakers took more direct action: when market interest rates again approached the legal ceiling on time deposits during the summer of 1966, the Federal Reserve held the ceiling firmly in place. The consequence of this decision was that banks faced an exodus of funds and businesses struggled to find financing, resulting in chaotic conditions in financial markets. The *Wall Street Journal* reported, "Banks are in the grip of the tightest money conditions since the 1920s, with so much of their deposits already on loan that they have little room to accommodate more loan demand."[17] Of course, banks were most eager to preserve their relationships to large corporate borrowers, and so reduced mortgage, consumer, and small business lending before turning away privileged business customers.[18] Ironically, this effect was amplified by the fact that the 1966 credit crunch impacted savings and loan associations even more severely than it did banks. Indeed, policymakers' attempts to defuse the escalating competition between banks and thrifts for funds only raised the likelihood that *both* institutions would lose funds to unregulated market instruments. As the American Bankers Association asserted, "The real culprit [in 1966] was the securities market, which attracted large amounts of individual savings."[19]

More generally, the 1966 credit crunch illustrated in dramatic terms the dilemma that confronted policymakers as they attempted to distribute capital between competing uses. As short-term business lenders, commercial banks were simply more nimble than the thrifts, whose portfolios were encumbered by long-term mortgage loans. As such, restraint that barely touched the banks could devastate the thrifts, strangling the housing industry. Duly chastened by this realization, the Federal Reserve soon resumed its practice of adjusting upward the ceiling on certificates of deposit whenever market interest rates began to pinch. The Federal Reserve also imposed a two-tier rate structure on certificates of deposit, applying a lower ceiling to the smaller-denomination instruments that would otherwise draw "hot" money from the household savers who *Business Week* noted had been newly sensitized to market rates of return.[20] In addition, legislation modifying Regulation Q by allowing thrifts to pay a slightly higher interest rate on passbook savings accounts than commercial banks—referred to as the "differential"—moved quickly through Congress.[21]

These measures provided marginal relief to the thrift industry, but they did little to resolve the underlying problem in the broader financial system: tight credit affected homeowners, consumers, and small business disproportionately, denying these sectors access to credit during periods of higher interest rates.[22] What is more, by the late 1960s another victim of inflation had joined the thrifts and also began clamoring for relief. State and municipal governments, whose bond sales were regulated by strict usury limits, discovered that they too confronted their own version of disintermediation. In Los Angeles, for example, the city charter placed a limit of 6 percent on the interest rate at which the city could market its debt. As market interest rates surged past this limit, bond issues to finance various infrastructure projects in Los Angeles failed to raise even a single bid. Construction of new facilities at the airport, improvements to the Los Angeles harbor, programmed expenditures for the water and power departments, and street repairs were all abruptly suspended as funds evaporated from the city's coffers.[23] In cities across the nation, the scenario was repeated, draining capital from the public sector. In New York City, Mayor John Lindsay complained that it had become almost impossible for the city to borrow to finance its public housing programs.[24] Although the cities had received an infusion of federal money following racial riots, now inflation was effectively washing away the money, leaving urban centers in as degraded a condition as ever. "There are emotions in the cities that can be as disruptive as 1967, 1968, 1969," San Francisco Mayor Joseph Alioto warned. "It would be a serious mistake to think the cities cannot erupt."[25]

As legislators examined the problem, conducting an endless series of hearings, they kept coming back to what seemed to be the very essence of the matter: *there was only so much money.* Only so much money for business. Only so much money for housing. Only so much for the cities. As such, legislators directed their efforts toward locating new sources of capital that could be channeled toward housing, urban problems, and small business. "Unless we find some money, *big money,* there is not much we can do about housing," Chairman Patman soberly assessed.[26] But legislators' most innovative attempts to tap new sources of financing sooner or later ran into the same inescapable reality: capital was available in a strictly limited supply.

A particularly telling episode was Congress's creation in 1968 of a new federal agency, the Government National Mortgage Association (GNMA), to support a market for mortgage-backed securities.[27] Mortgages are long-term loans; for this reason, they are not attractive to investors such as pension funds that require liquidity. Policymakers reasoned that one way to bring new capital into housing would be to transform the mortgage instrument from a loan into a security that could be traded in the capital markets. This was done by assembling a pool of mortgages, standardizing them by requiring that they meet certain criteria, and then selling participations entitling each investor to a prorated share of the cash flow generated by the underlying mortgages (Sellon and VanNahmen 1988: 9). The securitization of housing finance was enormously successful, and as policymakers had hoped, it helped to stabilize the mortgage market. But, as always, there was a complication: policymakers soon realized that rather than drawing new capital into housing, mortgage-backed securities were pulling money out of the thrifts.[28] In addition to Treasury bills or corporate bonds, savers could now choose from a range of agency securities in which to invest when market interest rates rose above regulated rates on passbook savings accounts. *There was only so much money.*

In fact, the inexorable logic of inflation suggested that even had legislators somehow managed to conjure up new capital for housing, small business, or the cities, they would have only added to price pressures. "Can the housing problem be solved with more money?" Congressman Chalmers Wylie asked his colleagues. "We have to be careful when we are weighing these priorities as to how much money we put into the housing industry. We do not want to increase inflation again. This is the edge Congress finds itself on."[29] Economists agreed. The iconic liberal Lester Thurow told policymakers, "You can't [increase] housing expenditures without cutting something else." He added, "And you gentlemen are the ones essentially who determine national priorities."[30] In a world in which capital was inherently scarce—a condition policymakers accepted with a certain amount of existential angst—everything pointed to the role of Congress in exerting the authority that Thurow bestowed on it.

Reflecting this imperative, credit allocation schemes were continually on the legislative agenda from the mid-1960s to the mid-1970s, with nearly 100 separate bills under consideration in the 1974 legislative session alone.[31] Although the details of these schemes varied, the basic premise was the same: if government controls in the form of Regulation Q ceilings were distorting flows of credit in the economy, then government actions could be devised to counteract the distortion, directing scarce capital where it was needed. In 1966, Congress passed legislation authorizing the Federal Reserve to purchase the obligations of the federal housing agencies, channeling capital directly into mortgage finance.[32] The Federal Reserve failed to act on this authority, however.[33] In 1969, frustrated legislators threatened to strip the Federal Reserve of its new powers and instead pass authority to purchase agency securities to the Treasury Department, which they hoped would make better use of it.[34]

In the same year, Congress gave standby authority to President Nixon to impose a voluntary credit restraint program such as had been used in the Korean War.[35] Nixon also demurred. In 1971, Congress extended this authority to the Federal Reserve,[36] which grudgingly drew up guidelines for priority lending in consultation with the banks.[37] In a bizarre turn of events, Federal Reserve Chairman Arthur Burns was later called before legislators and accused of attempting to exercise suasion on the banks in an inappropriate manner.[38] The experience only confirmed Burns's view that credit allocation was a distasteful activity that would inevitably plunge the Federal Reserve into politics.

Over the years, this game of hot potato highlighted the basic problem with credit allocation. Even when policymakers agreed that allocation was necessary, they also agreed it was better for *someone else* to do it. Congress insisted that the Federal Reserve was using the "Nation's credit" and therefore had an obligation to establish priorities;[39] the Federal Reserve argued that setting priorities was the proper responsibility of the president or, preferably, Congress.[40] The final showdown came over a legislative proposal that would have required the Federal Reserve to impose variable reserve requirements on bank loans for different purposes.[41] Banks belonging to the Federal Reserve System were required to set aside a certain percentage of the deposits they collected as reserves held in the Federal Reserve's vault. Because these reserves were "sterile"— they did not earn any interest while sitting in the central bank's vault— they represented a cost to the banks. Each dollar in the vault was a dollar not on loan and therefore not earning money for the bank. In 1970, Andrew Brimmer, a Federal Reserve governor, had suggested that setting reserve requirements in a discretionary manner offered policymakers a useful device for allocating credit. Banks engaged in loans supporting speculative activities would face higher reserve requirements; policymakers would impose lower reserve requirements on loans directed to housing or small business. The Federal Reserve could use this tool to make some loans more profitable than others, directing credit to appropriate uses. Congress seized on the idea, quickly drawing up legislation.

But as had occurred with other forms of credit allocation, the proposal drew intense opposition. Chairman Burns repudiated Brimmer, insisting that the Federal Reserve should not determine social priorities.[42] Involvement in the scheme would draw the Federal Reserve into politics, compromising the ability of the Federal Reserve to control inflation. In addition, Burns suggested that business could easily evade the controls. One control would lead to another, until the whole jerry-built structure collapsed, an ill-conceived bureaucratic disaster. Treasury Secretary William

Simon was even more unequivocal, warning that the proposal would create "a national credit police state."[43] The treasury secretary proceeded to paint a chilling portrait of a totalitarian society in which a "credit czar"[44] controlled all citizen initiative, dictating financial choices down to the last minute detail. Simon queried:

> Would a businessman who wanted to add a wing to his store and hire a dozen people be able to obtain a loan? Under this law, he would have to stand in line behind low-income housing, even though the tenants in low-income housing might be looking for a job.
>
> Would a housewife who wanted to buy a new refrigerator at a department store be denied the use of her charge account because someone in Washington thinks she can do just as well with the old refrigerator?
>
> Would a family of six that wanted a station wagon be able to borrow the money, or would it be limited to a smaller car that Federal officials thought would be better for the country?[45]

The answers to Simon's questions were clear: "Some borrowers could not obtain funds at any price, creating serious hardships for them, while others could obtain larger amounts of money than they actually needed."[46] Ironically, these questions were already being answered in much the same way, day after day, under the existing system of financial regulation. In the context of inflation, Regulation Q constrained some borrowers severely, while providing others virtually unlimited access to credit. In fact, Simon had gone to the crux of the matter: either policymakers would have to return to a world in which credit restraints bound all borrowers tightly—the direction in which Brimmer's proposal pointed—or housing and other similarly constrained sectors such as state and local government would have to be unshackled from these restraints. The former choice would place policymakers in the position of continually having to decide how to allocate the burden of restraint—with access to credit becoming increasingly politicized as policymakers weighed the claims of competing social groups. The latter choice meant that, at least within certain limits, the *market* could do the choosing, relieving policymakers of an unpalatable task.

It was perhaps not surprising that, as the debate over credit allocation ran its tortured course in Congress, deregulating interest rates became an increasingly attractive option to policymakers. What was surprising was that deregulation would alter the very nature of the political logic that policymakers applied so assiduously to the problem before them. In the context of deregulation, capital would not be limited, but *abundant,* transforming political constraints. Ironically, the struggle for the deregulation of interest rates would politicize credit more intensely than ever before, only to subsequently remove credit from the reach of politics in ways that policymakers could not have imagined.

The Struggle to Deregulate Interest Rates

As policymakers turned their attention to deregulating interest rates in the early 1970s, they faced a daunting challenge. Although interest rate ceilings on large corporate certificates of deposit had been removed without controversy in response to the bankruptcy of the Penn Central Railroad in 1970,[47] the deregulation of consumer savings deposits would be a different story. Nearly every major interest group was staunchly opposed to the removal of interest rate ceilings from consumer savings deposits. For commercial banks, interest rate ceilings on consumer savings accounts represented an inexpensive source of deposit money. For thrifts, who under Regulation Q were allowed to pay a small differential over the rate offered by commercial banks, interest rate ceilings offered a modest degree of protection from bank competition. For homebuilders and organized labor, the interest rate differential for thrifts was the last bastion shielding housing from the chaos of the free market. In short, policymakers did not have a constituency for interest rate deregulation, and they faced some very powerful opposition. To prevail, policymakers would need a new protagonist in the unfolding deregulation battle.

Initial attempts at financial deregulation drew on President Nixon's influential Hunt Commission, which provided a blueprint for several successive legislative attempts to reform financial institutions in the 1970s.[48] The Hunt Commission report proposed a relatively straightforward formula for dealing with the nation's financial woes. Because the malfunctioning of the financial system involved interest rate ceilings strangling some sectors of the economy while leaving other sectors virtually unrestrained, the solution quite clearly was to remove the ceilings so that market forces, rather than price controls, determined the allocation of capital between competing uses. The difficulty was that, once unencumbered from interest rate ceilings, thrifts' concentration on long-term mortgage lending would not allow them to pay interest rates on deposits that would be competitive with rates paid by commercial banks and other competitors.[49] The Hunt Commission's solution was to gradually liberalize the restrictions that required thrifts to concentrate a certain percentage of their portfolio in mortgage lending. By increasing their involvement in more lucrative consumer loans and other short-term lending, thrifts would be able to augment their earnings such that they could afford to pay competitive rates on deposits.

But this proposal—introduced in the Senate as the Financial Institutions Act of 1973—pleased almost no one. The thrifts were in favor of broadened powers to make consumer loans and otherwise diversify their portfolios, but they were emphatically unwilling to give up the differential they were allowed under Regulation Q over the interest rates that commercial banks could pay on savings deposits.[50] The commercial banks, for their part, also showed no great enthusiasm for the Financial Institutions Act.[51] Although the larger money center banks were prepared to compete aggressively for deposits, smaller banks were in a position that was similar to that of thrifts, without the earnings that would support a more expensive deposit base. They also did not welcome the increased competition from thrifts that would result from extending thrifts' lending activities into areas typically dominated by smaller banks.[52] The housing industry disliked provisions that would allow thrifts to diversify out of mortgages for fear that this would restrict financing available for housing.[53] Organized labor opposed the provisions for related reasons; unemployment in the construction trades was higher than 10 percent at the time, and anything that further reduced employment in these sectors would be detrimental to the labor movement.[54]

Enter the consumer-saver. This new, almost mythic figure on the American economic landscape first came to policymakers' attention in the summer of 1973 as another episode of disintermediation threatened to wreck havoc on the financial system.[55] In the years since the credit crunch of 1966, thrift institutions aided by the differential had recovered their position relative to commercial banks.[56] In this context, the Federal Reserve deemed it appropriate to take a series of measures specifically aimed at assisting commercial banks that were losing funds to market instruments at an alarming rate.[57] Regulators allowed commercial banks to introduce what was colorfully named the "wild card" certificate: this four-year time deposit was offered in denominations as small as $1,000 *and carried no interest rate ceiling.*[58] Because money market mutual funds typically required a minimum investment of $10,000, the wild card was something truly novel in American financial life: an instrument that offered competitive rates of return to the small saver.[59] The response to the wild card was nothing short of phenomenal: savers of modest means rushed to cash in their passbook accounts to purchase wild cards.

Predictably, the new certificates resulted in a hemorrhage of funds from the thrifts. Introduced in July, the wild card certificate was withdrawn by alarmed regulators in October. The scenario repeated itself in the following year, however, when Citicorp marketed a variable rate security similarly aimed at savers of modest means: the note carried an interest rate that fluctuated with the Treasury bill rate and could be purchased in denominations of $1,000 after an initial purchase of five notes. Ironically, in introducing the note, Citicorp was simply reaping the fruits of its own labor years earlier—it was the creation of the negotiable certificate of deposit that "encouraged the growth of a class of savers relatively more aware of financial market developments and more willing to respond to them."[60] In the years since National City Bank had introduced the negotiable certificate of deposit, however, the bank had reorganized itself as a holding company consisting of a larger parent corporation, Citicorp, which owned a bank, among other businesses. Restructuring itself as a bank holding company allowed Citicorp to take advantage of a loophole in the law that had neglected to place these entities under the control of financial regulators.[61] Thus, in introducing the variable rate note, Citicorp was not bound by Regulation Q or other banking regulations; it simply exercised its prerogative, like any nonbank corporation, to market its debt. There was of course a critical difference between Citicorp and a corporation like Sears, which similarly planned to tap into consumer savings to fund its growing financial services business. When savers purchased the Citicorp note, they assumed—*wrongly*—that the (federally insured) bank stood behind it, and therefore that the investment was more secure than in fact was the case.[62] A seemingly safe investment carrying a competitive market rate available in small denominations was irresistible: Citicorp initially planned a $250 million offering, but soon raised the issue to $850 million—at the time, the largest corporate securities offering to the public ever made.[63]

Policymakers again faced a choice between bringing errant market innovators back under the umbrella of regulation and further liberalizing the regulations that constrained Citicorp's competitors. The first course of action was difficult, given strong public enthusiasm for the issue. "It is hard to believe that responsible people would seriously advance the thesis that large investors are somehow entitled to a higher return on their money than consumers," Citibank complained loudly, invoking the consumer-saver.[64] Yet further deregulation presented the same problem that had stalled earlier financial reform efforts: encumbered by long-term mortgage lending, thrifts did not have the earnings capacity to pay market interest rates for deposits, even if legal ceilings on allowable interest rates were eliminated.[65] But the fact that the value of the Citicorp issue *floated* with the market offered policymakers an important lesson. Citicorp's loan portfolio was essentially on a variable basis—short-term assets al-lowed the bank to quickly adjust earnings to changing market condi-tions.[66] It was this flexibility in earnings that now enabled Citicorp to offer a variable rate of return to savers. *If one side of the balance sheet floated, the other side could, as well.* Applying the same logic to the thrifts suggested a way to finally break the impasse in Congress: if thrifts' earn-ings from their mortgage portfolios could fluctuate along with the cost of attracting and retaining deposits, policymakers reasoned, they could re-main mortgage lenders *and* compete successfully with commercial banks for household savings.[67]

When in 1975 the Federal Home Loan Bank Board, the thrift industry regulator, introduced a proposal to allow variable rate mortgages for federally chartered savings and loan associations, a resolution to the stalemate on financial reform seemed to be in the offing. The thrift lobby hinted that, if given variable rate mortgages, it would consider support-ing the repeal of Regulation Q—and, along with it, the differential that protected housing.[68] The American Bankers Association similarly indi-cated a willingness to consider exchanging expanded powers for thrifts for the elimination of the differential.[69] The housing industry maintained its opposition to the elimination of interest rate ceilings, but manifested some enthusiasm for variable rate mortgages, suggesting the outline of a possible compromise.[70] Indeed, the financial deregulation story might have ended here, with the consumer-saver as its hero, except that the consumer-saver turned out to be a somewhat fickle creature. In fact, the consumer-saver was little more than a convenient fiction: consumers were *borrowers,* as well as savers.

Initially, it seemed, financial deregulation could serve both consumers equally well: the same individuals who *as borrowers* were denied access to credit when the financial system seized up were also eager *as savers* to receive market rates of return on deposits. Motivated by such concerns, consumer organizations such as the Consumer's Union, the Consumer Federation of America, and Ralph Nader's Public Citizen had begun to actively campaign for the repeal of Regulation Q. But the proposal for variable rate mortgages revealed that consumers were in fact deeply con-flicted about financial deregulation. In the mid-1970s, the prospect of a world in which *all* interest rates could fluctuate freely was still foreign to the average consumer—and not a little sinister. In such a world, an unex-pected shift in the economic climate could saddle consumers with an obligation that they had not planned for, threatening financial ruin. As one community organizer asked,

How many steelworkers, how many autoworkers, how many public service employees, how many people working in any area can commit themselves to a 35-year mortgage with a fluctuating interest rate? As his mortgage goes up, will his employer raise his hourly rate to help meet the unanticipated, inflationary increased cost? If this answer is no, then where does he get the increased money? From another loan? Perhaps a second fluctuating variable mortgage?[71]

Confronted with such objections, advocates of the variable rate mortgage insisted that what was required was a process of consumer education.[72] Just as the consumer had learned—through advertising and constant media coverage—to be attentive to formerly esoteric concepts such as the yield on an investment, so consumers could also learn that the variable interest rate mortgage was an aid—not a threat—to personal prosperity. Unfortunately, this educational campaign was already under way at the state level—where some states had been experimenting with variable rate mortgages for a number of years—and it was not going well. Part of the problem was that in many states where adjustable rate mortgages had been approved for state-chartered savings and loan institutions, these institutions had instituted variable rate mortgages that could only be adjusted in one direction: *up*. As thrift institutions attempted to increase their customers' mortgage payments, these "escalator clause" provisions provoked spirited protests around the country.[73] In one such episode, in September 1966, Prudential Savings and Loan of Los Angeles informed customers that their mortgage rates were being "escalated," prompting 7,000 irate borrowers to band together to form the Homeowners Anti-Escalation Association. For three weeks the association picketed Prudential during the day and filled high school gymnasiums for mass protest meetings at night, forcing the bewildered savings and loan association to both rescind the increases and promise to never again include an escalator clause in a mortgage contract.[74]

Similar incidents were reported in scattered locations across the country, but the largest and most sustained protest occurred in Wisconsin, where the state trade association had written an escalator clause into its standard mortgage application.[75] In 1973 and 1974, Wisconsin thrifts began to exercise these clauses, especially in the Milwaukee and Racine areas, where approximately 20,000 homeowners received notices that their mortgage payments would be increased.[76] In Milwaukee, a local Catholic priest affiliated with the community organization Taxes and Taxpayers (TNT), led a social movement protesting these increases. TNT had been involved in property tax and street safety issues, but it quickly made the escalator clause its primary focus of attention, sending angry members to the shareholder meetings of several Milwaukee savings and loan associations. When savings and loan executives rebuffed demands to strike the escalator provisions from mortgage contracts, TNT joined with a newly formed Racine organization, Customers United to Oppose First Federal (CUTOFF), in organizing a mass protest at the State Capitol in Madison.[77] Fifty-five chartered buses transported 2,500 demonstrators to the capitol rotunda. With cries of "De-escalate! De-escalate!" these protestors brought the issue to the attention of state legislators, who introduced two bills into the 1974 legislative session demanding elimination of the escalator clauses from Wisconsin mortgages.[78] As these bills worked their way through committee hearings, CUTOFF took more direct action, securing commitments from members who collectively agreed to withdraw more than $1 million in deposits from First Federal of Racine.[79]

Although the Wisconsin protest may have been unusual in its vigor, the sentiment into which it tapped was widespread, making the variable rate mortgage a dead letter in Congress in 1975.[80] The Federal Home Loan Bank Board did not need formal congressional approval to implement its variable rate mortgage proposal, but the Board was unlikely to proceed without congressional support and quietly dropped the proposal when legislators responded sympathetically to popular outrage. Without the variable rate mortgage, the progress of financial deregulation slowed: a somewhat more populist version of financial reform legislation emerged in the House following the release of the massive Financial Institutions and the Nation's Economy (FINE) study in 1976,[81] but quickly encountered resistance from virtually the same configuration of interest groups as had opposed the earlier Financial Institutions Act.[82] To some degree, pressure for immediate action on financial reform was lessened by the fact that institutional responses to earlier rounds of disintermediation had made the housing sector more resilient in the face of high market interest rates. The securitization of housing finance, initiated in the late 1960s to draw new investors into mortgage lending, had proceeded apace in the intervening years. In 1970, policymakers created another agency, the Federal Home Loan Mortgage Corporation, with responsibility for purchasing conventional mortgages from thrifts and repackaging them as securities for sale in developing secondary markets. This process of securitization of mortgage finance increased the liquidity of the mortgage instrument while paradoxically creating another source of competition to the thrifts, with agency paper providing an alternative investment option.[83]

The thrifts, as a result, continued to suffer the consequences of disin-termediation, although the housing industry was increasingly insulated from sudden changes in the direction of credit flows. The newest challenge to the thrifts was Merrill Lynch's introduction in 1977 of its Cash Management Account, a money market mutual fund that for the first time allowed consumers to write checks against their accounts. Money market mutual funds had been available since 1972, but before Merrill Lynch attached a checking account to its fund—an innovation that was deliberately intended to suggest "bank" to nervous investors (Nocera 1994)—consumers had shied away from these instruments. Now, with a massive advertising campaign, the era of the money market mutual fund had begun. Regulators saw the threat to the thrift industry immediately and quickly authorized depository institutions to offer an instrument that mimicked the features of the money market mutual fund: the money market certificate was a six-month time deposit that paid an interest rate tied to the yield on Treasury bills, available in a minimum denomination of $10,000.

Critically for the evolving struggle over financial deregulation, the introduction of the money market certificate stirred the consumer-saver to action. At the time regulators introduced the money market certificate, consumer frustration with limited investment opportunities was growing. In the mid-1970s, the passbook savings account available at thrift institutions remained locked at 5.25 percent—5 percent for the comparable account at a commercial bank—and certificates of deposit purchased in denominations of less than $100,000 offered only marginally higher rates. Treasury bills had long been the investment of choice for savers of modest means, but this investment opportunity was curtailed in 1970 when Treasury officials increased the minimum denomination on Treasury bill notes from $1,000 to $10,000. The wild card certificate issued in 1973 had similarly offered small savers a brief taste for market rates, but was quickly withdrawn by regulators. Money market mutual funds provided the only exception to these restrictions, but in recent years regulators had discussed proposals to subject these instruments to new rules, threatening to place market interest rates once again out of the reach of the small saver.[84] It was this last development that prompted Dorothy Lichty of Port Edwards, Wisconsin, to write to Senator Proxmire in March 1976. As Mrs. Lichty explained to the senator, she did not "happen to have $100,000 laying around," but had been able to invest her small capital in a money market mutual fund, earning 11 or 12 percent, "just like the big guys." She observed, "Now the government is galloping to someone else's rescue—*certainly not mine*—and will tell me that I can only put my money in savings deposit if I want to be liquid—none of those high interest rates for me!"[85]

By limiting money market certificates to a minimum denomination of $10,000, regulators unwittingly fed into the popular resentment that Dorothy Lichty expressed so pointedly. Regulators viewed the $10,000 minimum denomination as striking a balance between the thrifts' need to retain deposits—it was the more affluent savers who were likely to be "interest-rate sensitive"—and what thrift institutions could reasonably afford to pay for deposits.[86] As it happened, regulators miscalculated on both sides of this equation. Within eight months of the introduction of the money market certificates, $100 billion had flowed into these accounts, providing thrift institutions with ample funds, but placing the institutions in a severe profit squeeze as they struggled to manage the cost of these new deposits.[87]

An even greater surprise came when the Gray Panthers, a grassroots organization advocating on behalf of older Americans, filed suit in federal court against the Federal Reserve Board, the Federal Home Loan Bank Board, the Federal Deposit Insurance Corporation, and the treasury secretary for discriminating against small savers. The Panthers' suit argued that, in an environment in which inflation was running in the double digits, requiring individuals of modest means to place their savings in passbook accounts paying 5.25 percent meant that their money was actually *losing* value over time.[88] The suit was joined by the California Legislative Council for Older Americans and the Council for Economic Democracy. A variety of other citizen action groups, from the American Association of Retired Persons (AARP) to Ralph Nader's Public Citizen, were not formally party to the suit, but endorsed the campaign. The Gray Panthers demanded that the regulators introduce the money market certificates in minimum denominations as low as $500.[89] If regulators were unwilling to create such an account, then the Panthers demanded that financial institutions inform the public that the interest rate paid on deposits was lower than the inflation rate by placing the following notice on all advertising: "WARNING: SAVINGS DEPOSITS MAY BE DANGEROUS TO YOUR WEALTH!"[90]

While none of the regulatory agencies took the Panthers' suit seriously, they did recognize the underlying inequities in the financial system to which the Panthers were responding.[91] More critically, the Panthers' suit provided frustrated legislators much-needed momentum on the issue. Congress wasted no time in seizing the issue—six separate hearings were held in the spring and summer of 1979. In short order, the regulators introduced a series of proposals designed to deal with the "small saver

problem." The centerpiece of regulators' proposals—a five-year certificate that offered an interest rate indexed to but *below* the Treasury bill
rate—was rejected by the Gray Panthers as wholly inadequate.[92] The
Federal Home Loan Bank Board was adamant that lowering the denomination on money market certificates would bankrupt the thrift industry
and in this context reintroduced its variable rate mortgage proposal, now
promoted as an instrument to enable thrifts to meet the costs of the new
money market certificates.[93] President Jimmy Carter intervened, using an
address before Congress to urge legislators to phase out interest rate ceilings, authorize variable rate mortgages, liberalize lending powers, and
allow depository institutions to provide interest-bearing checking accounts.[94] This last issue had become entangled in a court ruling that
determined that the popular interest-bearing checking accounts offered
by some New England savings associations were in violation of the 1933
prohibition against the payment of interest on demand deposits. A U.S.
Court of Appeals decision prohibited the accounts unless they were ex-
pressly permitted by Congress and gave legislators a deadline of January
1, 1980, to resolve the issue or face suspension of the accounts.[95] This
ruling became a vehicle for the much broader deregulation agenda outlined in Carter's address. Spurred on by the courts, the Depository Institutions Deregulation and Monetary Control Act became law in the spring
of 1980.[96]

The elimination of interest rate controls from consumer deposits was
the culmination of developments that had begun years before with the
introduction of the negotiable certificate of deposit. The result was an
economy that was increasingly inoculated from periodic episodes of credit
restraint. Interest rate ceilings no longer acted as "speed limits" for the
economy: credit simply flowed to the highest bidder. Similarly, the advent
of variable rate financing contributed to a world in which, as financier
Henry Kaufman (1986: 52) observed warily, "credit has no guardian."
When lending was based on fixed-rate contracts, rising interest rates constrained credit expansion as loans extended at lower interest rates quickly
became unprofitable, imposing a financial burden on institutions that
held these loans in their portfolios.[97] With variable rate financing, there
was no such restraint as lenders immediately passed on the costs associated with higher interest rates to borrowers. In these circumstances, lenders were free to do a volume business, pressing new loans on borrowers
without limit (Kaufman 1986: 21). The securitization of credit—the practice of purchasing loans from financial intermediaries and repackaging
them as securities for resale in secondary markets—similarly changed the
nature of the credit relationship. If a lender did not hold a loan for thirty

years, but perhaps only for a few days as the loan was repackaged and sold off as a security, there was no need to pore over every detail of a loan application and no need to make inscrutable judgments regarding the "character" of the borrower—long the stock-in-trade of the banker.[98] As one mortgage banker reported, "We can make a loan today, and we can sell it into the GNMA markets tomorrow. We can sell it by snapping our fingers and making a telephone call and in blocks of one million dollars."[99] The ability to sell mortgage (and eventually consumer) loans in the second-ary market also meant that financial intermediaries could now afford to offer depositors a competitive rate of interest. The whole circle came to a dizzying close: Vivian Cates would get her mortgage loan, Dorothy Lichty her market rate of return. The credit expansion had begun.

Prelude to Financialization

Since the early 1970s, the U.S. economy had undergone a remarkable transformation. In 1973, Milton Stewart, the president of the National Small Business Association, told legislators, "We live, and will live for the rest of our lives, in a capital-short and credit-short society. Everybody wants more money than there is available." He added soberly, "That is not going to change."[100] Stewart followed this prediction with another. Unless housing, small business, municipal finance, and consumers re-ceived relief, Stewart suggested, legislators would see a surge of popular anger so potent that they would wonder whether they had time-traveled back to the late nineteenth century—an era when agrarians, laborers, and Western miners made common cause in vigorously contesting the East-ern money trust.

Notwithstanding Stewart's dramatic imagery, he was wrong on both counts—and for related reasons. Even as Stewart uttered these words, the U.S. economy was undergoing a subtle shift that would fundamen-tally alter the political terrain for decades to come. As housing experts noted, beginning in the mid-1970s, the problem for the housing sector was not so much the availability of credit as its price. The development of agency securities, enabling housing to tap into capital markets during periods of credit restraint, contributed to the change. So too did the new money market certificates. As credit markets tightened in 1978, money market certificates allowed thrifts to adjust the interest rates they offered savers to changing market conditions, and housing rode the storm. But it was the removal of interest rate ceilings from consumer savings deposits that definitively marked the transition to an economy in which price, not availability, would determine access to credit: "Borrowers are able to

obtain credit if they are able and willing to pay the going rate," Federal
Reserve Governor Lyle Gramley observed in 1981.[101]

They mostly *were* willing. One of the great surprises of financial deregulation was how high interest rates could climb before consumers or
businesses pulled back from borrowing (Wojnilower 1985: 352; cf. Greider 1987). Without the mechanism of Regulation Q excluding borrowers from markets, *all* could seek credit, with the result that interest rates
in the economy were bid sharply higher. The presumption, of course, was
that the higher cost of credit would discourage some borrowers from
obtaining loans, imposing restraint as the economy accelerated. In this
manner, the price mechanism would ration individuals from the market
in much the same way as had formerly been achieved by rickety interest
rate controls. Indeed, the notion that the price mechanism could substitute for more heavy-handed means of rationing credit had been part of
policymakers' gambit in endorsing the deregulation of interest rates. But
the price mechanism largely failed to ration as Americans continued borrowing regardless of price. In the context of institutional innovations
occurring in financial markets, the taps on credit were opened wide.

The result was a kind of paradox. Policymakers had hoped that in removing interest rate ceilings they would relieve themselves of responsibility for overseeing the distribution of scarce capital between competing
uses, leaving this politically difficult task to the market. Ironically, rather
than offering an indirect means to allocate credit between uses, deregulation made the entire problem of allocation a moot issue. In a deregulated
environment, credit flowed freely across the economy, no longer constrained by interest rate ceilings nor, it seemed, by any reluctance on the
part of borrowers to meet its high price. But the high price of credit made
for very different politics than had the shared rationing experience that
Stewart so vividly described. There would be no reconvening of the Populist Party in the late twentieth century after all.

This was evident in the fate of the consumer movement, which was effectively demobilized by its very success in achieving the deregulation of
interest rates. The neutralization of the consumer movement reflected
both aspects of the brave new financial world in which consumers suddenly found themselves. First, freely flowing credit no longer constricted
by interest rate ceilings disorganized the broad-based coalition that had
initially stirred legislators to action. In a regulated financial environment,
Mrs. Cates's plight had extended from urban ghettos to tree-lined streets
in the suburbs. Only a few years later, Mrs. Cates lived in a starkly different world: financial deregulation divided individuals into those who,
with proper credit histories and formalized relationships to financial

institutions, had unrestricted access to credit, and those, euphemistically referred to as the "unbanked," who did not. Credit activism moved from the town hall and the labor union to the soup kitchen, developing from a preoccupation of middle-class homeowners into a movement directed primarily at issues of urban poverty.[102]

The second outcome of removing interest rate ceilings from consumer savings deposits—the sharply higher cost of credit—narrowed the scope of consumer activism in a different way. Importantly, it was not credit-constrained borrowers, such as Mrs. Cates, who had carried forward the struggle for deregulation. Instead, it was the *consumer-saver* who was the leading advocate of deregulation. These consumers, led by organizations such as the Consumer Federation of America, Ralph Nader's Public Citizen, and the AARP, confidently asserted that Americans were ready to accept higher loan costs in exchange for a better return on savings. This position, of course, reflected the consumer movement's calculation that the gains accruing to the consumer-saver following deregulation were likely to offset any losses to the consumer-borrower. But consumer advocates did not anticipate how high interest rates would climb in a deregulated economy. They also mistakenly assumed that the consumer-saver and the consumer-borrower were *different* people.[103] Indeed, the image of elderly ladies in retirement communities subsidizing (presumably more affluent)[104] homeowners had driven the consumer movement to a near frenzy. But as interest rates increased not only selectively on mortgage loans but *across* the economy, and as elderly ladies faced a plethora of new fees on their bank accounts, a belated realization set in: the interests of savers and borrowers blurred in a deregulated environment.[105] The Consumer Federation of America sheepishly acknowledged that it had been "mistaken" in supporting interest rate deregulation;[106] other community and public interest organizations called for the reimposition of interest rate controls.[107] Confronted with this new, more complex reality, the agenda of the consumer movement constricted, turning away from a broad concern with the structure of the financial system as a whole to focus on narrower issues such as disclosure requirements and financial privacy.[108]

The experience of the consumer movement reflected a broader political shift in U.S. society as the alchemy of financial deregulation transformed constraints into new opportunities. But if it seemed that all the grim certainties of the 1970s had been somehow suspended, this judgment was premature. As the decade closed, two nagging worries lingered on the horizon. The first was that inflationary pressures would accelerate in a deregulated environment, once again forcing difficult decisions on policymakers who appeared to have momentarily escaped them. Indeed, financial economists who observed credit working itself free from institutional constraints predicted that inflation would accelerate sharply in the 1980s (Kaufman 1986; Wojnilower 1980).[109] The second worry was closely related. Although financial deregulation allowed policymakers a reprieve from decisions about how capital should be distributed between competing uses, large projected government deficits in the early 1980s threatened to revisit these pressures on policymakers with a vengeance. Observers feared that government deficits would swamp capital markets, forcing the cost of credit so high that the market's rationing mechanism would finally slam into place, excluding all other users of capital. As it turned out, neither of these scenarios materialized. The tenuous balance would hold, although the resolution to each of these problems would reinforce the shift to a high interest rate regime and an accelerated pace of credit expansion, both developments in turn contributing to the turn to finance in the U.S. economy.

CHAPTER FOUR

The Reagan Administration Discovers the Global Economy

CHAPTER 3 DESCRIBED how policymakers responded to the social tensions resulting from the eruption of inflation in the 1960s and 1970s by turning to the market. Deregulation of financial markets offered policymakers a reprieve from difficult political choices, while also creating conditions conducive to the financialization of the U.S. economy. This chapter continues the story but shifts the focus from social crisis to the emerging fiscal crisis that confronted the state in the Reagan era. If the experience of the 1960s and 1970s first presented policymakers with the problem of capital scarcity, this problem would re-emerge with a vengeance in the 1980s. While in the 1960s and 1970s the government had been one of a number of borrowers competing with business and housing for funds in crowded capital markets, in the 1980s government deficits on an unprecedented scale threatened to preempt all other borrowers. Government deficits also threatened to ignite inflationary pressures that policymakers were struggling to contain.

In this chapter I analyze how policymakers' response to fiscal crisis restructured the relationship between the U.S. economy and global financial markets in the 1980s, reinforcing the turn to finance set in motion by domestic financial deregulation in the 1970s. The mechanisms connecting changes in global financial markets to the financialization of the U.S. economy parallel those associated with domestic financial deregulation described in the previous chapter. In the context of large projected deficits, a collision between Reagan administration and Federal Reserve policymakers produced a shift to a high interest rate regime in the U.S.

economy in the early years of the 1980s.[1] Extraordinarily high interest rates—with short-term rates climbing as high as 20 percent in the early 1980s—created punishing conditions for productive investment and drew economic activity inexorably toward finance.[2] Critically, high interest rates also attracted foreign capital inflows to the U.S. economy in unprecedented volumes, financing the deficit while contributing to a dramatic expansion of credit in the U.S. economy that inflated financial sector profits and fueled financialization.

Here, too, the creation of a macro-economic environment conducive to financialization was not the result of a deliberate policy on the part of policymakers. When, in his 1985 State of the Union address, President Reagan proclaimed the United States "the investment capital of the world," he was describing an inadvertent discovery rather than the culmination of a carefully executed plan to draw the world's savings to U.S. financial markets. Although unplanned, foreign capital inflows into the U.S. economy were a propitious development. Policymakers in the 1960s and 1970s had searched tirelessly for new sources of capital to finance competing social priorities, but they found that directing credit to one purpose necessarily required denying it for other uses. Financial deregulation offered relief from the zero-sum nature of this political calculus, but freeing credit also threatened to unleash inflationary pressures. Reagan's unusual policy mix would provide a solution to this problem, as the extraordinarily high interest rates that drew abundant capital to the United States avoided inflationary pressures by channeling this capital into financial markets and suppressing the productive economy (Greider 1987; Konings 2008; cf. Hutton 1995).[3]

Thus this chapter tells the story of how Reagan administration policymakers harnessed developments in global capital markets to domestic political objectives, escaping the fiscal constraints that first began to impinge on policymakers beginning in the late 1960s and 1970s. As deficits mounted, policymakers expected that the disciplinary mechanism of the market would force a confrontation between the government and all other users of capital. But as policymakers learned to their surprise, at least as far as the U.S. economy was concerned, global financial markets represented an erratic source of discipline, when they were a source of discipline at all (cf. Gowan 2001). If the deregulation of domestic financial markets had allowed policymakers to momentarily escape politically difficult decisions regarding the allocation of scarce resources between competing social priorities (Chapter 3), access to global capital markets would allow policymakers to defer these choices indefinitely.

The Rise and Fall of Bretton Woods

Scholars have typically treated the dissolution of the Bretton Woods system in the early 1970s as the key event that allowed the U.S. state new freedom vis-à-vis global capital markets, preparing the ground for the subsequent rise of finance in the U.S. economy (e.g., Arrighi 1994; Gowan 1999; Helleiner 1994; for a countervailing view, see Konings 2008). This view is largely correct: without the gold-dollar standard operating as a constraint on global economic imbalances, the discipline exerted over countries choosing to run large deficits loosened considerably, with no state more emboldened by this change than the United States (Gilpin 1987).[4] But this fact has led some scholars to overstate the degree to which the resulting restructuring of the global economy was a conscious objective of U.S. policymakers.[5] Peter Gowan (1999), most notably, argues that President Richard Nixon engineered the "escape" of capital from regulatory controls because he clearly foresaw—in a still quite distant future—the consequences of the liberalization of global financial flows in allowing U.S. policymakers to freely tap into the world's savings (cf. Hudson 2003). In contrast, the account presented here suggests that even if Nixon had perfect foresight about how the liberalization of global capital flows would create new opportunities for U.S. policymakers, this knowledge was clearly lost by the time Reagan was confronting fiscal crisis. Deficit financing on the scale achieved in the 1980s and later decades was a theoretical possibility as soon as Nixon closed the gold window, but it took Reagan's bold blunder to fully realize the potentialities contained in a reorganized global system. In this regard, placing the Reagan-era developments in the context of the earlier dissolution of Bretton Woods underscores the inadvertent nature of Reagan's encounter with a recently restructured international monetary system.

The international monetary system exists to solve a very basic, though vexing, problem. To the extent that citizens living in one country consume the products of other countries, domestic means of payment must be fully convertible into all other currencies (Williamson 1977). Otherwise, the citizens of a country that exports goods to another country (and therefore receives payment in the currency of the importing country) would be obliged to spend their earnings *only* in that country—hardly the basis for a multilateral international trading system such as envisioned by the architects of the Bretton Woods system (Block 1977; Helleiner 1994). In the late nineteenth century, and intermittently in the first part of the twentieth, this problem was solved by making all currencies convertible into gold, which then served as the *numeraire* for settling transactions. Such a solution imposed a necessary discipline on countries, which would suffer depleted gold stocks if they persistently ran balance of payments deficits,[6] but it also contained some well-known limitations as a basis for organizing world payments. The most important of these limitations is that the supply of gold is inelastic and hence cannot easily accommodate an expanding economy; under a gold-based system, the growth of world trade would always be limited by new discoveries of gold stocks. For this reason, the gold standard tended to have a contractionary bias, and it was rejected on these grounds as a suitable basis for the international monetary system following the disruption of the Great Depression and World War II (Block 1977). Instead, the British and American delegation who met at the Bretton Woods Hotel in New Hampshire in 1944 to plan the shape of the new economic order sought a compromise between the discipline exerted by gold and the flexibility of a paper money (or fiat) system by putting the international monetary system on a dollar standard, but making the dollar fully convertible into gold (Cohen 1977; Williamson 1977). Under this system, all currencies were pegged to the dollar at fixed exchange rates,[7] and the dollar in turn was convertible into gold at an exchange rate of $35 per ounce.

While freeing the world economy from what John Maynard Keynes (1963: 288) famously referred to as the "gold fetters" of the nineteenth-century gold standard, a dollar-based international monetary system created other problems. Most importantly, if the dollar was to replace gold as the *numeraire* currency, other countries would have to dispose of a stock of dollars to use as a means of payment. To provide liquidity to the world economy, the U.S. economy was consigned to inject dollars into the rest of the world by running deficits. Initially, these were deficits on government account: through the Marshall Plan and subsequent European rearmament, the U.S. government transferred dollars to the recovering European economies that these economies could then use to purchase U.S. exports. In the 1950s and 1960s, as American multinational corporations channeled increasing amounts of foreign direct investment abroad, U.S. deficits on the capital account were added to these government transfers. By the late 1960s, as European (and to a lesser extent, Japanese) recovery proceeded apace, the U.S. trade account also moved into deficit (Block 1977). This last development was worrisome to the international creditors of the United States, as it signaled a deterioration of the competitive position of the U.S. economy, with possible implications for the ability of these creditors to redeem accumulated dollar reserves for gold. In 1968, these worries materialized in a "run" on the dollar, as foreign holders of U.S. currency moved en masse to exchange dollars for gold while the opportunity was still available (Collins 1996).

Effectively, the dilemma that international economist Robert Triffin had described in his influential book, *Gold and the Dollar Crisis* (1961), was at hand. Triffin observed a fundamental flaw in the dollar-based international monetary system created at Bretton Woods: the expansion of world liquidity required the United States to run chronic balance of payments deficits, yet these deficits undermined confidence in the dollar, ultimately shaking the stability of the world monetary order (cf. Block 1977). Triffin argued that this problem was inherent in any monetary system that rested on a single currency. For many of the same reasons, at the Bretton Woods conference Keynes had urged the creation of an international clearing house that would issue its own reserve unit—the *bancor*—to avoid dependence on the dollar or gold to settle international transactions.[8] Even U.S. banking interests opposed to the Bretton Woods settlement had supported a "key currency" system in which Britain and the United States would share responsibility for organizing the international economy, with the dollar and sterling each serving for settlement purposes. With U.S. approval of the British Loan in 1945, which was intended to restore sterling convertibility, this initiative became the official policy of the Truman administration (Block 1977; Helleiner 1994). But for a variety of reasons, Britain was not in a position then or later to take up this role, and the dollar standard was inaugurated by default. Ever since, U.S. deficits have been a source of controversy in international monetary relations, with Europeans suggesting that the ability of the United States to freely issue its own currency, when other countries must earn dollars for international transactions, has provided Americans with a free ride. The American view, in contrast, has tended to stress the obligations associated with the dollar's role in the global economy, which effectively consigns the U.S. economy to run deficits simply to meet the liquidity needs of the rest of the world (Gowa 1983: 43–44).

These tensions over the role of the dollar in the international system reached a breaking point in 1971. In that year, Nixon relinquished gold cover for the dollar in response to a further deterioration in the U.S. trade balance—a decision that prefigured in important ways Reagan's own, very different response to declining U.S. economic fortunes in the 1980s (see Gowan 1999; cf. Helleiner 1994; Hudson 2003). The requirement that dollars be freely convertible into gold had placed an important degree of restraint on the United States: even if foreigners rarely sought to convert their dollar assets into gold, the threat that they might do so exerted considerable pressure on policymakers (Hudson 2003). When

Nixon suspended convertibility—intended initially as a stop-gap measure while the United States negotiated a currency realignment that would enable it to improve its trade position (Calleo 1982; Williamson 1977)—this threat was effectively removed. Now foreign dollar holders were faced with a choice: either hold these dollars (preferably in the form of U.S. Treasury securities) or sell them for other currencies. In the former case, foreigners would again be footing the bill for U.S. deficits (without, however, the threat of conversion into gold); in the latter case, the resulting depreciation of the dollar would both erode the value of accumulated dollar assets and increase the competitiveness of U.S. exporters. It was, in effect, a choice between continuing to finance U.S. deficits and wreaking havoc on the international economy (Hudson 2003).

As we will see, Reagan would later exploit this feature of the U.S. economy's relationship to its foreign creditors in the context of an unprecedented buildup of state debt in the 1980s. However, the account offered here cautions against reading Nixon's monetary maneuvering too seamlessly against the later experience of the Reagan administration. If freeing the United States from its obligation to convert dollars for gold allowed the accumulation of U.S. deficits without limit, this was hardly the goal of President Nixon (as Gowan [1999], for example, implies),[9] who sought a reprieve from the pressure of gold sales to depreciate the currency and eliminate the trade deficit (Calleo 1982; Williamson 1977). Critically, the Nixon administration was anxious to retain the central role of the dollar in the world economy, but it was *not* anxious to accept the deficits that this role necessarily entailed (Williamson 1977: 77).[10] Thus, in unilaterally ending Bretton Woods, the Nixon administration hoped that the dollar's role in the international economy could be preserved, but in the event that this was not possible, Nixon's primary objective was to gain control over the trade deficit and minimize associated job losses in the U.S. economy (Gowa 1983; Williamson 1977: 167). This was still an effort to escape the constraints of the global system and not yet an effort to harness global capital markets to domestic political objectives.

As it happened, international negotiations held between 1971 and 1973 failed to produce any acceptable alternative to a dollar system (Williamson 1977), and what Michael Hudson (2003) refers to as the "Treasury Bill Standard" was inaugurated by default. In the absence of convertibility, foreign economies exporting to the United States had little choice but to recycle export earnings into U.S. financial assets or face a deterioration of their competitive position vis-à-vis U.S. producers (Murphy 1997). But, as the following narrative makes clear, it would require both the gradual liberalization of global (especially Japanese) capital markets and the Reagan administration's unusual marriage of supply-side economics and monetarism to fully unlock the potential of the Treasury Bill Standard. Initially, Reagan administration policymakers did not anticipate, much less plan, the inflows of foreign capital that resulted from this policy. But once they stumbled upon this outcome, Reagan policymakers welcomed capital inflows, even if the policy mix that drew foreign capital also pushed interest rates sky high and accelerated the pace of credit expansion in the U.S. economy, creating macro-economic conditions conducive to the turn to finance. In the financialization of the U.S. economy, the Reagan administration would discover an unexpected resolution of the fiscal crisis that had marked the late 1960s and 1970s.

The Reagan Administration and the Fiscal Crisis of the State

The "fiscal crisis of the state" refers to a structural gap between government expenditures and the tax revenues needed to cover these expenditures (Block 1981). For Marxist theorists such as James O'Connor (1973), the fiscal crisis was a result of the state's dual imperative to underwrite capitalist profits and at the same time engage in social expenditures to protect those disadvantaged in the market (cf. Habermas 1973).[11] As long as there was strong underlying momentum in the economy, tax revenues would be sufficient to cover both types of spending. Once the rate of growth in the economy slowed, however, taxes levied on business sapped private investment and therefore future revenues that the state could claim, trapping state officials in a vicious cycle of slowing growth and cumulating debt burdens. Under such circumstances, what Daniel Bell (1976) evocatively called "the public household" would find itself in disarray, with a deteriorating budget situation placing a strain on the broader economy.

Considered in historical perspective, the event that established the contours of the fiscal crisis of the U.S. state was the Vietnam War. Most critically, an escalation of the conflict in Southeast Asia coincided with an expansion of domestic anti-poverty social programs—President Lyndon Johnson's ill-fated policy of "guns and butter."[12] While such extravagances may have been possible in an earlier era of American affluence, by the mid-1960s profit margins of U.S. firms were under pressure both from new producers in Germany and Japan and from an increasingly militant labor movement at home.[13] As these challenges mounted, the Johnson administration deferred a tax hike to finance its war budget, introducing what in retrospect were mild but persistent inflationary pressures into the U.S. economy.[14] These pressures steadily built over the following decade, particularly in the wake of oil price hikes in 1973 and 1979.[15] The inability of state managers to effectively respond to economic malaise in this period posed, in general terms, the problem formulated by O'Connor (1973): How could the state promote economic growth without itself becoming an albatross, weighing down the economy and stifling accumulation?

The answer, it seemed increasingly in the Carter years, was that it could not. Indeed, it was this growing conviction on the part of liberal and conservative economists alike that gave rise to a general rethinking of the proper role of the state in the economy. Initially, "supply-side" economics referred to a broad range of policies, from worker training programs to deregulation schemes, which aimed at removing obstacles to the smooth functioning of markets. In this sense, Carter—who had forsaken the Keynesian idea that the state should attempt to stimulate (or restrain) aggregate demand[16]—was the first supply-sider, before the radical Reagan tax program usurped the mantle. Nevertheless, during the Reagan administration the term came to have a much narrower meaning: that tax cuts (and other reforms aimed at changing incentives) would stimulate economic activity and drive an investment boom. Under the most extravagant claims of the supply-siders, tax cuts would "pay for themselves," generating sufficient new economic activity so as to offset revenue losses.[17] Notwithstanding such claims, tax cuts were to be accompanied by an aggressive program of expenditure slashing. It appeared that the supply-siders had found their answer to the fiscal crisis of the state: by withdrawing from the market, the state not only could reduce its expenditures, but it could actually support accumulation more effectively.

Events transpired differently: the result of the supply-side program was the return of the fiscal crisis with a vengeance. The failure of supply-side economics was aptly characterized by Reagan's director of the Office of Management and Budget (OMB), David Stockman (1986), as "the triumph of politics." Stockman discovered, to his dismay, that in a society in which elections are won and lost by competing parties, the needed expenditure cuts would be difficult, if not impossible, to obtain. The electoral imperative, in short, trumped ideology for all but a small band of dedicated revolutionaries isolated inside the Reagan administration. Exacerbating the situation was the fact that Reagan remained stubbornly wedded to his program of military expansion even as increasingly grim fiscal projections began to impinge on American power pursuits abroad. As a result, when the 1981 tax cuts were passed in advance of any agreement on offsetting (social or military) expenditure reductions, the budget deficit ballooned to levels that made previous U.S. deficits seem trivial by comparison.

By late 1981, the budget projections showed, as Stockman (1986: 370) later put it, "deficits as far as the eye can see." While the supply-siders remained confident that Reagan's tax proposals would unleash a vigorous recovery and that the economy would "outgrow" the deficits, the financial markets were less certain. The forecast that haunted Wall Street— and increasingly, policymakers inside the administration who fell off the supply-side bandwagon—was that of an imminent collision between the federal government and private borrowers in the credit markets. Under this scenario of "crowding out," the government would preempt capital from private borrowers; as private borrowers bid among themselves for the remaining funds, interest rates would rise so high as to price these borrowers out of the market. That unhappy outcome, analysts feared, would grind economic activity to a halt, suffocating the nascent recovery by making it impossible for firms to obtain financing for new investment. For most of 1981 and 1982, the stock and bond markets lurched along in anticipation of this crowding-out scenario, causing considerable consternation among Reagan officials.[18]

To the surprise of both Washington and Wall Street, no such scenario materialized. Several factors kept the dreaded calamity in the credit markets at bay. First, recovery proved elusive for many months, and private demand for investment funds remained sluggish well into 1983. Second, firms were able to fund investment projects directly out of retained earnings, which had received a significant boost as a result of the liberalized depreciation allowances associated with the 1981 tax cut.[19] Finally, most importantly, just as the recovery was finally under way in mid-1983, a major new source of capital emerged, quite unexpectedly, to finance the federal budget deficit: international—especially Japanese—investors had developed a voracious appetite for Treasury securities.

Reagan administration officials did not anticipate this development for three primary reasons. First, while Japan's status as a "high-savings" economy—reinforced by a financial system that provided restricted access to consumer credit[20]—was widely recognized, Japan's large pool of savings had until recently been channeled toward supporting high levels of domestic investment. Only as Japan's economy matured and rates of domestic investment slowed were these savings directed to other purposes. During the 1970s, these funds financed the Japanese government's own sizable budget deficit. After 1979, when the Japanese government's fiscal position swung sharply into surplus, Japan's savings became available to global markets in a way that had not been the case previously. This coincided with the deregulation of Japanese financial markets in 1980, allowing capital to flow more easily into foreign lending (Murphy 1997).

A second reason that the Reagan administration failed to foresee the way in which the economic program would be rescued by Japanese savers was that, in the early 1980s, policymakers had not fully adjusted to thinking of the world in terms of a sea of open capital flows. International financial integration was a work in progress, the implications of this process still unfolding. David Stockman later admitted that no one among Reagan's close advisers had anticipated the role that foreign capital flows would come to play in financing the budget deficits (Murphy 1997: 148). Even Paul Volcker, perhaps more attuned to the international economy than any Federal Reserve chairman before or since, did not predict the magnitude of the capital flows that would emerge, out of nowhere and seemingly overnight, to finance the budget deficits (Volcker and Gyohten 1992: 178–179).

To be sure, the economists in the Treasury Department and at the Council of Economic Advisers (CEA) were equipped with the familiar macro-economic formula that suggested that a savings shortfall (in the form of a budget deficit) would, by definition, be offset by (negative) net exports, and hence a capital inflow, but even here the linkages were stated rather tenuously.[21] In a memo written in the fall of 1981, for example, CEA chairman Murray Weidenbaum noted that "foreign portfolio flows are *potentially* useful in easing deficit financing pressures in domestic markets."[22] Similarly, in December 1981, during a speech given at the American Enterprise Institute, CEA member William Niskanen (1988: 110) hypothesized that the opportunity to import capital meant that the deficits then on the horizon might not place the strong upward pressure on interest rates that observers at the time were expecting. Niskanen recalled that his audience was highly skeptical that capital inflows of any significant magnitude were possible, however.[23]

In addition, while these relationships may have been understood—in abstract terms, at least—by the economists on Reagan's staff, the notion that in an open economy a deficit could be financed by importing capital from abroad did not penetrate far into the broader cabinet. As late as October 1984, Niskanen wrote a memo for the cabinet Council on Economic Affairs, explaining that the gap between domestic saving and domestic investment was necessarily equal to foreign borrowing.[24] Niskanen recalled, "That was a surprise to nearly everybody in the Cabinet meeting!"[25] Contrary to Niskanen's free market intentions, his presentation gave greater force to protectionist voices in the cabinet who were alarmed to learn of the growing dependence of the U.S. economy on foreign capital.

Finally, a third reason that many members of the Reagan administration did not fully anticipate the role that foreign capital inflows would come to play in financing the budget deficit was that these flows were drawn in by the extraordinarily high interest rates associated with Volcker's embrace of monetarism[26]—conditions that were widely expected to be temporary. In fact, while the monetarist experiment was short-lived (see Chapter 5), high interest rates were not.[27] While this was in part a result of structural change in the economy associated with financial deregulation,[28] the persistence of higher rates also reflected Volcker's resistance to the Reagan program. Volcker observed the budget wrangling going on inside the administration and feared that the large deficits would reverse the progress he was making on inflation (Volcker and Gyohten 1992; cf. Greider 1987: 358). As a result, he stubbornly refused to do what central bankers before him had done in similar circumstances—to "monetize" the deficit by steering the economy toward a more accommodative monetary policy that would create inflation and thereby reduce the current-dollar value of the debt (Greider 1987: 560).[29] Instead, Volcker ratcheted interest rates higher, determined to smother any inflationary spark.

In principle, such a development was not unwelcome by Reagan administration economists. Their version of supply-side economics was married to a particular brand of monetarism, the theory being that a high-growth, noninflationary economic policy could be achieved by combining stimulus, in the form of tax cuts, with restraint, in the form of tight monetary policy. The idea that the two policy levers could pull in opposite directions was, to say the least, an odd one: journalist William Greider (1987) aptly called it "a car with two drivers."[30] But Volcker took the policy to an extreme that alarmed even the hard-core monetarists in the Reagan administration. Treasury Undersecretary for Monetary Affairs Beryl Sprinkel noted, "We had hoped that this movement toward tighter money could be done very gradually, so that we would have a reasonable possibility of eating our cake and having it too. . . . We [wanted] the Fed [to] come down gradually over a period of two to three years and . . . do it without creating a recession. [But] we got a full dose of monetary restraint, regardless of what we had urged."[31] Volcker's goal was not to usher in the triumph of Reaganomics, but as Jane D'Arista, a senior staff member of the U.S. House Committee on Banking, Housing, and Urban Affairs, commented, "to defeat and embarrass the administration's policies."[32]

What Volcker did not envision was the way that such a plan would backfire in the context of open global capital flows. As D'Arista elaborated, "Volcker wanted to counter the effects of the easy fiscal policy, but *compounded* them by an interest rate policy that encouraged capital inflows."[33] Rather than producing the crowding out that would force the administration back on to the path of fiscal austerity, high interest rates—as much as five percentage points higher than comparable risk-free government securities sold in Japan (Murphy 1997: 144)—brought capital pouring into the U.S. economy: $85 billion in 1983, $103 billion in 1984, $129 billion in 1985, and a staggering $221 billion in 1986.[34] It was the best of all possible worlds: the state virtually unchained from hard budget constraints,[35] inflation kept at bay, and abundant liquidity in U.S. financial markets to ensure that the much-dreaded collision of private and public borrowers in the credit markets never occurred.

The Caterpillar Report

If crowding out was not occurring in the textbook fashion, another, more insidious form of crowding out was reshaping the American economy. In the 1980s, the textbook form of crowding out was mitigated by the fact that rising interest rates attracted funds from abroad, allowing private borrowers continued access to capital even as the deficit grew. But the capital pouring in from abroad introduced another distortion into the economy of the 1980s: the dollar began to appreciate rapidly. To invest in the U.S. economy, foreigners had to exchange their currencies—yen, marks, francs, and so on—into dollars, with the result that the demand for the dollar on foreign exchange markets increased, driving up its price. This, in turn, placed American exporters at a competitive disadvantage in foreign markets for the reverse reason: to sell in those markets, exporters converted dollar prices into local currencies, which became more expensive as the value of the dollar rose.[36] The results of this process were soon evident in the intense pressure on U.S. manufacturing and agriculture as American producers steadily lost market share to foreign competitors.

Domestic opposition to the strong dollar came from all quarters, but was spearheaded by the Business Roundtable and its very vocal leader, Caterpillar Tractor chairman Lee Morgan (Destler and Henning 1989). In 1982, Morgan commissioned two academics, David Murchison and Ezra Solomon, to study the causes of the strong dollar and propose appropriate policy responses. Their report, officially released in September 1983 but widely circulated the year before, argued strongly in favor of the view that the Japanese had taken deliberate steps to hold down the value of the yen to gain a competitive advantage in U.S. markets. In particular, they argued that restrictive capital market policies discouraged inflows of capital into Japanese markets, thereby suppressing demand for the yen, and increasing demand for other currencies, such as the dollar. As such, the Caterpillar report called for correcting the strong dollar by further opening Japanese financial markets.

This analysis turned out to be erroneous. In fact, the most significant controls in the Japanese capital market restricted *outflows,* not inflows, of capital.[37] As a result, liberalizing Japanese financial markets would have the effect of increasing capital flows from Japan to the United States. As Paul Krugman, then a staff economist at the CEA, noted in a memo, "It is hard to believe that liberalization of Japan's capital markets would make Japan a major importer of capital. Japan has the world's highest savings rate. With free movement of capital we would expect it to invest some of these savings abroad, i.e., become a capital exporter rather than a capital importer."[38] Nevertheless, prompted by the Caterpillar report, in November 1983 the Treasury Department launched a diplomatic offensive aimed at liberalizing Japanese financial markets (Frankel 1984).

Did Treasury adopt the Caterpillar report knowing that the report's conclusions were faulty and that in fact opening Japanese capital markets would augment capital flows to the United States, assisting the Treasury in financing the budget deficit, but further strengthening the dollar? Or did Treasury, along with Caterpillar, simply miscalculate the effect of liberalizing Japanese markets on the direction of capital flows? This is difficult to know definitively, but there can be no doubt that the convoluted economic logic of the Caterpillar report solved a number of sticky problems for Treasury.

The first of these was Secretary of State George Shultz's insistence that the high dollar was creating a strain on U.S.–Japan relations. Indeed, it was Shultz who first proposed that the United States and Japan engage in a series of high-level talks with the aim of jointly managing the exchange rate problem. The project was passed off to Treasury, which, given its free market predilections, had no interest in targeting the level of the exchange rate,[39] as Shultz (and Caterpillar) intended. Fortunately for the Treasury Department, the Caterpillar report could be used to justify redirecting the State Department initiative toward something that generated considerably greater enthusiasm at Treasury: removing barriers to the free flow of capital internationally. As Fred Bergsten, director of the Institute for International Economics, commented, "The whole thing was a perversion of the initial objective."[40]

The Caterpillar report also solved a second problem for the Treasury Department: that of needing to appear to respond to the increasingly vociferous complaints of the business community without, however, compromising the laissez-faire principles of the Reagan administration. As Jeffrey Frankel, an economist then working at the CEA explained, "For Treasury, this seemed like a way of responding to this pressure [from business] without abandoning free trade principles."[41] It is here that the interpretation of events becomes somewhat challenging, for the public and private pronouncements of the Treasury Department regarding the likely effect of Japanese capital market liberalization diverge. In public—especially in the statements of Treasury Secretary Donald Regan[42]—the Treasury appeared to adopt the view expressed in the Caterpillar report that steps taken to liberalize Japan's capital markets would result in increased capital flows to Japan, putting upward pressure on the yen and downward pressure on the dollar. In private, Treasury knew better. At a cabinet council meeting in which Krugman's memo was discussed, Treasury Undersecretary Beryl Sprinkel agreed with the CEA that the immediate result of pressuring the Japanese to further open their financial markets would be to *weaken,* not strengthen, the yen.[43]

Whether this implies that the Treasury Department deliberately played both sides of the issue to deflect political pressure to "do something" about the strong dollar, or whether it simply reflects the fact that the treasury secretary was out of step with his staff, is difficult to know with certainty.[44] It is possible that Treasury was engaged in an entirely Machiavellian ploy: Treasury loudly proclaimed that it was dealing with the exchange rate problem, all the while knowing that the effect of its negotiations with Japan would be the *opposite* of what the business community believed. Even more plausible, though, is the proposition that Treasury's interest in liberalizing Japanese capital markets was purely ideological: Treasury saw the initiative as bolstering the liberalization of international financial markets, rather than having an effect one way or the other on the exchange rate. As Bergsten noted of the Reagan Treasury Department, "They didn't care where the dollar exchange rate was, they just believed let the market do it, we don't care if it's up, down, or sideways, no, that's for the market."[45] Sprinkel's self-presentation was similar: "The direction of capital flows resulting from the yen/dollar agreement was not a major factor in my mind. Most of the people in the Reagan administration were free market people with a very strong conviction that that's the way we ought to run our economy."[46] Not for the first time in the Reagan administration did ideology fit hand-in-glove with more practical imperatives.

Finally, the analysis developed in the Caterpillar study was welcome at Treasury because it deflected attention away from an alternative explanation of the strong dollar articulated within the CEA. The CEA argued that the dollar had appreciated because the budget deficit contributed to high interest rates; high interest rates, in turn, made the dollar a desirable asset, attracting a capital inflow.[47] For Treasury, this analysis—with its unpleasant emphasis on the budget deficit—amounted to "selling short" the Reagan program.[48] From Treasury's perspective, foreign capital was attracted to the U.S. economy because the rate of return on investment was higher here than elsewhere.[49] Even if the logic was a little erroneous, then, the Caterpillar study at least put the emphasis where it belonged: the dollar was strong because deregulated U.S. markets drew capital in, whereas shackled markets abroad repelled capital.[50] For the Treasury economists, if not for Caterpillar Tractor, the soaring dollar was a sign not of some underlying pathology but of all that was right in Reagan's America.

But there was one thing on which Treasury and the CEA could agree: whatever their cause, the capital inflows associated with the high dollar represented a beneficial development.[51] This position was elaborated most explicitly in what came to be known as the "Feldstein Doctrine," after CEA chairman Martin Feldstein.[52] Feldstein argued that, issues of allocation aside,[53] foreign capital inflows provided a significant supplement to national savings. Thus, taking the budget deficit as given, the rise of the dollar and associated capital inflow acted as a "safety valve" for the U.S. economy, avoiding the crowding out of domestic investment.[54] Treasury concurred: "The capital inflows to the United States . . . will permit interest rates to be lower here than they otherwise would be, preserving jobs in interest rate sensitive industries, and [allowing] more capital formation than would otherwise be the case."[55]

In short, over the course of two years, the Reagan administration economists had learned that they lived not in a closed national economy, but in a world of global capital. Consequently, when the Reagan recovery began to accelerate in mid-1984 and fears again turned to an imminent crowding out of private borrowers in the capital markets,[56] the Treasury Department was prepared. While Volcker startled the financial markets by repeating, loudly, his earlier warnings that he would not, under any circumstance, accommodate deficits—and hence that "the day of reckoning" was close at hand—administration economists calmly analyzed the role that foreign capital would play in financing the coming investment boom.[57]

Whether efforts to liberalize Japanese financial markets represented a deliberate attempt on the part of the Treasury to harness Japanese capital flows to finance U.S. deficits—or, as some have argued, was simply a policy "mistake"—there can be no ambiguity about Treasury's intentions as economic recovery progressed.[58] Beginning in July 1984, Treasury took several concrete steps to make U.S. financial instruments more attractive to foreign borrowers (Frankel 1994: 301–302). First, the 30 percent withholding tax imposed on interest earned by foreigners on U.S. investments was eliminated. *Business Week* remarked, "A desire to expand the pool of buyers of U.S. government debt was a major reason the [tax] was finally repealed."[59] Second, in the fall of 1984, Treasury initiated its foreign-targeted securities program, in which several special issues were prepared for European and Japanese markets. In September, David Mulford, Undersecretary of the Treasury for International Affairs, traveled to Europe to generate interest in the new issue. Beryl Sprinkel visited Tokyo to market the bonds to Japanese investors. The auction was extremely successful; I. M. Destler and C. Randall Henning (1989: 29) called the Reagan Treasury Department "The greatest bond salesmen in history." Finally, in October, after a battle with Congress, Treasury obtained permission to issue so-called bearer bonds, consistent with the preference of international investors for unregistered securities that could be held anonymously.[60]

The result of these various initiatives was to transform the zero-sum relationship between the government and all other borrowers competing for capital in crowded markets. Remarkably, only a few years had passed since the perennial capital shortages of the 1970s, and yet the dilemmas confronted by policymakers in that decade seemed to belong to another era entirely. Reagan's record deficits notwithstanding, fiscal crisis had been averted. At least for the moment, the stock market ceased to gyrate on every budget number. As *Business Week* noted in an incredulous tone:

> The nation's financial foundation was supposed to shake when a growing economy collided with the huge budget deficit. Credit demand would soar, driving interest rates into the stratosphere. Instead, after being intimidated for two years, the stock market is pressing boldly ahead to record levels. . . . The experience of the last two years [has] shown that the U.S. does not have a closed system. Inflows of foreign capital can sustain private and public borrowers alike.[61]

What the Reagan policymakers discovered in the early 1980s, then, was that they lived in a world in which capital was available in a potentially *limitless* supply. Access to global financial markets would allow the state to defer indefinitely the difficult political choices that had confronted previous administrations struggling to allocate scarce capital between competing social priorities. As the administration economists gradually came to understand this, they endeavored to harness global capital flows to domestic policy objectives. Beryl Sprinkel expressed this sentiment quite explicitly in a memo written for Chief of Staff Donald Regan in October 1985.[62] In commenting on the desirability of reforms to the monetary system that would restore fixed exchange rates and therefore restrictions on international capital flows,[63] Sprinkel observed:

> Consider the international investment of the past three years. We have experienced a marked increase in the world demand for dollar-denominated assets. This increased demand has generated a rise in the . . . value of the dollar. The resulting net capital inflow into the U.S. has helped to finance an unprecedented domestic investment boom and a robust expansion that has dramatically improved our standard of living. What would have happened if the exchange rate were fixed? As the incipient capital inflow placed upward pressure on the . . . value of the dollar, the [Federal Reserve] would be forced to supply dollars to prevent this rise. In effect, then, the [Federal Reserve] would prevent the capital inflow from occurring. Consequently, the growth of domestic investment, output, and our standard of living would not have been as large as we experienced.[64]

Sprinkel was acknowledging that the United States had been extremely well served by unregulated global capital markets because inflows of foreign capital underwrote increasing U.S. standards of living. As a result, in the Reagan era, budgets ceased to bind state officials in the same way they had under the Bretton Woods regime of fixed exchange rates and controls on capital movements. Put in the starkest terms, in the absence of foreign capital inflows, deficits of the magnitude generated by the Reagan administration would have precipitated a full-blown financial crisis. Instead, the financial strains imposed on the economy by the Reagan deficits were deferred until the October 1987 stock market crash, which, while calamitous, was very quickly contained. Paradoxically, integration into the global economy brought not the discipline of the market, but freedom from constraint (cf. Gowan 2001).

From Fiscal Crisis to Financialization

With the Reagan administration's inadvertent discovery of the global economy, the policy regime supporting the financialization of the U.S. economy was put firmly in place. Reagan-era economic policies thus completed—and in a sense, *perfected*—the process begun with the deregulation of domestic financial markets in the previous decade (Chapter 3). Financial deregulation had removed barriers to the free flow of credit in the U.S. economy, sparing policymakers the politically difficult task of allocating capital between uses. But as the process of financial deregulation culminated with the elimination of interest rate ceilings in 1980, the resulting expansion of credit in the economy threatened to contribute to accelerating inflation. Public tolerance for inflation was wearing decidedly thin by the late 1970s, and Volcker had assumed leadership of the Federal Reserve with a mandate to suppress steadily climbing prices. As such, Volcker's adoption of monetarism was intended to force a bitter pill down the throats of capital-starved American businesses and consumers by squeezing credit *hard*. This was a policy designed for a closed economy, however, and foreign capital inflows washed out any effect high interest rates might have had on restricting the growth of total credit in the U.S. economy (Greider 1987; Konings 2008). In an era of deregulated *and* globalized financial markets, neither the mechanism of disintermediation from the banking system, nor the crowding out of private borrowers from capital markets functioned to choke off seemingly limitless demands for credit.

The key to understanding this outcome was the dual nature of capital inflows. Volcker's imposition of high interest rates drew foreign capital into the U.S. economy, but as Reagan policymakers quickly learned, by increasing the supply of capital circulating in U.S. financial markets, these inflows also placed a limit on how high interest rates would climb.[65] While interest rates reached levels that were unprecedented in the postwar period in the 1980s, they did not rise so high as to shut borrowers out of credit markets, as Reagan administration officials had feared would occur. Instead, credit remained available to those who could meet its high price. Naturally, the soaring price of money directed capital to increasingly speculative uses, alarming some observers who worried about the long-term prospects of the U.S. economy as firms withdrew from investment in plant and equipment for more lucrative financial ventures.[66] A parallel transformation was evident in the investment behavior of American households, who no longer sought refuge from inflation by investing in housing, land, works of art, jewelry, and other tangible goods sure to *increase* in value as money *decreased* in value. Instead, as Volcker decisively restored the value of money, firms and households alike quickly abandoned the economy of goods and services, channeling capital into financial markets (Greider 1987: 552, 661). The result was to transfer inflation from the nonfinancial to the financial economy—where it was not visible (or conceptualized) as such.[67]

Of course, vanquishing inflation to the financial markets introduced other distortions. In particular, surging asset prices encouraged a debt-financed consumption boom in the U.S. economy—the foundation of the "belle époque" of the 1980s, 1990s, and 2000s (Arrighi 1994). Critically, the growing indebtedness of the U.S. economy changed patterns of accumulation, not only domestically but in the global economy as a whole, by providing suppliers of foreign capital with a virtually guaranteed market for their exports. As long as foreign capital continued to find its way to the U.S. economy, and as long as American firms and households served as "buyer of last resort" for foreign creditors, the resulting system appeared to be self-sustaining—and in fact proved surprisingly resilient to changing economic and political conditions.[68] In particular, while Volcker's high interest rate regime was necessary to initially draw foreign creditors into the orbit of the U.S. economy, later even this inducement was not necessary. The experience of the 2000s showed that Asian central banks would accept paltry returns on accumulated dollar reserves to finance their exports and maintain access to the seemingly insatiable American consumer. In Taggart Murphy's (2008) memorable phrase, Asia was the enabler allowing the U.S. economy to imbibe "endless dollar cocktails."

But, to extend Taggart Murphy's metaphor, it was not only American firms and households that were partying hard. In fact, the U.S. government was going on the biggest bender of all. With the growing integration of the U.S. economy into global capital markets, policymakers had stumbled on an unexpected resolution to the fiscal crisis of the state: access to foreign capital provided ample financing for mounting U.S. deficits, while a restrictive monetary policy suppressed the inflationary pressures associated with excess credit expansion (cf. Greider 1987: 562, 565). No wonder that the policy regime underpinning financialization offered irresistible temptations to policymakers, even as it also severely distorted the structure of the U.S. economy. No longer would the state face seemingly impossible trade-offs between fiscal austerity and ever-mounting inflation—once a bedrock principle of American political economy that had assumed the immutability of something like the law of gravity. Instead, foreign capital inflows would allow state officials to avoid difficult political decisions about how the burden of declining affluence would be shared.

Of course, Reagan officials did not so much avoid these decisions as transfer them to other parts of the state apparatus, where they were less visible and therefore less likely to be subject to political contestation. Critically, reliance on foreign capital to finance U.S. deficits required letting go of an important lever used to regulate the expansion and contraction of the economy. Deprived of control over the *supply* of credit, policymakers would have to manipulate the *price* of credit to exert restraint on a society that was living well beyond its means. This was the proper domain of monetary policy, which became the ultimate source of restraint in an economy that seemed to have thrown off the yoke of market discipline. The challenge for monetary policymakers, of course, was to exercise this restraint lightly and avoid politicizing the management of the economy, as the Volcker episode threatened to do. Here, too, policymakers would learn to use developments in financial markets to their advantage, in the process deepening and extending the turn to finance.

CHAPTER FIVE

The Making of U.S. Monetary Policy

I N CHAPTERS 3 and 4 I examined the political origins of the turn to finance of the U.S. economy in the responses of policymakers to social crisis and fiscal crisis, respectively. A common thread running through both chapters was policymakers' belated discovery that relying on market mechanisms to restrain consumers, corporations, and governments all vying for scarce capital imposed no such restraint. In eliminating interest rate controls in the U.S. economy, policymakers hoped to pass the politically difficult task of allocating capital between competing social priorities to the market (Chapter 3). Instead, policymakers inadvertently freed the expansion of credit from institutional constraints, avoiding the need for allocation altogether. In a closed economy, of course, freeing borrowers to compete for a finite amount of capital would have eventually pushed the price of credit so high as to force some borrowers to drop out of the market or, failing this, would have contributed to accelerating inflation, imposing austerity by other means. But in a newly open economy, such an outcome was forestalled, as high interest rates drew abundant foreign capital to U.S. financial markets, suppressing inflation while avoiding credit rationing in domestic capital markets (Chapter 4). Neither domestic nor global financial institutions were sources of the much vaunted discipline of the market (Blecker 1999; Greider 1987: 660).

This inability of the market to exert discipline reflected the fact that in deregulating financial markets both domestically and internationally, policymakers effectively removed quantitative restrictions on the flow of credit in the U.S. economy. Critically, this development shifted the locus of economic restraint from regulatory policies that operated on the *supply* of credit to policies that influenced the *demand* for credit by controlling its price, the interest rate. Of course, letting go of the one lever meant that policymakers would have to lean much harder on the other, and, accordingly, the era of financial deregulation ushered in a period of high and volatile interest rates (Kaufman 1986). The Federal Reserve is the institution that determines the level of interest rates in the economy, and as such its role in imposing restraint became more central after regulators abandoned responsibility for directly determining how capital would be allocated between competing social priorities. But if monetary policy was to be the ultimate arbiter of the hard decisions that politicians had evaded, here too policymakers would succumb to familiar temptations, with now familiar results.

As monetary policy assumed greater importance in the exercise of economic policy generally, so it also became the terrain on which the state sought to maintain—and was threatened with losing—tenuous public confidence in its ability to govern the economy. In this chapter, I examine how Federal Reserve officials negotiated this terrain by analyzing policymakers' evolving response to the legitimation crisis, the third face of the crisis of the state. In general terms, the legitimation crisis reflected the loss of public confidence in the state's ability to maintain conditions supportive of economic growth while also managing the social imbalances associated with growth (Bell 1976). As conditions supporting broad-based prosperity in the U.S. economy eroded over the course of the 1970s, these two tasks necessarily came into conflict. For Marxist theorists, the conflict was inherent in the capitalist nature of the state (Habermas 1973; O'Connor 1973; Offe 1974), but navigating these contradictory imperatives could equally be interpreted as a generic problem of democratic polities (Bell 1976). Put simply, voters would reject any government that proved itself to be an ineffective economic manager or that governed the economy in a manner indifferent to the social consequences of growth. By the late 1970s, with steadily climbing inflation and rising unemployment, such voter retaliation seemed an increasingly likely prospect.[1] In this context, policymakers were confronted with a dilemma: How could policymakers guide market outcomes while avoiding responsibility for lackluster economic performance (cf. Burnham 2001; Carruthers, Halliday, and Babb 2001; Pauly 1995)?

Monetary policymakers confronted a particularly acute version of this dilemma. Although the implementation of monetary policy is generally presented as a purely technical, apolitical exercise, the level of interest rates in the economy shapes distributional outcomes—both directly by shifting economic resources from debtors to creditors and indirectly by regulating the rate of growth in the economy (Greider 1987; Kirshner 2001). As such, the Federal Reserve has a strong incentive to obscure its role in determining economic outcomes, and it generally has done so by redefining economic events as the product of "market forces" rather than the activities of state officials. As numerous scholars have observed, this strategy represents a reversal of the overt politicization of economic policy that accompanied the expansion of state management of the economy in the early postwar decades (Burnham 2001; Flinders and Buller 2006; Hay 2007). One paradoxical consequence of the expansion of the state's role in managing the economy was that the state actors increasingly appeared responsible for economic outcomes (Offe 1974). Where there was an inflation policy, for example, inflation was interpreted as a product of misguided economic management, rather than resulting from randomly occurring "shocks" akin to a natural hazard. Where there was an employment policy in place, similarly, unemployment could no longer simply be attributed to the regular fluctuations of the business cycle. As these and other policy failures accumulated with the deterioration of economic performance beginning in the 1970s, policymakers sought to depoliticize economic policy by returning to the market aspects of policy implementation formerly attributed to the state.

Most notably, the Federal Reserve's adoption in 1979 of monetarism—the policy of targeting the money supply rather than directly setting interest rates to control the rate of growth in the economy (see below)—represented an attempt to present policy choices as arising automatically from market-generated fluctuations in the supply of money in the economy. The monetarist experiment was beset with problems, however, and it quickly unraveled, but in later years policymakers would continue their efforts to govern the economy "at a distance" through varied techniques (Rose and Miller 1992). In the following pages, I analyze the evolution of monetary policy after monetarism was abandoned in 1982, tracing policymakers' attempts to enlist market mechanisms to avoid responsibility for economic management. Paradoxically, these efforts have continually revisited the same dilemma on policymakers: transferring policy implementation, and its attendant political risks, to the market has successfully deflected attention away from the active role of policymakers in guiding the economy, but it has also in varying degrees compromised policymakers' control of policy (cf. Burnham 2001). As this chapter shows, and consistent with what we observed in earlier chapters, the Federal Reserve's efforts to depoliticize its activities by turning to the market has placed control over the expansion of credit in the hands of a particularly lax master, creating conditions conducive to the financialization of the economy.

A Primer on Central Banking

Monetary policy is one of the least accessible domains of economic policymaking. Thus, in this section, I explain precisely how the Federal Reserve implements monetary policy, providing the necessary technical background for understanding the following narrative.[2] (Readers who are already well versed in the intricacies of monetary policy may want to proceed directly to the historical analysis.)

The Federal Reserve exercises a number of functions in the economy, but the most important is using monetary policy to smooth fluctuations in the business cycle.[3] In pursuing economic stabilization, the Federal Reserve attempts to influence economic activity by changing the level of interest rates. Interest rates affect the behavior of businesses by making it expensive or inexpensive to borrow to finance investment or consumption. Thus, in an "easy" (low) interest rate environment, economic activity will be stimulated; in a "tight" (high) interest rate environment, economic activity will contract. The Federal Reserve uses these relationships to conduct a countercyclical policy, stimulating a declining economy or slowing an economy that is in danger of overheating.

The process is not quite as straightforward as this brief description suggests, however, because the interest rate controlled by the Federal Reserve, the federal funds rate, is a *short-term* rate, whereas the interest rates that really matter for the economy are *long-term* rates.[4] Conventionally, the way economists relate the short-term rate that the Federal Reserve controls to the long-term interest rates that influence economic behavior is through the "expectations theory of the term structure" (Blinder 1998). Suppose a firm is undertaking a project that is expected to return the initial investment over a period of one year. The firm can finance the investment by issuing a one-year bond at the going rate or by taking out and renewing a loan with a one-day maturity 365 times in a row. This potential for arbitrage between short- and long-term rates requires that they move together, such that through setting a short-term rate, monetary policy should be able to control longer-term rates. The problem with this theory is that although it is infallible theoretically, its empirical performance leaves something to be desired. In short, economists do not have a good understanding of the mechanism through which monetary policy affects long-term interest rates. In this sense, the ability of monetary policy to ultimately affect economic behavior rests, in the words of one prominent economist, "on a minor financial miracle."[5]

Bracketing the problem of how the short-term interest rate controlled by monetary policy determines longer-term interest rates—and ultimately economic behavior—a brief explanation of the procedure through which the Federal Reserve determines the federal funds rate is necessary. The appropriate place to begin is with the realization that the levers pulled by the central bank in setting interest rates "work" because banks are required to maintain reserves against their deposits at the Federal Reserve.[6] That is, when a bank customer makes a deposit—in essence, a loan from the customer to the bank, redeemable on demand—the bank is required by law to set aside a certain percentage of the value of the deposit as a reserve, kept either as cash in its vault or in a special account maintained for the bank at the Federal Reserve. Banks failing to maintain reserves at the prescribed level over a two-week "maintenance period" are assessed a penalty (Edwards 1997). Depending on their activities over this period—and on their desire to maintain clearing balances *above* the required level of reserves—some banks will periodically find themselves short of reserves; others will have a surplus. The federal funds market is the market for reserve balances held at the Federal Reserve; it enables banks temporarily facing a shortfall in reserves to borrow overnight from banks with a surplus to meet reserve requirements and to avoid overdrafts.

The federal funds rate is the price charged for these overnight loans, determined—at least as an approximation—by the supply and demand for federal funds. In setting the federal funds rate, the Federal Reserve does not itself conduct transactions in this market—traders in the market are banks, other depository institutions, and their largest customers—but what it does do is manipulate the supply of bank reserves. It does so by executing what are called "open market operations"—the sale and purchase of Treasury securities—through the Trading Desk at the Federal Reserve Bank of New York. When the Federal Reserve purchases Treasury securities, it creates new reserves by crediting the account of the seller's depository institution at the Federal Reserve (Edwards 1997: 862). Similarly, when the Federal Reserve sells Treasury securities from its own portfolio, it extinguishes reserves by debiting the account of the buyer's depository institution at the Federal Reserve. In either case, the open market operation has changed the amount held in reserve at the depository institution's account at the Federal Reserve—and thus the amount that the bank will need to purchase, or have available to sell—in the federal funds market. This alters the level of activity in the federal funds market, changing the interest rate in this market.

In addition to engaging in open market operations to make it more or less difficult for banks to meet those requirements, there is another lever used by the Federal Reserve in setting policy: the discount window is the facility established by the Federal Reserve for the purpose of providing liquidity to the banking system, especially during times of acute financial stress. Thus, in addition to borrowing in the federal funds market, banks facing shortfalls in reserves may also seek to borrow directly from the Federal Reserve through the discount window. Surplus reserves borrowed from other banks through the federal funds market and funds borrowed directly from the Federal Reserve through the discount window are functional equivalents in terms of their role in enabling banks to meet reserve requirements. But when there is a significant price differential between the federal funds rate and the discount rate—which is controlled directly by the Federal Reserve, by fiat—borrowers may prefer to use the discount window (Clouse 1994). There are limits to the extent that such preferences are set by price considerations alone, however—a certain stigma is attached to borrowing at the discount window because of its association with distress lending.[7] But, within limits, the Federal Reserve can administer the discount rate—lowering or raising the cost of funds—in such a way as to either encourage or discourage borrowing at the window. Because banks meet whatever part of their borrowing is not satisfied in the federal funds market at the discount window, this too is another way of influencing prevailing interest rates.

Another way of understanding the relationship between the federal funds market and discount window borrowing is that when the demand for bank reserves rises, the federal funds market allows individual banks to trade reserves, but cannot remedy the aggregate shortage of reserves for the banking system as a whole (Meulendyke 1998: 141). This shortage can only be resolved when the Federal Reserve supplies new reserves through open market operations *or* when pressure in the federal funds market increases the federal funds rate, widening the differential between the federal funds rate and discount rate and inducing some banks to borrow at the discount window. This discount window borrowing adds new reserves to the banking system, expanding the money supply, just as occurs when open market operations are conducted. For our purposes, the important point is that a given level of borrowing at the discount window will tend to be (at least loosely) associated with a specific federal funds rate because they are approximately substitutes and both respond in the same direction to shifts in demand for bank reserves.[8]

A final tool at the Federal Reserve's disposal is to adjust the level of required reserves. The preceding discussion of both open market operations and the discount window presumed that the percentage of reserves that banks must set aside against deposits is locked firmly in place. In fact, the Federal Reserve has the option of setting required reserves at higher or lower levels, contracting or expanding the economy in a much more direct fashion than through conducting open market operations or changing the discount rate. In practice, however, the Federal Reserve does not make regular changes in the level of required reserves, relying on its other two tools to make incremental adjustments in the stance of policy on a day-to-day basis. When reserve requirements are adjusted, the long-term trend has been to lower rather than raise them as policymakers have sought to make membership in the Federal Reserve System less onerous for banks.[9]

To understand how these various mechanisms work together, consider a stylized example. Suppose that the economy is in the midst of a brisk expansion. As economic activity increases, individuals need a place to store new wealth, and banks take in additional deposits. As bank deposits grow, so do the reserves that banks are required to hold at the Federal Reserve against these deposits. If the Federal Reserve is conducting a countercyclical policy, it will "lean against the wind" by *not* supplying these reserves to banks through open market operations. That is, the Federal Reserve refrains from injecting reserves into the banking system by purchasing Treasury securities, but instead requires banks that are short of reserves to enter the market to bid for federal funds (or to borrow at the discount window). This activity in the federal funds market puts upward pressure on interest rates, "tightening" monetary policy and exerting a dampening influence on economic activity. If the Federal Reserve wants to impose further tightening, it can drain reserves from the banking system by using open market operations to sell Treasury securities. Because the accounts of the banks maintaining reserves at the Federal Reserve are debited by the amount of the Treasury sales, banks will find themselves short of reserves, placing additional pressure on the federal funds market and the discount window.

This process also works in reverse. Suppose the economy is languishing and the Federal Reserve wants to take steps to stimulate economic activity. The Federal Reserve can once more engage in open market operations to purchase Treasury securities. As a result of these purchases, the accounts of banks maintaining reserves at the Federal Reserve are credited, and reserves are made available to support new loans.[10] Simultaneously, bank borrowing in the federal funds market and at the discount window is reduced, easing pressure on interest rates and encouraging households and businesses to borrow to fund new consumption and investment.

As should now be evident, the Federal Reserve relies on a number of different methods of policy implementation. Although it is possible to differentiate between these methods on purely technical grounds, the Federal Reserve's choice between them has also been shaped by policymakers' attempts to negotiate a series of dilemmas as the performance of the U.S. economy has deteriorated in the period since the 1970s. In this regard, three discrete policy regimes should be distinguished from each other in the following historical analysis. Under the first policy regime examined below, the monetarist experiment in effect from 1979 to 1982, the Federal Reserve inverted its traditional procedure by targeting the money supply instead of interest rates. More specifically, under monetary targeting, policymakers attempted to hold what are known as "nonborrowed reserves" (so called because open market operations allow banks to meet reserve requirements without having to resort to borrowing, either in the federal funds market or at the discount window) at a constant level, allowing interest rates to move up and down as changes in economic activity increased or decreased the demand for reserves. Under a second regime, in operation between 1982 and 1987, the Federal Reserve resumed its use of an interest rate target, but attempted to control the amount of bank borrowing from the discount window (called "borrowed reserves"), relying on the special relationship between the discount window and the federal funds market to implement policy. Finally, under a third regime, in effect from 1987 to the present, the Federal Reserve has returned to its traditional procedure of directly targeting interest rates, but policymakers are now increasingly open about using this procedure. Most critically, beginning in 1994 policymakers began publicly announcing their interest rate target, a radical departure from the Federal Reserve's prior practice of keeping information about its activities a closely guarded secret. In what follows, I examine the evolution of monetary policy from the late 1970s to the late 1990s, suggesting that the development of transparency offered policymakers a means of reconciling contradictory imperatives to both guide the market and avoid responsibility for unfavorable economic outcomes. Paradoxically, this evolution has also progressively loosened policymakers' control over the expansion of credit, creating conditions conducive to the financialization of the economy.

The Evolution of U.S. Monetary Policy: 1979–2001

For many years, central bankers took it as an article of faith that monetary policy could only be effective when the Federal Reserve protected information about its activities from public knowledge (Goodfriend 1986; Greider 1987).[11] Most notably, monetarism represented a covert method of policy implementation in which Federal Reserve officials concealed policy choices behind the veil of market forces as drastic action to control inflation became necessary. Given the Federal Reserve's well-known penchant for secrecy, the gradual shift toward greater policy transparency in the period following the monetarist experiment represents a rather puzzling development. Central bankers' own explanation of this development revises the conventional wisdom to argue that more open disclosure makes monetary policy *more*—not less—effective (Blinder 2004; Woodford 2002). In particular, because transparency enables policymakers to credibly commit to objectives, market expectations can be enlisted in pursuit of policy goals. Although this argument is undoubtedly correct, transparency is not merely a technical aspect of policy implementation, but also represents a political strategy that enables policymakers to emphasize some aspects of their activities and not others (cf. B. Friedman 2002).

Thus, if monetary policy has become more effective under transparency, this greater effectiveness reflects the fact that policymakers have managed to avoid becoming embroiled in political contests over their basic objectives and how to best achieve these objectives. Such a situation could hardly be said to obtain at the outset of the period under examination. Paul Volcker's appointment to the chairmanship of the Federal Reserve in August 1979 occurred at a moment of intense politicization of economic policy, with policymakers struggling to appease both disgruntled consumers and financial markets veering toward panic. It was in this context that Volcker announced his "conversion" to monetarism in October 1979, perhaps the key event in the evolution of monetary policy over the past two decades.

The central claim of monetarism is that the role of the government in stabilizing the economy ought to be limited to ensuring a steady rate of growth of the money supply (M. Friedman 1968). Any other form of government intervention would quickly be "priced in" by omniscient markets, eventually resulting in more—not less—inflation. As such, monetarists argued that rather than narrowly targeting interest rates (the price of money), the Federal Reserve should set its sights on controlling the *quantity* of money in circulation. Milton Friedman, a key proponent of monetarism, liked to use the following analogy to explain monetary targeting: if the government wanted to control the number of cars produced, it could either set a price for automobiles *or* it could ration the quantity of steel available in the economy (Greider 1987: 107–108). In the former case, producers would determine how many cars to manufacture based on the mandated price, ordering the appropriate amount of steel to meet this production; in the latter case, the quantity of steel available would guide production, determining the prevailing price. Similarly, the Federal Reserve could contract or stimulate the economy either by controlling interest rates, in which case the money supply would adjust as borrowing became more or less expensive, or by directly controlling the money supply, so that interest rates would be bid up and down as economic conditions changed (Wallich 1984).

Although the two policy instruments are equivalent in a *technical* sense, monetarists endorsed monetary targeting because they believed that under a policy regime targeting the money supply, the Federal Reserve would refrain from the constant (and counterproductive) tinkering in the economy engendered by a policy that targeted interest rates (M. Friedman 1968). Policymakers were attracted to monetarism for other reasons, however. When the Federal Reserve directly set interest rates, the political blame for a recession was clear. But it was less widely understood that, in targeting the money supply, the Federal Reserve was also setting interest rates, albeit indirectly (as Friedman's automobile analogy made clear). Thus monetarism provided the Federal Reserve with the political cover it needed to push interest rates high enough to sharply contract the economy and suppress the inflationary pressures that had troubled policymakers for more than a decade.

When it became necessary (for reasons that are explored below) to end monetary targeting in 1982, Federal Reserve officials confronted questions about how to return to traditional operating procedures without sacrificing the flexibility acquired through the use of covert methods of policy implementation. These questions were not easily resolved: over the following two decades, policymakers engaged in an intensive process of experimentation in which they sought to construct changes in policy as the product of market mechanisms rather than deliberate policy actions (cf. Offe 1974). This chapter traces these developments historically by examining changes in the implementation of monetary policy at the

Federal Reserve between 1979 and 2001, culminating in the adoption of policy transparency.

The "Volcker Shock": 1979–1982

In embarking on its remarkable experiment with monetarism in October 1979, the Federal Reserve set on a course that would shape the evolution of the U.S. economy over the next two decades. By the time Paul Volcker assumed leadership of the Federal Reserve, there were any number of academic economists—Allan Meltzer and Karl Brunner, not to mention the ubiquitous Milton Friedman—carping at the Federal Reserve policy-makers to reform their techniques of policy implementation. These ideas began to receive a serious hearing at the Federal Reserve shortly after Volcker's arrival—not because Volcker believed in monetarism per se, which he considered "extreme" (Volcker and Gyohten 1992: 167)—but because, whether one believed in the theory or not, "the operational relationship between [bank] reserves and [the] money [supply] . . . was direct" (Volcker 2002: 9). That is, to control the money supply—M1, defined as currency in circulation plus demand deposits—the Federal Reserve needed only to hold so-called nonborrowed reserves at a constant level. A fixed quantity of reserves would support a given quantity of bank deposits and hence a fixed amount of money in circulation. As Volcker later explained, there was something psychologically appealing about clamping down on the money supply. "People don't need an advanced course in economics to understand that inflation has something to do with too much money," he wrote (Volcker and Gyohten 1992: 167). Anyone could grasp that inflation was related to the amount of money in circulation; by controlling money directly, the Federal Reserve would be seen to be taking direct action against inflation.

Equally important was what the Federal Reserve would *not* be seen to be doing. Advanced training in economics is also not necessary to grasp that interest rates have something to do with recessions. Critically, by claiming it was targeting the money supply and no longer concerned with interest rates, the Federal Reserve obscured its role in influencing interest rates. As Charles Schultze, President Carter's chairman of the Council of Economic Advisers, explained: "In a world in which the Fed runs policy by . . . setting the interest rate target, they are the ones who did it. Whereas if you get to exactly the same place by squeezing the money supply . . . [there's] nobody here but us chickens!"[12] Notwithstanding Volcker's argument about the "psychological appeal" of controlling money, the money supply remained an esoteric concept, far removed from everyday intuitions about the economy.[13] In this sense, as Schultze argued, even if the economic foundations of the monetarist experiment were dubious, "Volcker was fundamentally right about the politics of it."[14]

Although Schultze's retrospective analysis of the political significance of the policy shift is an apt one, this understanding of the rationale for monetary targeting fully emerged only after the policy was implemented. In particular, it was not salient as a motive for the adoption of the procedure. At the time the policy change was announced, the discussion in the Federal Open Market Committee (FOMC)[15] centered on the need to reverse inflationary psychology by making a dramatic move that would be seen as a departure from past methods of operating.[16] More practically, Volcker also hoped that the new technique would help committee members overcome the inherent inertia built into their policy deliberations where even wide swings in economic activity brought forth incremental adjustments in policy stance.[17] Only Governor Henry Wallich,[18] perhaps the most hawkish member of the committee, observed that under the cover of monetary targeting, the Federal Reserve would be able to raise interest rates more aggressively than otherwise possible. He noted, "We were very much more constrained in the [former] technique by the appearance of very high interest rates."[19] But such thoughts were not at the forefront of the concerns expressed by the other committee members or the chairman. There is a simple reason for this: in the fall of 1979, with the economy careening toward recession, committee members simply did not anticipate how high interest rates would have to go to suppress inflation.[20]

The political cover provided by monetary targeting quickly became evident, however. In controlling the money supply, the committee set a path for the rate of money growth that it deemed consistent with declining inflation. Should demand for reserves exceed the FOMC's projected growth in the money supply—indicating an acceleration in economic activity—the Trading Desk would hold steady to its path by refusing to supply additional reserves through open market operations, forcing banks to bid for funds in the federal funds market or to borrow from the discount window.[21] As a result, interest rates would rise, exerting a dampening influence on economic activity and gradually bringing money supply growth back within its target. Unlike academic monetarists, the FOMC staff was never under any illusion that it would be possible to precisely control the money supply using this procedure, but policymakers hoped that the technique would prove serviceable.[22]

In fact, during the first few months of monetary targeting, the new procedure seemed to function largely as anticipated. But this performance was short-lived: the money supply began to exceed its targets in February and March 1980. In the space of two months, the federal funds rate climbed from 13 to almost 20 percent—an unprecedented rate of increase. This rise was reversed just as quickly, as economic activity plunged precipitously in the following months.[23] The sudden collapse in economic activity in 1980 was exacerbated by President Carter's credit control program. Carter wanted to signal the shared sacrifice that fighting inflation would entail and asked the Federal Reserve to impose restrictions on consumer credit. Volcker opposed the controls and purposely designed them to be weak—large ticket items, such as auto financing and installment credit, were exempted. Nevertheless, Carter's plea to the American people resonated deeply, and borrowing in the U.S. economy came to an abrupt halt (Greider 1987).

Committee members were adamant that they had followed the money supply on the way up, and they should adhere to their targets just as closely on the way down.[24] By the first week in May, the federal funds rate had fallen to 13 percent; in subsequent weeks, it would fall further to around 9 percent, before the economy turned and started vigorously up again in mid-summer. Policymakers quickly discovered that in mechanically following movements in the money supply, the new policy produced surprisingly violent gyrations in the economy. With one more tap and release on the brakes—the FOMC applied restraint in the autumn of 1980 and then relaxed its grip again in the early months of 1981—the committee grew frustrated with the lack of progress against inflation.[25] President Gerald Corrigan asked his colleagues, "We've hit these targets for [a year] . . . so where are the results?"[26] If policymakers immediately offset each upward and downward movement in the money supply from its projected path, then policy restraint would never have a chance to take effect before policymakers turned the dial toward ease.[27] Like the restless hotel guest who continually tinkers with the thermostat as the room temperature alternates between extremes of hot and cold, policymakers realized that to achieve their desired objective it would be necessary to apply a consistent policy of restraint.[28]

In this context, the political logic of monetary targeting was immediately apparent to all. In an FOMC meeting in the winter of 1981 in which the effectiveness of the new operating procedures was assessed, Governor Lyle Gramley noted, "There really is only one reason why we should have abandoned the federal funds target procedure to go to the [nonborrowed] reserve target. And that is because if we operate on federal funds, we explicitly take responsibility for what is happening to interest rates and then this becomes a very difficult world to live in."[29] By the summer of 1981, the U.S. economy had entered a deep and grueling recession—with unemployment exceeding 10 percent, the most severe contraction since the 1930s—that would extend into the autumn of the following year. Interest-rate-sensitive industries—especially construction, automobiles, and agriculture—came to a grinding halt, throwing the agro-industrial heartland of the country into a near depression. The burden of Volcker's policy fell especially heavily on American exporters, who were squeezed out of foreign markets as the value of the dollar climbed with interest rates (see Chapter 4). Congress occasionally bared its teeth at Volcker, as did the Reagan administration, but, importantly, neither intervened, even as the economy plummeted.[30]

But if money supply targeting allowed the Federal Reserve to raise interest rates to record levels to suppress inflation, M1 proved elusive even as an approximate guide to policy. At the time monetary targeting was introduced in the early 1980s, a great deal of financial innovation was occurring in the U.S. economy, complicating policymakers' tasks immeasurably. In particular, the introduction of negotiable order of withdrawal (NOW) accounts—interest-bearing checking accounts—drew flows of savings away from traditional time deposits. NOW accounts were considered "currency-like" and therefore were included as a component of M1, rather than the broader measure of money, M2, as was the case for traditional time deposits. Thus one result of the movement of funds into NOW accounts was that M1 suddenly exploded. In this context, it was virtually impossible to determine whether M1 growth over its target reflected an acceleration in economic activity or merely a change in consumer preferences for different savings vehicles.

As a result, the relationship between the money supply and interest rates became erratic, making it difficult to calibrate changes in the money supply to real economic outcomes. In particular, if such overshoots in money growth targets reflected the fact that households were shifting assets into new savings vehicles rather than any real change in economic activity, holding fast to the targets would imply a greater degree of restraint than policymakers intended. Yet if the committee relaxed its targets, it would be seen to be reneging on its commitment to control inflation at any cost. The committee experimented with a variety of responses to this problem—"rebasing" the targets, widening the publicly announced ranges around its targets, and continually finessing the language explaining its actions—but none proved satisfactory. When serious financial strains began to emerge as a result of a prolonged period of high and volatile interest rates,[31] and with somewhat faster progress in reducing inflation than expected, the committee decided that, in Staff Director

Stephen Axilrod's words, "it was finally enough."[32] In the summer of 1982, with considerable internal dissent and confusion, the committee returned to relying on the federal funds rate as a guide to policy.[33] No explicit statement of the change in policy was made; the committee merely noted that somewhat more rapid monetary growth would be permissible in the context of "financial and economic uncertainty."[34]

Although the retreat from money supply targeting might have represented a kind of tactical defeat for the FOMC, the episode had nevertheless provided invaluable lessons. While the economy was left in a perilous position, inflation had been reduced from 13 percent when Volcker assumed his post to a quite respectable 4 percent; it would remain in this range through the end of Volcker's tenure at the Federal Reserve in August 1987. It was quite an accomplishment, particularly given the fact that only a few years previously, policymakers were seriously beginning to doubt that they possessed the tools to bring inflation under control. In the end, the most critical tool belonged as much to the art of politics as it did to economics. Volcker and his colleagues had learned that if the Federal Reserve could evade responsibility for setting interest rates, they could obtain "the flexibility to do what has to be done," as President Corrigan urged.[35] In Claus Offe's (1974) terms, policymakers had managed to "re-naturalize" the economy, returning to the market what had previously been attributed to the state: the Federal Reserve only determined a noninflationary growth rate for the money supply; markets did all the rest. If the Federal Reserve was to return to some form of interest rate target, as appeared inevitable given mounting difficulties in calibrating M1 to real economic outcomes, then every effort would be made to retain this lesson of the monetary targeting episode.

"Letting the Market Show Through": 1982–1987

Central to the Federal Reserve's strategy for maneuvering through this difficult period was the manner in which it communicated its policy intentions to the market and to the public. The heart of each FOMC meeting was an often lengthy session in which committee members laboriously drafted what was called the Directive—instructions to the manager of the Trading Desk at the Federal Reserve Bank of New York, whose job it was to interpret these instructions and observe market conditions to determine whether to conduct open market operations on behalf of the system. The Directive was purposely vague, with committee members often deliberating over such minutiae as whether to include an explicit reference to "weakness in the economy" in the Directive[36] or where to include M1 in the list of variables monitored by the committee.[37] The Directive was not made public immediately, but was released a few days after the following FOMC meeting, approximately six weeks later. During the period of monetary targeting, the most important information in the Directive included the targets set by the committee for M1, as well as for the broader monetary aggregates M2 and M3.[38] The Directive also included upper and lower limits for the federal funds rate that would trigger a committee consultation if interest rates moved higher or lower.

The problem for the FOMC in the summer of 1982 was how to ease policy without providing any indication to the public that the committee had returned to targeting interest rates. Although the Federal Reserve had won the battle against inflation, committee members were not certain that they had won the war. In the event of a resurgence of inflation, policymakers worried that they would be poorly positioned to raise interest rates if they had to do so openly, fully exposed to public criticism for slower growth and higher unemployment. President Frank Morris noted, "I think it would be a big mistake to acknowledge that we were willing to peg interest rates again. The presence of an [M1] target has sheltered the central bank from a direct sense of responsibility for interest rates, and this has contributed to a stronger policy posture."[39] But Morris acknowledged that M1 no longer provided a reliable guide for steering interest rates lower; along with other committee members, he worried that another miscalculation could crack the economy.

In these circumstances, the committee continued to report the monetary aggregates in the Directive, but as Governor Gramley bluntly put it, this was now done "to keep up a façade."[40] To be sure, the committee did closely monitor the aggregates along with broader developments in financial markets, but operationally the emphasis of policy had shifted. Rather than operating on a nonborrowed reserves target (and allowing the federal funds rate to adjust with changes in economic activity), the Trading Desk would now attempt to use discount window borrowing as its policy instrument. Because a fixed amount of discount window borrowing was associated with a given level of the federal funds rate, this procedure was functionally equivalent to targeting interest rates. But there was a subtle difference. In fact, Volcker was adamant in insisting that the Federal Reserve was *not* targeting interest rates: it was targeting borrowed reserves.[41] What Volcker meant was that the committee was not aiming at a *specific* interest rate—intervening in the market as much and as often as was necessary to maintain that rate—but instead was allowing the rate to fluctuate a little more broadly around an (unstated) target. The distinction was useful inside the committee—where there was considerable disagreement regarding appropriate operating procedures—but it was even more useful outside of it.

For the result of targeting the level of borrowing at the discount window was to tie down the federal funds rate—but not *too* tightly. As Volcker described it, borrowed reserves were a "loose steering wheel"[42]—the association between a given quantity of borrowing at the discount window and a specific level of the federal funds rate was only an approximate one. As such, compared with a procedure in which the federal funds rate was directly pegged, targeting borrowed reserves allowed market forces to "show through."[43] The term had a double meaning: on the one hand, it simply meant that looser control of the federal funds rate allowed policymakers to garner some information about market conditions from movements in the rate rather than merely gazing into the "mirror" of their own actions.[44] The second sense was perhaps more critical. In allowing some fluctuation in the rate, the Federal Reserve produced a market-like effect, making "the rate appear a bit more market determined than Fed determined," as Stephen Axilrod (2000: 72) observed. Marvin Goodfriend (1991: 29), an economist at the Federal Reserve Bank of Richmond, elaborated: "The resulting noise . . . obscures the underlying target and makes the federal funds rate appear free of Fed influence."

Thus the results of the modified procedure were analogous to the policy adopted in October 1979. As President Robert Black remarked, "The most important argument for using the borrowed reserve target is that it gives us a certain amount of political insulation so that we can let the funds rate move more than we otherwise would be able to do."[45] Under the procedure, Black elaborated, policymakers could claim that "we're not moving the funds rate, we are targeting [borrowed] reserves and the markets have driven the funds rate up."[46] Governor Wayne Angell concurred that it was important that the technique used by the committee "have the camouflage of market forces at work."[47]

Unfortunately, and also much like the earlier experience, the procedure of targeting discount window borrowing soon ran up against developments in the financial sector of the economy. In 1984, Continental Illinois, the ninth largest bank in the United States at the time, failed, itself a casualty of the collapse of the Penn Square Bank two years earlier. The distressed institution began a massive program of emergency borrowing at the discount window as it attempted to restructure its loans. As a result, other institutions, wary of being "tarred with the same brush," avoided borrowing at the discount window (Axilrod 2000: 72). This meant that the rough rule employed by policymakers—each additional $100 million of borrowing at the discount window represented approximately one quarter point increase in the federal funds rate[48]—was no longer reliable. In particular, if policymakers continued to aim at the same borrowing target, money would be much tighter than intended. Although policymakers were aware of this difficulty, they were reluctant to relax their target for fear it would be read by the market as an easing move.[49] Under the circumstances, Federal Reserve policymakers opted to keep money tight.

But if the Continental failure made using the borrowed reserves procedure difficult, it was the stock market crash that occurred in October 1987—a mere two months after Alan Greenspan assumed the chairmanship of the Federal Reserve—that finally brought an end to borrowed reserves targeting. In the context of an extremely fragile situation in financial markets, the Federal Reserve had to be sure that its position supporting the market was absolutely clear. Suddenly the ambiguity associated with "the camouflage of market forces"[50] was a liability. In the weeks following the crash, the Federal Reserve reverted to directly targeting interest rates, conducting whatever volume of open market operations was needed to maintain the federal funds rate within a narrow band.[51] Policymakers intended this change as a temporary response to crisis conditions. Over the next several months—months that gradually stretched into years—committee members looked for an opportunity to return to borrowed reserves targeting.[52] Yet every attempt to move away from narrowly targeting interest rates involved introducing more "ambiguity" into the federal funds rate and, as a result, risked unsettling financial markets. Increasingly, it appeared that policymakers would have to find a way to adapt interest rate targeting to new political and economic realities.

Toward Policy Transparency: 1987–1994

The stock market crash of 1987 signaled the limitations of a deliberate policy of obfuscation. It also inaugurated a period of experimentation that would lead inexorably, if indirectly, toward policy transparency. As committee members considered their options in the wake of the turmoil in financial markets, they vacillated between targeting interest rates narrowly and relying on the borrowed reserves procedure. Neither technique, however, offered policymakers a resolution of the dilemma they confronted. On the one hand, policy intentions needed to be conveyed clearly to be effective. On the other hand, the Federal Reserve's political position was compromised when it was perceived to be "setting" interest rates. President Thomas Melzer noted, "[When] the public and the politicians attribute to us having control over interest rates, we are on dangerous ground."[53] What would happen when inflationary pressures returned and policymakers once again felt the need to clamp down on the economy—perhaps as severely as they had in 1981 and 1982?

As the expansion of the 1980s approached record length, such concerns were increasingly on the minds of policymakers, prompting an intense debate on operating procedures within the Federal Reserve. In particular, the nature of reactions in the market to the Federal Reserve's policy adjustments became a focus of discussion among committee members. Under a procedure that targeted borrowed reserves, looser control of the federal funds rate meant that there was greater scope for the market to move interest rates. These market reactions tended to be stabilizing—the rate moved to desired levels in anticipation of policy moves—because market participants formed expectations of the Federal Reserve's likely response to incoming data on prices or economic activity.[54] As Board Advisor Donald Kohn explained to his colleagues, under borrowed reserves targeting, "the market can push us toward a higher or lower funds rate in anticipation of something we might be doing."[55] This situation could, of course, be quite advantageous to policymakers, facilitating needed policy adjustments.[56] The tendency of the federal funds rate to fluctuate with market expectations made it less likely that market participants would overreact to a small policy adjustment, as had often occurred when policymakers narrowly targeted interest rates.[57] As President Roger Guffey explained, "You have to keep it fuzzed up a bit to permit the Committee to operate."[58]

But the other side of keeping policy "fuzzed up" was that the market might misread policy intentions. Policymakers remained frustrated by the lack of a stable relationship between borrowed reserves and the federal funds rate. Straying too far from a narrow interest rate target could confuse markets—as policymakers learned in dramatic fashion following an incident in November 1989. Near-pandemonium broke out in the market after traders incorrectly interpreted Trading Desk activity—a "technical" adjustment with no intended implication for the stance of policy—as indicating an easing move by the Federal Reserve.[59] When incidents like this occurred, the market's tendency to "ease or tighten on its own"[60] could be destabilizing rather than stabilizing, working counter to policymakers' intentions.

As these discussions progressed, it became evident that more was at stake than the level at which federal funds would trade. For it was not only traders in the federal funds market who read off future policy moves from incoming data on prices and economic activity; increasingly, traders in the bond market did too. This was helpful to policymakers on a number of scores, not least because it offered the possibility of "shortening the lags" in monetary policy.[61] The conventional notion of monetary policy is that its hydraulics work slowly; a change in the short-term interest rate is only gradually transmitted to the long-term interest rates that "matter" for economic activity (Blinder 1998). If, in contrast, long-term rates moved immediately in response to an expectation of tightening or easing by the Federal Reserve, then restraint or accommodation would take hold in the market more quickly. Thus market expectations could amplify policy moves, providing valuable leverage over economic outcomes in the process.

Although policymakers had always observed occasions in which the bond rate anticipated policy moves, the notion that policymakers might attempt to manipulate market expectations as a deliberate part of policy strategy was novel. In part, this idea reflected the growing influence within academic economics of the notion of "credibility," which asserted that policy would be more effective if the central bank committed to its objectives in a fashion that was convincing to market participants (e.g., Barro and Gordon 1983a; Barro and Gordon 1983b; Cukierman 1992; Kydland and Prescott 1977).[62] Staff economists developed simulations in which they considered policy outcomes under scenarios where the committee had "strong" versus "weak" credibility.[63] In the first scenario, market actors would alter their current behavior on the basis of announcements of future policy plans; in the second scenario, credibility had to be earned anew with each policy action. The lesson of these simulations was that under a fully credible policy, market actors believed stated policy intentions and would therefore respond to these intentions immediately, helping policymakers to achieve their goals.

Credibility was often discussed in such general terms, but in practice the concept referred more narrowly to the central bank's commitment to low inflation (B. Friedman 2002). Credibility could be a double-edged sword, however, as committee members soon discovered. If establishing its inflation-fighting credentials meant that the Federal Reserve would react in a predictable fashion to incoming data on the economy— enabling markets to "move ahead" of policy because traders could anticipate the Federal Reserve's response—*markets were not the only audience for monetary policy.* In particular, policymakers worried about how the broader public would interpret a tightening move that was perceived to be a reaction to "good" news on the economy—especially if that news was in the form of strong employment numbers.[64] This was especially the case when the Federal Reserve made policy adjustments between meetings in response to the release of economic data. These occasions reinforced the impression that "the data led to the action," as Trading Desk Manager William McDonough noted.[65] In this context, committee members wondered how they could build credibility with markets while avoiding the unfortunate inference that in pursuing price stability the Federal Reserve was anti-growth and anti-employment. Greenspan fretted, "How do we develop [public] support for the policies we need?"[66]

Greenspan's question went unanswered, but it would assume even greater significance as the Federal Reserve became embroiled in a deepening political controversy regarding its disclosure policy in the following months and years. In the fall of 1992, Henry Gonzalez, chairman of the U.S. House Committee on Banking, Housing, and Urban Affairs, began pressing the Federal Reserve for greater openness in its deliberations. Gonzalez asked committee members to consider recording their votes, releasing minutes more promptly, and videotaping the FOMC meeting for eventual public release.[67] Committee members resisted these requests for the better part of a year, but in October 1993 Greenspan inadvertently acknowledged in testimony before Congress that the FOMC had made and retained transcripts of all its meetings.[68] Meetings were recorded to assist the secretary in preparing minutes, but until Greenspan's awkward admission, it was commonly assumed—by the public, as well as by most members of the committee—that the tapes and transcripts were destroyed following the publication of the minutes.[69] The admission unleashed a congressional fury.[70] Gonzalez demanded that the transcripts of the meetings be released to the public *and* that the committee release its policy Directive immediately following each meeting.

Although committee members seemed to take the congressional pressure largely in stride—there had been innumerable incidents like this in the past—the episode caused them to conduct an internal review of their disclosure policy. A subcommittee was formed,[71] which ultimately decided to protect the Directive from immediate release,[72] even as the committee moved toward voluntary release of lightly edited transcripts of FOMC meetings.[73] Initially, the committee resisted immediate release of the Directive because publishing it would involve revealing the so-called bias.[74] The bias referred to specific wording in the Directive that indicated whether the committee maintained a neutral ("symmetric") outlook for policy or was leaning ("asymmetric") toward an easing or a tightening move. The operational significance of an asymmetric Directive was that it authorized the chairman to take unilateral action—without a committee vote, if circumstances warranted—during the six-week period between FOMC meetings. Policymakers worried that the immediate release of an asymmetric Directive would tip the Federal Reserve's hand to markets, compromising policy by locking the committee into a given course of action.[75]

The notion that the release of information about future policy intentions would constrain policymakers was close to an article of faith among central bankers. This received wisdom was tested by a remarkable event in May 1993, however, when the committee's adoption of an asymmetric Directive toward tightening was accidentally "leaked" to the press. Although the use of the asymmetric Directive provided flexibility by allowing the chairman to respond immediately to developing conditions in the economy, committee members had become increasingly disenchanted with intermeeting moves that could be "linked to statistics on economic growth or unemployment."[76] But the accidental revelation that the Federal Reserve was biased toward tightening proved serendipitous, offering much-needed reassurance to the markets that the Federal Reserve was on guard against inflation. Following the incident, Greenspan reported that the growing fear in the bond market that the Federal Reserve was "behind the curve" on inflation had completely dissipated. "It's dead," he gloated to committee members.[77] Perhaps more importantly, the leak avoided the need for an intermeeting move—the news "[had] the market raising rates," Board Advisor Donald Kohn observed.[78] Here, it appeared, was a convenient way to both burnish the Federal Reserve's credibility as being "serious" about inflation and avoid the potentially damaging association between policy moves and incoming data on the economy.

In the following months, the unexpected impact of the accidental disclosure encouraged further experimentation in policy. At a highly unusual FOMC session held on February 4, 1994, Greenspan asked his colleagues for permission to announce an increase in the federal funds target.[79] It is impossible to read Greenspan's intentions from the transcript of the session—in suggesting the move, he was reversing both his publicly and privately stated opinions on disclosure policy. It does not, however, appear that Greenspan was merely folding to congressional pressure. By February 1994, the Federal Reserve had weathered the worst of the congressional storm; the FOMC had also already decided to release transcripts of its meetings, taking pressure off the policy decision. As Greenspan explained to his colleagues, "There's nothing forcing us to do [this]; I can't believe there will be legislation requiring [immediate release.]"[80]

Rather, it appears that Greenspan was taking seriously the suggestion made by several committee members that congressional requests for greater transparency should be complied with where disclosure made policy more effective.[81] As Trading Desk Manager William McDonough noted, "I think there would be an additional benefit [to announcing policy moves] because sometimes it isn't altogether clear how much we've eased [or tightened] and it takes us a day or two of fiddling around in order to convince the market exactly what was done."[82] The favorable response to the May 1993 leak provided the immediate context for Greenspan's change of stance, but in addition something akin to what McDonough articulated seemed to be motivating the chairman. This was the first tightening move in five years, and with inflationary pressures again on the horizon and an emerging speculative bubble in the equity market, Greenspan did not want the move to be "missed" by the market. "I would like to stand up and be counted. We are the central bank and we are making a major move. . . . To do so in an ambiguous manner I think is unbecoming of this institution."[83]

One thing is certain: Greenspan did not intend for the announcement to set a precedent. But the reaction to the announcement—a relatively trivial quarter-percentage-point move—in the market was startling.[84] Bond prices fell sharply and the stock market's upward climb came to an immediate halt, leading Greenspan to note in late February that "our action . . . had far greater impact than we anticipated."[85] The committee followed the February move with two additional quarter-percentage-point increases in quick succession, both of which were revealed to the public with statements similar to the February 4 announcement. By the end of March, the subcommittee charged with disclosure policy had formally reversed its earlier position, noting: "The February 4th experience . . . does suggest the possibility that there might be stronger reactions to announced moves both in the markets and in the public which could complicate the implementation of open market operations from time to time. But . . . the balance of costs and benefits in the view of the subcommittee has shifted toward the notion of announcing changes in instrument settings."[86]

The change in disclosure policy signaled a radical new direction for monetary policy. It also came at a critical juncture: given continued difficulties in implementing borrowed reserves targeting, for the first time since the "Volcker Shock," the Federal Reserve would be raising interest rates *without political cover*. As Staff Economist David Lindsey noted, "As the [federal] funds rate has become more discretionary, the less it [can] be characterized as responding to market forces. Sustained increases in the funds rate are more likely to be seen as a *deliberate policy choice* than as a by-product of obtaining other objectives."[87] But the experiments—planned and unplanned—of 1993 and 1994 raised intriguing possibilities. Perhaps it was possible that "markets could do the work of the Fed." The notion that the bond market could "help" policymakers was not new, of course; it had been central to the debate on operating procedures that occurred within the committee in the years following the stock market crash of 1987. But in those discussions it was presumed that the federal funds rate would move with the bond market, providing needed flexibility for the market mechanism to do its work. Somewhat ironically, the ingenuity of the current innovation in policy was precisely that the federal funds rate would hold still. One lesson of the May 1993 incident had been that an indication of a policy intention could in some circumstances *substitute* for action—without any loss of credibility in the market. Fully exploiting such possibilities would require another period of experimentation in which the Federal Reserve attempted to reap the benefits of its now considerable credibility with market participants, all while avoiding the familiar political liabilities of directly targeting the federal funds rate.

The Era of the Fed? 1994–2001

Monetary policymakers faced a number of novel challenges in the second half of the 1990s. Perhaps inevitably, the return to openly targeting interest rates dramatically increased the visibility of monetary policy.[88] "Our new policy is being watched with incredible intensity, not just by market participants but perhaps for the first time by the man in the street," noted Governor Edward Kelley.[89] Increased public attention to monetary policy reflected not only the committee's new policy of transparency, but also unprecedented volatility in financial markets as the decade progressed. This volatility itself represented a major constraint on policymakers. Although Greenspan's February 1994 announcement had been intended to "prick" an emerging bubble in the stock market, the response to the move had startled policymakers, who worried that further surprises could unsettle markets, perhaps with disastrous results. In this context, the committee's new disclosure policy allowed policymakers a means to restore confidence to jittery financial markets, while at the same time reducing the salience of each discrete change in policy. Under transparency, policymakers learned to follow rather than lead markets, restricting adjustments in the interest rate target to "validating" changes that had already occurred in the market. Of course, following behind market expectations meant that policymakers would increasingly abdicate control over the pace of credit expansion to the market, accelerating financialization and also sowing the seeds of a devastating financial crisis.

As tightening commenced in 1994, the immediate problem for policymakers was how to reassure financial markets following Greenspan's unexpected February announcement. Greenspan observed that because the increase in the interest rate target was intended as a "preemptive" strike against speculative activity in financial markets, it was not closely timed to incoming data on the economy. "When we were perceived as moving on the basis of economic data," Greenspan explained, "the markets had a certain sense of what we were doing. . . . Now they are worried that they don't know when we are going to move, and so we have this Sword of Damocles hanging over the market." In this regard, Greenspan emphasized the importance of making future moves predictable "with respect to timing as well as dimension." Greenspan recommended the third in a series of quarter-percentage-point moves: "The markets, having seen two moves in a row, will tend to suspect that the next move will be at a meeting. If the markets perceive that we are going to 4 percent by mid-year, moving only at meetings, then we will have effectively removed the Sword of Damocles."[90]

Greenspan's recommendation appeared to be a specific response to market conditions in the wake of the February 1994 announcement. In fact, Greenspan was writing a script that committee members would adhere to closely in the coming months and years, for it encapsulated a concise diagnosis of the committee's latest difficulty in implementing policy. Predictability was essential to enabling the bond market to "move ahead" of the Federal Reserve. However, the standard procedure for making policy predictable—responding to incoming data on the economy, typically through an intermeeting move—was no longer viable. In addition to appearing to position the Federal Reserve against growth, intermeeting moves in response to data releases were not effective in a context in which policymakers were increasingly committed to moving before price pressures were visible in the economic data. In this context, Greenspan's new practice of making policy adjustments only at scheduled FOMC meetings offered policymakers an alternative means of establishing predictability: traders no longer had to "guess" when a change in policy was likely to be implemented (Poole and Rasche 2000: 16–17).[91] In addition, statements accompanying a change in the interest rate target helped to contextualize policy adjustments. Was the move the first in an "installment plan," or was the Federal Reserve effectively "on hold" for the foreseeable future?[92] In this manner, committee members endeavored to inform markets of their intentions, making policy as predictable as possible.

But this strategy also raised a familiar problem in a new guise: if the market was informed, was not the public, as well? How could policymakers avoid surprising financial markets, without also broadcasting more widely that the Federal Reserve was initiating a series of tightening moves, especially at a time when inflationary pressures were nowhere visible in the economy? Paradoxically, transparency contained an unexpected solution to this well-worn dilemma. As committee members gained experience with the new disclosure policy over the course of 1994, they observed a curious result. When the Federal Reserve announced where it intended the federal funds rate to go, traders immediately moved the rate in anticipation of the move, and as a result the Federal Reserve actually had to conduct fewer operations in the reserve market to obtain the desired rate.[93] British central banker Charles Goodhart (2000; emphasis added) referred to this as the advent of "open *mouth* operations."[94] Perhaps more important than the effect of open mouth operations on the federal funds market, policymakers' increasingly expansive explanations of FOMC actions in statements, speeches, and congressional testimony provided opportunities to "condition" responses in the bond market. As a result, it was not necessary to adjust the federal funds rate as frequently or by as much to achieve necessary adjustments in long-term interest rates. As Board Adviser Donald Kohn explained, "Because the bond market anticipates your actions, long-term rates rise to the levels needed to counter the inflation impulse with *much less movement in the funds rate.*"[95]

Kohn's observation encapsulated transparency as policy strategy and as political logic. Ironically, if the central bank's communication strategy effectively prepared markets for a policy move, then sometimes *no* adjustment in policy was necessary. The notion was first introduced into committee discussions as policymakers considered whether monetary policy should be eased as President Bill Clinton's deficit reduction program exerted a restraining influence on the economy. Staff economist Thomas Simpson presented a model suggesting that if the bond market was fully "forward-looking," declines in long-term interest rates would provide needed stimulus to the economy and "no reduction in the federal funds rate would be necessary until the turn of the century."[96] The proposition was a radical departure from past operating procedures, and several committee members expressed skepticism of Simpson's model. Vice-Chairman Alan Blinder pressed Simpson, "If I'm reading this [chart] right, it says that . . . the fed funds rate stays fixed for four or five years. Is that what it says literally?"[97] Simpson affirmed. President Jerry Jordan objected, "This is like saying, if the bond market rallies enough, we don't have to lower the funds rate."[98] On another occasion, as policymakers contemplated the need for a tightening move in May 1996, President J. Alfred Broaddus observed that the staff's forecast relied on an increase in long-term interest rates to moderate a surging rate of growth in the economy. Broaddus explained, "What worries me is the impression that all of this can happen without an increase in short-term rates."[99] Broaddus insisted that to the extent that changes in long-term interest rates reflected expectations of policy rather than fundamental economic conditions, policymakers would eventually have to "validate" these expectations with an adjustment in the federal funds rate.

Notwithstanding these objections, over the course of the 1990s, the federal funds rate was held at fixed levels for extended periods of time, including a three-and-a-half-year period between January 1996 and June 1999 in which the federal funds rate was left virtually unchanged (Blinder 2005: 285).[100] But the logic described by President Broaddus was inescapable: the danger in relying on Federal Reserve statements to communicate the committee's objectives was that the market could become fixated on policy statements in and of themselves rather than for what they indicated about the committee's evolving view of conditions in the economy. If policymakers feared "disappointing" market expectations, they could quickly become locked in a game of mirrors with financial markets.

Such a prospect was especially worrisome following the East Asian financial crisis that unfolded in the autumn of 1997. Markets interpreted policy statements in the immediate wake of the crisis as indicating that the Federal Reserve would be "on hold" for an extended period of time.[101] In fact, the U.S. economy proved resilient and continued to perform strongly even as global financial turmoil spread. But markets refused to revise expectations in light of this performance. President Broaddus observed, "Even very strong economic reports are not getting much reaction in bond markets."[102] He continued, "The insensitivity of longer-term rates to growing momentum in the economy may prevent them from playing their usual [stabilizing] role." Governor Laurence Meyer drew the unavoidable conclusion for the committee: "If we want financial conditions to become less [accommodative], we will have to do the dirty work ourselves."[103] But doing the "dirty work" meant that the Federal Reserve would have to get *ahead* of market expectations, leading rather than following the market. This was almost inconceivable under current conditions. In addition to "grabbing headlines" and drawing unwanted attention to the committee, policymakers feared that an unanticipated move could cause stock markets that were dangerously overvalued to plummet, destabilizing the broader economy.

Under the circumstances, policymakers waited, hoping that long-term interest rates would begin to climb upward as the economic expansion continued to gain momentum. But such hopes were continually disappointed. As the months passed, the key question in the committee became how to best put markets on notice that an adjustment in policy would be made in the near future. Once again, navigating between the twin shoals of fragile financial markets and a potentially resistant public pointed in the direction of greater transparency—this time, in the form of the immediate release of the policy bias contained in the Directive. When committee members had last contemplated such a change during their review of disclosure policy in 1993 and 1994, it had been rejected for fear that the release of information about the future direction of policy would "pre-commit" policymakers to a given course of action. Now policymakers weighed this concern against the possibility that some indication of the likely future direction of policy might cause markets to refocus their attention on incoming economic data in light of the committee's assessment.[104] If markets had known that the committee had adopted an asymmetric Directive toward tightening in the early months of 1998, for example, the release of strong employment numbers might have garnered a more immediate response in the market.[105]

After discussing these issues for several months, the committee decided to allow the immediate release of the policy bias, first revealing its adoption of an asymmetric Directive toward tightening in May 1999. The announcement brought the long-awaited increase in market interest rates, which policymakers "validated" with their own move in June. Over the following year, the committee proceeded to tighten policy in a series of incremental steps, signaled to the market in advance with the aid of the asymmetric Directive. As a result, each move was already discounted by market participants and hence generated little or no reaction when it was implemented. In this respect, the new policy functioned exactly as desired: by letting market expectations run ahead of policy, and then validating these expectations with an occasional adjustment in the federal funds rate, policymakers had rediscovered a means of "quietly" changing their target (Goodfriend 2005).

In other respects, the latest innovation in policy implementation proved frustrating. Although policymakers had hoped that the release of the policy bias would sensitize markets to incoming data on the economy, market participants remained fixated on what the statement revealed about *policy* rather than about shifting economic conditions.[106] In this circumstance, committee members' earlier fears that narrowly targeting the funds rate would leave policymakers "looking in a mirror" were confirmed.[107] Committee members were adamant that they would not blindly follow the market with the new procedure—where the market departed from their own view of economic conditions, policymakers would refuse to validate market expectations, with the result that anticipatory moves by the market would quickly unravel.[108] But in addition to the perennial worries about disappointing nervous financial markets, there was now a potentially even more serious problem. How would policymakers know when the market was wrong? *Or when policy was?* If markets moved mechanically in response to the signals sent by policymakers, and policymakers in turn read off the appropriate stance of policy from changing market conditions, then both would move in a dizzying dance that could quickly become decoupled from underlying economic conditions.[109]

Such concerns led policymakers to make one final adjustment to their disclosure policy in December 1999, when they replaced the policy bias with a statement of the "balance of risks" in the economy. Policymakers hoped that in releasing a statement that referred to the risks policymakers saw in the forecast—weighted toward inflation or toward economic weakness—rather than the likely policy action, they would succeed in removing "our finger off the trigger," as Chairman Greenspan put it. Greenspan observed that central bankers had often made mistakes in the past by believing too much in their own infallible judgment. As such, the shift in orientation represented by the balance of risks language placed "more burden on [the market] to be certain and less on ourselves."[110] Given the feedback between policy actions and market reactions, policymakers had little alternative. As Greenspan explained, "In our meetings we are required to evaluate not only the balance of risks but also what our statement about the risks will do . . . which feeds back on our assessment of what the balance of risks is."[111] Such a chain of logic turned on itself endlessly, as markets dialed up and dialed down. If policymakers were consigned to look in a mirror, they preferred to turn the mirror at the market rather than have it reflect their own imperfect image. Policymakers, it increasingly appeared, did not set policy: they merely validated market expectations of policy, consistent with the balance of risks in the economy.

Economic Policy in an Era of Financialization

The crisis of legitimation faced by policymakers in the 1970s set the stage for developments in economic policy in subsequent decades. The evolution of monetary policy can be understood in terms of a key dilemma that confronted policymakers as public confidence in the state eroded with the general deterioration of economic conditions in the post-1970s period: markets require regulation to function, and yet the state is under pressure to escape responsibility for unfavorable economic outcomes. Under monetary targeting, policymakers attempted to negotiate the terms of this dilemma by relying on covert methods of operation. The Federal Reserve concealed its responsibility for the federal funds rate; as interest rates climbed, policymakers could claim that the market had propelled them there. When monetary targeting proved untenable, the use of a borrowed reserve target provided similar political cover for the committee. Policymakers deliberately allowed fluctuation in the federal funds rate in order to work behind the "camouflage of market forces."[112] But when the relationship between the federal funds rate and the borrowed reserves target became unreliable—with potentially severe consequences in financial markets—a return to directly targeting the federal funds rate seemed inevitable. Over the course of several years, policymakers vacillated between targeting borrowed reserves and targeting the federal funds rate, without a clear resolution of the dilemma that confronted policymakers. How could policymakers communicate their intentions to markets without at the same time compromising the political position of the Federal Reserve?

Transparency provided an unexpected solution to this problem—one which inverted the political lessons of the "Volcker Shock." Under monetary targeting, the Federal Reserve cloaked its policy instrument behind a veil and then used that instrument to manipulate the economy. Under transparency, the Federal Reserve threw back the veil on its policy instrument—but used it less and less as a lever to move the economy. Instead, the announcement of the federal funds rate target was deployed merely as a signal. Of course, the Federal Reserve had always signaled markets (e.g., Borrio 1997), but in the past policymakers had viewed this phenomenon a little ambivalently. There was a worry that markets might somehow slip policymakers' control, or worse, that the Federal Reserve might "follow" rather than "lead" the market.[113] Now such worries were set aside as policymakers became intrigued with the notion that "markets could do the work of the Fed." Not only was the committee able to use its disclosure policy to avoid moving under circumstances in which the Federal Reserve might be cast as anti-growth or anti-employment, but even when an adjustment in policy *was* necessary, the release of the asymmetric Directive allowed policymakers to "pave the way" for the move. As a result, when the chairman announced the committee's decision, markets had already moved in anticipation of the policy change, and the change in the interest rate target was a non-event when it occurred. As Vice

Chairman Roger Ferguson explained, "When [the Federal Reserve] is . . . predictable in its policy timing, its decisions are likely to raise fewer questions . . . When policy achieves a high level of transparency in this sense [of predictability], unexpected or rapidly evolving economic events and not policy changes are the news."[114] Committee members took the regime of transparency to its logical conclusion when, in the final months of 1999, they replaced the language of "symmetry" and "asymmetry" with a blander statement of the "balance of risks" in the economy, attenuating any direct implications for policy at all.[115]

Once the political logic of such a regime was clear, policymakers were effusive in celebrating the magic of market expectations. Critically, policymakers' claim that in moving interest rates they were simply "validating" changes that had already occurred in the market allowed the Federal Reserve to shield itself from potential criticism of its policies (cf. Burnham 2001; Flinders and Buller 2006; Hay 2007). But if such a formulation held great promise for policymakers, it also contained new dangers. It is only a small step from the idea that "markets do the work of the Fed" to the notion that the Federal Reserve doesn't do any work at all. Most prominent of those making that logical extension was Treasury Secretary Robert Rubin, who argued in meetings of the National Economic Council that the Federal Reserve was "redundant."[116] Because it was the market that ultimately determined prevailing interest rates, clumsy central bankers could only serve to impede this process, undermining market efficiency. More insidious than Rubin's attack on the Federal Reserve was the fact that this idea found an echo inside the institution itself. If in the past, central bankers had erred by placing too much weight on their own infallible judgment, as Greenspan suggested, now they would err by trusting too much in the infallible judgment of the market.

Although the Federal Reserve under Chairman Greenspan's leadership had acted quite "consciously and purposively"[117] to contain an emerging speculative bubble in the stock market in 1993 and 1994, by the end of the decade the now infamous idea that central banks should not attempt to control soaring asset prices had become the unofficial doctrine of the Greenspan era. We do not know precisely what led to the shift in Greenspan's thinking on this question, and undoubtedly there were multiple determinants.[118] But the analysis presented in this chapter suggests that the Greenspan doctrine evolved organically from the new methods of policy implementation adopted in the 1990s. In particular, as policy moves and market moves became more closely synched, central bankers gave up their ability to independently determine the correct stance of policy and thus had little choice but to trust the market to be right.[119] In one telling episode, committee members worried about the Federal Reserve's "exit strategy" as the market led policymakers in a string of easing moves following the stock market sell-off in 2001. As policymakers followed the market lower, each easing move caused market participants to build in expectations of greater easing to come, inviting policymakers to meet these expectations and turn the wheel again. In this context, committee members wondered how they would "get off the treadmill" when credit expansion in the economy became excessive.[120] Chairman Greenspan had an answer for his colleagues: "I think the market [will] take us off the treadmill."[121]

And so it did, although undoubtedly not in the manner that Greenspan imagined. Greenspan was expressing confidence that the market, in its infinite wisdom, would discern when policy easing had gone too far and lead policymakers to resume a more restrictive policy. Instead, as we now know, the Federal Reserve's failure to restrain the growth of credit in the economy ended the speculative bubble through other means—a devastating financial crisis whose effects are still reverberating in U.S. and global financial markets. Although most accounts of the financial implosion that began in the summer of 2007 pin the blame on Greenspan's decision to leave interest rates at low levels after 2001, the analysis presented here suggests that the conventional view offers only a very proximate explanation of the crisis. Greenspan's lax monetary policy was the culmination of a much longer-term evolution in which policymakers gradually abdicated control over credit to the market. The turn to the market was based on the notion that it would be possible to impose a more restrictive policy through the market than if such a policy were implemented directly and visibly by state officials. But as it turned out, the market was not a very effective source of restraint, and transferring control to the market ultimately served to loosen rather than restrict credit, propelling financialization to its most intense phase before bringing it to what appears to be a precipitous end. In the final chapter of this book, I consider the challenges facing U.S. society after the limits of financialization as a strategy for deferring social and political conflicts appear to have been reached.

CHAPTER SIX

Conclusion

The ineluctable fact about any society, as we now recognize, is that there is no escape from economics.
   —Daniel Bell (1976)

D ANIEL BELL'S STATEMENT above provides a fitting, if paradoxical, coda to the dramatic turn to the market in the past three
decades, a development that achieved perhaps its fullest expres-
sion in the processes I have explored under the rubric of financialization.
Bell intended to suggest that the post-industrial dream of an era of abundance in which scarcity was overcome could never be realized. But ironically, for Bell, the inability of society to "escape" economics did not imply
the ultimate triumph of the market (Brick 2007: 198). Instead, Bell suggested that novel forms of organizing the economy under post-industrialism
would pose new forms of scarcity,[1] requiring policymakers to assume an
ever more active role in allocating resources in a context in which claims
on the state proliferated seemingly without limit. In this sense, if economics
presented society with an inescapable reality, this was a *political* economics in which market processes were firmly embedded in the polity.

Bell's special brilliance was that he was prescient even when his predictions missed their mark. For most of the past three decades, U.S. society
did in fact appear to escape the resource constraints that first began to
press on policymakers in the late 1960s and emerged with full force in
the 1970s. In addition, this apparent escape from scarcity involved the
embrace of markets untethered from their political integuments. In the
financialization of the U.S. economy, policymakers avoided the difficult
choices that Bell suggested would increasingly embroil the state, present-
ing a series of impossible trade-offs between fiscal austerity, accelerating
inflation, and plummeting levels of public support. But critically, the turn
to finance did not play this role by virtue of unleashing a new era of

economic growth—long the American remedy for distributional conflict (Collins 2000). Rather, domestic financial deregulation, the restructuring of global capital markets, and changes in the implementation of monetary policy removed internal and external constraints on the expansion of credit in the U.S. economy, fueling financialization while also alleviating resource constraints. An economic model that rested on a rapid pace of credit expansion was necessarily a fragile one, however, and in this sense the policy regime associated with financialization *suspended* rather than eliminated scarcity.

It is therefore not surprising that, in the context of the still unfolding crisis in U.S. financial markets, economics has reasserted itself with a vengeance. State officials now face a set of trade-offs that are of a 1970s vintage: Will policymakers provide relief to homeowners caught by rising mortgage payments, perhaps blunting the recession in the short term but contributing in the longer term to inflationary pressures that threaten to erode the living standards of other social groups? Will policymakers impose new restraints on credit, returning to an era of administered markets in which some rationing mechanism (overt or covert) must be devised and legitimated? Or will policymakers continue to allow credit to flow freely, encouraging serial asset bubbles in which financial exuberance is transmitted from one market to the next, risking an even deeper financial crisis in the future? Whatever they choose, how can policymakers avoid public accountability for one or another of a series of unpalatable choices? Although it would be imprudent to offer any firm predictions here, it does appear that, as a response to the crisis conditions of the late 1960s and 1970s, the episode marked by financialization is coming to a close (cf. Fligstein 2005).

In this context, it is now clear that financialization did not resolve, but merely deferred, questions that first confronted U.S. society in the late 1960s and 1970s regarding which social actors should bear the burden of a fading prosperity. Either these questions will become increasingly fraught, the focus of intensifying social conflict, or it will become necessary to forge what Bell (1976) described as a new social compact about how to achieve social objectives with limited resources.[2] Bell was not overly sanguine about the possibilities for achieving agreement on such issues, but if anything the prospects for creating a public philosophy that could undergird collective decisions about distribution have become even more difficult in the years since he wrote. Bell (1976: 278) noted that such a compact must rest on "conscious decisions, publicly debated, and philosophically justified, in the shaping of directions for society," yet as I have argued, financialization has been a means to avoid such conscious decisions over the past several decades. More generally, the depoliticization of the economy that has been a key element of the turn to finance has atrophied the collective capacities that Bell called upon in *The Cultural Contradictions of Capitalism* (1976). In this chapter, after first drawing together the threads of a complex narrative, I elaborate on the process of depoliticization as a means of understanding the nature of the challenges confronting American society in an era after financialization no longer serves as a means of deferring distributional conflict.

Capitalizing on Crisis

This book has examined how policymakers' ad hoc responses to the economic crisis of the late 1960s and 1970s created conditions conducive to the turn to finance in subsequent decades. The state faced three interrelated difficulties as the era of postwar abundance came to an end: a social crisis associated with increased distributional conflict as growth slowed, a fiscal crisis that resulted from policymakers' attempts to meet proliferating demands with ever more limited resources, and a legitimation crisis that reflected sinking public confidence in the ability of the state to act as a steward for the economy. Inflation was the common denominator of all three crises, an outcome of policymakers' efforts to extend the fruits of economic growth beyond the limits that were becoming apparent beginning in the late 1960s. If the robust economic growth of the immediate postwar decades had eased latent distributional conflicts and financed an expansive state, inflation would accomplish these same tasks through other means when growth faltered. As numerous commentators observed, inflation served to mask open distributional conflict, allowing competing groups to dissipate social tensions in a game of leapfrog in which winners and losers continually traded places (Crouch 1978; Goldthorpe 1987; Hirschman 1980). Similarly, a permissive attitude toward inflation enabled policymakers to pursue their objectives without regard to budget constraints, at least for a finite period of time. But critically, the solutions that inflation offered to the end of growth became increasingly dysfunctional over the course of the 1970s, exacerbating rather than alleviating social conflict, contributing to deteriorating state finances, and embroiling the state in a full-blown legitimation crisis by the end of the decade. These developments set the context for the turn to finance.

Just as inflation had temporarily offered an answer to the dilemmas posed by slower growth, the turn to finance would answer the dilemmas posed by inflation, similarly allowing policymakers to avoid the constraints associated with declining affluence. Of course, policymakers did not pursue the financialization of the economy with this objective clearly in mind. On the contrary, the policy regime associated with the turn to finance initially reflected policymakers' efforts to impose new limits on the U.S. economy rather than evade these limits. By the late 1970s, policymakers viewed accelerating inflation as signaling the need for restraint in a society that had come to take for granted a continually improving standard of living, and yet state officials were understandably quite reluctant to impose this restraint directly. Critically, policymakers did not at this time conceptualize the turn to the market as offering a ready alternative. Outside of a few isolated proponents of the new laissez-faire economics, there was no general presumption that market outcomes would necessarily be accepted as legitimate (Crouch 1978; Goldthorpe 1987; Hirsch 1978). Because markets do not supply their own normative foundations—as Bell (1976: 277) wrote, "The market is a mechanism, not a principle of justice"—relying on the market to distribute the economy's less bountiful spoils threatened to exacerbate social divisions and deepen political conflicts. For this reason, observers on the left endorsed the reassertion of state control over distributional outcomes through the imposition of an incomes policy (or more radically, the reorganization of distributional politics altogether with the establishment of socialism), while observers on the right pinned their hopes on the restoration of traditional values that would encourage moderation, displacing the hedonism of Western consumer culture with family, community, and God.

When neither of these solutions proved workable, trial and error led policymakers to the embrace of the market that now appears in hindsight as the only possible route out of the 1970s. The notion that the ascendance of the market under neoliberalism was inevitable, however, pays insufficient attention to the inadvertent discovery made by policymakers who deregulated markets in the 1970s and 1980s. In particular, although policymakers turned to the market as a means of exerting discipline on proliferating demands on the state, in fact the market would deny these demands no more effectively than had state officials (cf. Greider 1987: 660). Paradoxically, the market was not the strict disciplinarian imagined by neoliberal visionaries, operating with the blunt force of unforgiving nature, but a surprisingly lax master. As a result, policymakers' reliance on market mechanisms did not plunge the state into divisive conflicts about how to allocate limited resources, as Bell (1976) feared would occur, but rather allowed policymakers to dissolve emerging political tensions into what for the moment appeared to be a return to prosperity.

Policymakers first made this discovery in the context of domestic financial deregulation. In the regulated financial environment that characterized the U.S. economy before 1980, mechanisms built into the financial system regulated the business cycle and channeled capital toward productive activity. But as inflationary pressures became embedded in the economy, these mechanisms began to malfunction, distorting flows of capital in the economy. As a result, policymakers were forced to make explicit choices about which sectors to favor in the allocation of credit: Would policymakers direct capital to business or housing, large corporations or small business, urban areas or struggling farmers? As these choices became increasingly politicized, the deregulation of financial markets offered a means to substitute the rationing mechanism of the market for the heavy hand of the state. In particular, the elimination of interest rate ceilings meant that the market could do the choosing in deciding which sectors to favor in the distribution of capital, sparing policymakers this unpalatable task. But in fact markets did *not* prove to be particularly effective rationing devices, and deregulation opened the taps on credit in the U.S. economy. The era of capital shortages was transformed into an era of freely flowing credit, allowing policymakers to escape a zero-sum political calculus where directing capital to one use necessarily meant denying it for another.

Of course, the danger in freeing credit was that financial deregulation would contribute to accelerating inflation (Wojnilower 1980)—a prospect that threatened to reintroduce the zero-sum considerations that policymakers seemed to have momentarily escaped. This threat was compounded as unprecedented government deficits in the early 1980s placed extraordinary pressure on credit markets, prompting the Volcker Federal Reserve to dramatically tighten monetary policy to counter inflation. In a closed economy, Volcker's draconian policy would have choked off demand for credit as private borrowers competing with government were crowded out of financial markets, likely forcing the Reagan administration back on to the path of fiscal austerity. In the context of newly liberalized global capital markets, however, the effects of the policy were quite different from what policymakers expected: high interest rates brought foreign capital pouring into the U.S. economy, providing ample capital to private and public borrowers alike. Critically, high interest rates also suppressed the productive economy, diverting inflationary pressures into financial markets where they fueled asset price bubbles, contributing to a debt-financed consumption boom in the U.S. economy (Greider 1987; Konings 2008).

In short, neither domestic nor global financial markets seemed capable of turning away the seemingly limitless demands of U.S. households, corporations, or the state for capital. As a result, the locus of policy restraint shifted from controlling the *supply* of credit to controlling its *price* as deregulation weakened quantitative restrictions on credit flows in the U.S. economy. This was the domain of monetary policy, which became increasingly central in the exercise of economic policy beginning in the early 1980s. But here too, the temptations of the market proved irresistible. Federal Reserve officials learned that when they operated behind the cover of market forces, they could impose a more restrictive policy than would be possible if they openly took responsibility for higher interest rates. This was the main lesson of the monetarist experiment, but even after monetarism failed, the strategy of "following the market" allowed state officials to avoid the appearance that they were acting against growth or employment in managing the economy. As was also true of efforts to rely on market mechanisms in other domains, however, policymakers ultimately ceded control over policy outcomes to the market, accelerating the expansion of credit in the U.S. economy.

Thus the basic elements that supported the financialization of the U.S. economy—most critically, a rapid pace of credit expansion associated with domestic financial deregulation, large foreign capital inflows, and a monetary policy regime that "followed the market"—were put in place over the course of the 1980s and 1990s. In the preceding chapters, I argued that these policy changes created conditions conducive to the financialization of the U.S. economy through two specific mechanisms. The first, arguably more important, mechanism was the effect of the uncontrolled growth of credit on increasing financial sector profits, particularly as free-flowing credit fueled asset price bubbles in financial markets. Wider availability of credit allowed investors to purchase assets with less money down, exerting upward pressure on asset prices and thereby encouraging further asset purchases in a self-reinforcing cycle. The second mechanism involved the role of the interest rate shock administered to the U.S. economy in the early 1980s in reorienting nonfinancial firms to financial markets. As I elaborated in Chapter 2, extraordinarily high interest rates discouraged nonfinancial firms from borrowing to finance productive investment and instead directed corporate treasurers toward higher-yielding financial assets that could return invested capital more quickly. The interest rate shock was itself relatively short-lived, but the volatility it introduced proved an enduring feature of the U.S. economic landscape. This volatility encouraged the expansion of financial activities, as finance entrepreneurs introduced a dazzling array of new products designed to allow firms to protect themselves from (or speculate on) fluctuations in interest rates (cf. Strange 1986).

These two mechanisms, of course, do not exhaust the manner in which state policies shaped the turn to finance. I have placed emphasis on these mechanisms because they emerged as salient in the research I conducted and because the complexity of the narrative necessarily requires some selectivity in focus. But even these two factors intertwine in a complex manner, with the relationship between the level of interest rates and the pace of credit expansion shifting in important ways over time. Initially, soaring interest rates in the U.S. economy accelerated the pace of credit expansion by drawing unprecedented quantities of foreign capital into dollar-denominated assets (Frankel 1988). Later, cause and consequence were reversed, as large inflows of foreign capital *reduced* interest rates in the U.S. economy by increasing the supply of credit circulating through financial markets. Notably, this evolution reflects an important element of path dependency: extraordinarily high returns on dollar-denominated assets drew foreign investors into the orbit of U.S. markets in the early 1980s, but maintaining access to the insatiable American consumer eventually became the more salient motive of the foreign central bankers who financed U.S. deficits (see Chapter 4). Accordingly, the high interest rates of the 1980s and 1990s turned to historically low interest rates in the 2000s, with both regimes associated with the rapid growth of credit that sustained financialization in the U.S. economy.

In the financialization of the economy, policymakers would find an unexpected resolution to the various policy dilemmas they confronted in the guise of social crisis, fiscal crisis, and legitimation crisis of the state. Paradoxically, this resolution was possible not because policymakers successfully transferred the task of disciplining unrestrained social wants to the market, but rather because the market *failed* to impose the discipline that policymakers sought. Under the policy regime that supported financialization, capital would no longer be scarce but available in abundant supply, with the result that incipient political conflicts over how to distribute limited resources between competing social priorities were effectively *depoliticized*. But much like the experience of inflation in the late 1960s and 1970s, which similarly allowed state officials a brief respite before deepening the very conflicts to which it appeared an answer, the turn to finance is likely to be self-defeating as a means of avoiding the difficult political choices that confront American society. In the discussion that follows, I consider the reasons why through an examination of the process of depoliticization.

The Depoliticization of the Economy

As Flinders and Buller (2006: 4) note, "Depoliticization is something of a misnomer." The term suggests the evacuation of politics from the realm of the market, and indeed has been celebrated as such by commentators who argue that transferring economic policy from deliberative bodies such as Congress to quasi-judicial bodies such as the Federal Reserve elevates technocratic considerations over political ones in the execution of policy decisions (e.g., Blinder 1997). But as Polanyi (2001) emphasizes, there can be no such excavation of politics from the economy, as this is the substratum on which all market activity—even that organized in "free" markets—rests. Rather than the removal of politics, depoliticization should therefore be understood as the reorganization of the boundary between the political and the economic so as to allow policymakers to govern the economy "at one remove" (Burnham 2001: 128). But while the state continues to guide economic outcomes (albeit using indirect methods) under this regime, depoliticization represents more than a sleight of hand in which nothing is changed other than the outward appearance of state action. To be sure, depoliticization operates by assigning social objects to one side or another of a conceptual divide that marks off state from market (cf. Somers 2008), but these ideational effects rest on what is an *actual* reorganization of material practices (Burnham 2001). In other words, depoliticization is accomplished not by fiat but through institutional innovation, which closely involves the state (Polanyi 2001).

Conceptualized in this manner, the depoliticization of the economy encompasses a number of processes occurring at different levels (see Hay 2007 for a more elaborate discussion). If for something to be "political" means that it is subject to human manipulation or control, then the most fundamental form of depoliticization is to remove some question from the realm of active decision to the realm of fate where the exercise of human agency is neither possible nor desirable. The implementation of economic policy is replete with examples of depoliticization that take this form, particularly when the market is invoked as a quasi-natural force that trumps all countervailing social considerations. Once a given problem area is admitted as belonging to the realm of human control (and therefore the subject of politics), then two less absolute forms of depoliticization are possible. One involves the transfer of a given problem from the direct control of elected officials to nonelected officials or to the nongovernmental public.[3] This is what Chorev (2007, 2009) refers to as "judicialization" and "bureaucratization" to describe the transfer of policy questions from arenas where they are subject to open deliberation to arenas that are insulated from such deliberation through legal protocols and layers of protective rules about who may access the proceedings. A classic example of this form of depoliticization is the removal of monetary policy from direct legislative oversight through the establishment of formal central bank independence. Traveling a further distance from the political, problem areas may migrate from governmental or nongovernmental publics to the *private* realm of domestic deliberation and consumer choice. Relegated to this realm, problems are still subject to human decision (and hence political in the most fundamental sense), but no longer subject to public scrutiny and deliberation. The depoliticizing effects of rendering some problem a "private" matter are so well known as to scarcely require elaboration (but see Weintraub 1997).

Although all of these forms of depoliticization involve the transfer of social problems between various social arenas, more or less subject to deliberation and influence, another dimension of depoliticization is concerned less with the social location of decisions than with their *content*. This is depoliticization by technocratic expertise, which involves the attempt to imbue decisions with objective knowledge, creating a gulf between these decisions and those that are said to reflect questions of values to be resolved in public, quasi-public, or private settings (Starr and Immergut 1987). Claims of technocratic expertise depoliticize by imposing both *social distance* as the exclusive authority of the scientist over a problem area is established and *temporal distance* as facts are gathered, ordered, and acted on in a methodical process that is foreign to the rhythms of political life (Offe 1984). These two dimensions need not develop in the same direction: health care represents a problem area that has been *politicized* in recent decades as questions regarding health have increasingly become a matter of public rather than private concern, but *depoliticized* to the extent that health care policy has been defined as a matter of technical knowledge rather than lay judgment (Starr and Immergut 1987). This example underscores the point that tendencies to depoliticize or politicize given areas of social life can move in either direction, extending or retracting the boundary of the political (Burnham 2006).

This raises the question of what, exactly, is at stake in these back-and-forth movements. As I have emphasized in the preceding chapters, the predominant tendency toward depoliticization in recent decades can be understood as a response to the overt politicization of the economy under the Keynesian regime of the 1950s and 1960s. However, the "political" character of Keynesian economic management was of a very particular kind. Keynesianism involved the state taking responsibility for aggregate economic performance, but removed the state from more interventionist forms of steering markets, such as had been under discussion during debates on the feasibility of national planning during the 1930s (Goldthorpe 1987).[4] Keynesian policies thus avoided the direct administrative control of particular industries and sectors, even as the state's endorsement of economic growth as an explicit national goal politicized management of the economy more broadly. As Offe (1974, 1984) observed, the mere promulgation of an official state policy aimed at sustaining growth changed the social definition of economic events that were now attributed to state action—or its failure. This was a boon to state managers under conditions of robust growth in the 1950s and 1960s, but it could become a liability when economic conditions deteriorated, as they did precipitously in the U.S. economy in the 1970s and later decades.

In this context, it is easy to understand the appeal of depoliticization and its significant limitations as a strategy of economic governance. Critically, as conditions supporting broadly based prosperity in the economy eroded, efforts to shift aspects of policy implementation from state institutions to markets allowed policymakers to shield themselves from responsibility for unfavorable events such as inflation or unemployment. Depoliticization thus offered an answer to the basic dilemma confronted by neoliberal policymakers who faced contradictory imperatives to regulate the economy while deflecting attention from their active role in guiding economic outcomes (cf. Burnham 2001). But while reliance on market mechanisms provided essential protection to policymakers, it also involved a significant loss of control over the outcomes of policy. We observed this in the case at hand in which policymakers' attempts to evade difficult decisions about how to allocate scarce capital between competing social priorities (Chapters 3 and 4) as well as the practice of making changes in the stance of monetary policy behind the cover of market forces (Chapter 5) were both associated with the loss of control of credit in the U.S. economy—with ultimately disastrous consequences.

But if neoliberal policymakers necessarily lose some degree of control over policy outcomes, an even more serious failing of depoliticization as a form of economic governance is the erosion of *consent* to economic outcomes (Goldthorpe 1987). Credit claiming and blame avoidance are in this sense asymmetric strategies of economic management (Weaver 1986). In the Keynesian era, the state's assumption of responsibility for sustaining growth exposed state managers to criticism, but also allowed the state to encourage normative commitments that legitimated economic policies, especially those aimed at securing broad participation in the labor market and a more equal distribution of resources across society. Under neoliberal economic management, in contrast, the state's avoidance of responsibility for economic outcomes may shield policymakers from public scrutiny, but it does not build a foundation for state action. As the state has withdrawn support from the goals of full employment and steadily improving distributional outcomes, the basis of consent is no longer clear. Nor is it obvious how state managers can organize consent on whatever basis by pulling market levers.

Of course, market ideologues have long assumed that markets do not require normative foundations—or at least supply their own through the encouragement of a kind of fatalistic acceptance of market outcomes. Fatalism is indeed one possible answer to the problem of consent, but the appeal to the market as quasi-natural force is likely to operate within well-defined limits. One such limit is defined by prior historical experience: although fatalistic acceptance of market outcomes may have been feasible in the pre-Keynesian era, it appears considerably more difficult following the Keynesian episode, as numerous theorists observed as Keynesianism was unraveling (Bell 1976; Hirsch 1978; Offe 1984). But even were the half-life of state intervention relatively short and expectations encouraged under Keynesianism easily reversible, fatalism would still appear to operate only within a restricted range of market outcomes. Most notably, in the wake of a severe financial crisis in the U.S. economy, few individuals appear ready to accept the sudden deterioration in their livelihoods as simply the hand that the market has dealt them.

In addition, although distressed homeowners, failing industries, and insolvent financial institutions have all turned to the state for assistance in the recent crisis, the experience of depoliticized economic management has left the state with few resources to navigate this complicated new terrain. To reiterate, depoliticizing economic management may have allowed policymakers to slip the blame for the last crisis, but this has hardly established a reservoir of public support for state action, and as a result the state's response to *this* crisis is from a considerably weaker position. The state's efforts to reassert a more active role in managing the economy under rather extraordinary circumstances have drawn reactions ranging from bewilderment to open hostility. From truncated discussions of bank nationalization, to failed efforts to regulate executive compensation, to widening resistance to the Federal Reserve's use of unorthodox techniques to supply liquidity to capital-starved businesses and households, there is ample evidence to suggest the state's options are becoming increasingly circumscribed, even as the need for bold action grows more urgent.

It should now be clear why the state's effort to avoid politics by governing through the market has been a self-limiting strategy in the context of the financialization of the U.S. economy. To the extent that the turn to the market has avoided the spreading conflicts that embroiled policymakers in the late 1960s and 1970s, this was a result not of a once-and-for-all cultural shift that elevated the market as the arbiter of human fates, but a rather more idiosyncratic (and likely less durable) feature of neoliberal statecraft. By managing the economy indirectly through market mechanisms, policymakers transformed an era of capital scarcity and perennial credit shortages into apparent prosperity, obviating the need for an emergent social consensus of the sort that Bell (1976) had urged. But we now know that financial exuberance rested on exceedingly fragile economic, as well as normative, foundations: just as free-flowing credit subjected the economy to the spasms of financial markets, so the moral life of the nation has also ridden surging and collapsing asset prices.

We should therefore be wary of diagnoses of the current crisis that focus narrowly on policy mistakes in the years leading up to the financial collapse—as though our current predicament might have been avoided had those mistakes not been made (cf. Goldthorpe 1987). To be sure, Federal Reserve Chairman Alan Greenspan's lax monetary policy in the early 2000s, as well as the broader failure of the Federal Reserve and other regulatory agencies to rein in shady mortgage dealings, accelerated the credit expansion and deepened the resulting crisis. But as the preceding chapters have demonstrated, our current problems rest on a deeper political economy than is suggested by such analyses. It is not only Greenspan's reckless policy that brought us to the abyss, but more fundamentally the inability of an affluent society to face the political challenges imposed by the end of affluence. In this regard, the analysis presented here reaffirms an observation that John Goldthorpe (1978: 211–212) made in the crucible of the 1970s: "Free market relations will in themselves be unable to provide a basis for their own stable continuance, [and] further they will be the source of divisions and antagonisms which may then lie at the root of what are experienced as economic problems."

Goldthorpe was referring to the inflation crisis, but he may just as well have been writing of the financial excesses that have become our generation's own economic quagmire. The important implication is that the problems confronting U.S. society, then as now, will not yield to merely technical solutions. This is not, of course, to underplay the magnitude of the economic difficulties facing the U.S. economy, where the unrestrained expansion of credit over nearly three decades has compromised financial institutions and burdened households with spiraling debts. In this regard, a resolution of the financial crisis will require clearing the tangle of bad loans from the books of financial institutions and restoring households to financial solvency—both extremely daunting tasks. Even more daunting, it will also involve reconstructing the regulatory architecture of domestic financial markets to prohibit the highly leveraged financial plays that featured prominently in the implosion of mortgage markets, as well as rebuilding the international financial system so as to prevent the buildup of the global economic imbalances that are the ultimate source of financial manias, panics, and crashes (Gao 2009). Once these tasks are completed, however, there remains a task for which we are far less equipped.

This task is, of course, to define a public philosophy to guide decisions about distribution. We are less equipped for this task because for more than two decades the problem of distribution has been eclipsed by financialization,[5] eroding collective capacities to engage questions of economic justice. "The problem of capital," Bell (1976: 230) observed in the mid-1970s, "will *always* be with us." Policymakers at the time concurred, and they viewed it as their responsibility to allocate scarce capital between competing social purposes (cf. Thurow 1980). In turning to the market, policymakers not only avoided this responsibility, but they also avoided taking up the question that Bell (1976: 278; emphasis added) suggested must be confronted: "How much do we want to spend, and *for whom?*" The market, Bell (1976: 277) understood, could not resolve such matters because these are questions for which the price mechanism has no metric. In fact, it was precisely the state's role as arbiter—to return to our point of departure—that threatened to plunge the state into ever more divisive conflict in a society in which boundless economic growth no longer provided easy answers to every social and political dilemma. This was the predicament presented by organizing allocation around political rather than economic power: political decision making *concentrated* responsibility, whereas the market *dispersed* it (Bell 1976: 197, 226). Accordingly, as questions regarding how resources are allocated and rewards distributed in our society once again concentrate in organized centers of political power, it will be necessary to ground these questions in a broader public debate regarding our social priorities and how these priorities will ultimately be financed. In short, in the era after financialization, there will be no alternative to the political management of the economy, with its attendant conflicts and crises.

APPENDIXES

NOTES

REFERENCES

INDEX

Appendix A: Notes on Sources

Chapter 2

A variety of different data sources were used to construct the measures of financialization presented in Chapter 2. For data on corporate profits, sectoral employment, and gross domestic product by industry, I used data provided in the *National Income and Product Accounts*. For data on portfolio income and foreign income taxes, I relied on information contained in the *Corporation Income Tax Returns*. I used the *Balance of Payments* to obtain data on U.S. profits earned abroad and the *Corporate Foreign Tax Credit* data to construct series for foreign-source interest income and foreign income taxes paid. A number of issues arise in the use of these sources that merit special discussion, and I address these separately in Appendix C.

Chapter 3

The examination of the social politics of U.S. financial deregulation presented in Chapter 3 is based on an analysis of hearings on nearly every major piece of financial reform legislation that came before the U.S. Congress between the early 1960s and the end of the 1980s. Congressional hearings on major legislation affecting the financial sector contain expert testimony by bankers, manufacturers, labor, urban advocates, and consumer groups. In this respect, congressional records provide an extremely useful data source: although the social actors impacted by monetary and financial policies remain veiled in many kinds of documentary evidence, these actors are quite literally written into the script of these hearings. An analysis of the shifting position of various social actors in debates concerning the structure of the financial system therefore offers a view of how state officials and non-state actors interpreted the economic problems confronting the country beginning in the 1960s and how policymakers' responses to these problems transformed the political constraints operating on the state.

Chapter 4

The analysis presented in Chapter 4 is based on archival research at the Ronald Reagan Presidential Library in Simi Valley, California. I used memoranda from Cabinet Council meetings and the papers of members of the Council of Economic Advisers to trace the evolution of various policy positions within the Reagan administration and to determine what Reagan officials knew regarding the likely outcome of several of these policy initiatives. To assist interpretation of these archival materials, I also conducted supplementary interviews with former Reagan administration officials and other "policy intellectuals" who were close observers of economic policy during the 1980s (see Appendix B). Because there were gaps and inconsistencies in the secondary literature discussing the events I analyze in the chapter, it was necessary to work across these various sources, putting events into sequence and using interviews to verify and provide a context for information contained in historical documents.

Chapter 5

For the analysis in Chapter 5, I relied on the verbatim transcripts of the meetings of the Federal Open Market Committee, the policymaking arm of the Federal Reserve. This document constitutes a fascinating source of data that is very likely unique in terms of the comprehensiveness of coverage.[1] Yet there are considerable challenges to using the transcripts. The first and perhaps most daunting is simply one of energy—at the time I conducted the research reported in this chapter, transcripts had been released for every year between 1979 and 2001, with each year containing approximately 500 pages of text. Because of the difficulty of interpreting a document of this sort—specific conversations contain references to prior debates and discussion—I read through the transcripts in sequence more or less completely rather than devising a sampling strategy. Beyond the sheer bulk of the transcripts is the nature of the speech they contain: monetary policy is conducted in what can accurately be described as its own particular—and highly inaccessible—language. After a first pass at the transcripts in which I was unable to penetrate beyond a surface-level understanding of what was being discussed, I delved into the technical literature published by the journals of the various Federal Reserve Banks. This literature became a data source in its own right, providing a separate record of the evolution of policy regimes within the Federal Reserve System. In addition, I conducted a series of supplementary interviews with former and current members of the Federal Reserve Board, as well as with academic experts on monetary policy (see Appendix B). These interviews provided essential preparation for using the transcripts as they directed my attention to particular issues in reading the transcripts, such as shifting understandings of how markets might be enlisted in the implementation of monetary policy.

Appendix B: Interview Subjects

The following is a list of individuals (and relevant current and former positions) interviewed for the research contained in this book.

Stephen Axilrod, Secretary, Federal Open Market Committee (1979–1986); Staff Director, Federal Open Market Committee (1978–1986); Staff Director for Monetary and Financial Policy, Federal Reserve Board (1976–1986). Interviewed in Lyme, Connecticut, on July 15, 2002.

C. Fred Bergsten, Director, Institute for International Economics. Interviewed in Washington, D.C., on July 19, 2002.

Ron Blackwell, Director, Department of Corporate Affairs, AFL-CIO. Interviewed in Washington, D.C., on July 22, 2002.

Alan Blinder, Professor of Economics, Princeton University; Vice-Chairman, Federal Reserve Board (1994–1996); member, President's Council of Economic Advisers (1993–1994). Interviewed in Princeton, New Jersey, on July 8, 2002.

Douglas Cliggott, hedge fund manager, Brummer and Partners. Interviewed in New York City on July 11, 2002.

Jane D'Arista, finance economist, U.S. House Committee on Energy and Commerce, Subcommittee on Telecommunications, Consumer Protection, and Finance (1983–1986); analyst, Congressional Budget Office (1978–1983); economist, U.S. House Committee on Banking and Currency (later renamed House Committee on Banking, Currency, and Housing and House Committee on Banking, Housing, and Urban Affairs) (1966–1983). Interviewed in Hadlyme, Connecticut, on July 15 and 16, 2002.

Jeffrey Frankel, Professor, Kennedy School of Government, Harvard University; member, President's Council of Economic Advisers (1997–1999); economist, President's Council of Economic Advisers (1981–1983). Interviewed in Cambridge, Massachusetts, on July 12, 2002.

Benjamin Friedman, Professor of Economics, Harvard University. Interviewed in Cambridge, Massachusetts, on July 12, 2002.

David Huether, Director of Economic Analysis, National Association of Manufacturers. Interviewed in Washington, D.C., on July 25, 2002.

Donald Kohn, Governor, Federal Reserve Board; Adviser to the Board for Monetary Policy (2001–2002); Secretary, Federal Open Market Committee (1987–2002); Director, Division of Monetary Affairs (1987–2001); Deputy Staff Director for Monetary and Financial Policy (1983–1987). Interviewed in Washington, D.C., on July 18, 2002.

Roger Kubarych, Senior Economic Adviser, HVB Americas, Inc.; Managing Member and Chief Investment Officer, Kaufman and Kubarych Advisors, LLC (1997–1999); General Manager, Henry Kaufman and Company (1988–1997); Senior Vice President and Chief Economist, New York Stock Exchange (1986–1988). Interviewed in New York City on July 9, 2002.

William Niskanen, Director, Cato Institute; member, President's Council of Economic Advisers (1981–1985). Interviewed in Washington, D.C., on July 18, 2002.

Martin Regalia, Vice President and Chief Economist, Economic Policy Division, U.S. Chamber of Commerce. Interviewed in Washington, D.C., on July 23, 2002.

Alice Rivlin, Vice-Chairman, Federal Reserve Board (1996–1999). Interviewed in Washington, D.C., on July 19, 2002.

Charles Schultze, Chairman, President's Council of Economic Advisers (1977–1981). Interviewed in Washington, D.C., on July 24, 2002.

Beryl Sprinkel, Chairman, Council of Economic Advisers (1985–1989); Treasury Undersecretary for Monetary Affairs (1981–1985). Interviewed in Chicago, Illinois, on August 16, 2002.

Albert Wojnilower, Chief Economist, Credit Suisse First Boston, for over 25 years. Interviewed in New York City on July 10, 2002.

Janet Yellen, President, Federal Reserve Bank of San Francisco; Professor of Business Administration, University of California, Berkeley; Chair, President's Council of Economic Advisers (1997–1999); Governor, Federal Reserve Board (1994–1997). Interviewed in Berkeley, California, on June 1, 2002.

Appendix C: Economic Data

In this appendix I provide more detailed information regarding definitions of concepts and methodological issues involved in the use of data in Chapter 2.

GNP versus GDP Conceptions of the U.S. Economy

There are two methods of compiling data on the U.S. economy. The first method corresponds to the definition of gross national product (GNP) and includes as part of the domestic economy all economic activity conducted by U.S. residents, wherever it is located. Thus, by this definition, the U.S. economy includes profits generated domestically and profits earned abroad by U.S. corporations. The profits of foreign corporations from activities undertaken within the geographic boundaries of the United States are excluded from this measure. The second method, corresponding to the definition of gross domestic product (GDP), counts all economic activity occurring in the territorial United States, regardless of ownership. Thus this conception of the U.S. economy includes the profits earned by foreign firms from their U.S. operations but excludes the profits of U.S. corporations earned abroad.

Except where noted, the data in Chapter 2 are reported on a GDP basis. Economic data reported on a GNP basis are not disaggregated by industry, so it is only possible to do the analyses in Chapter 2 using data that reflect the GDP-conception of the U.S economy. As noted, this leaves the analysis vulnerable to the objection that the results reported in Chapter 2 are generated by the offshore activities of U.S. corporations—a hypothesis that is examined systematically. While I do incorporate U.S. profits earned abroad in that analysis, I do not remove foreign profits earned in the United States, as would be required to put the measure on a GNP-basis. Due to data limitations, this is not possible, and hence I cannot fully discount the possibility that the findings reported in Chapter 2 are generated by foreign investment in the U.S. economy. However, while foreign (financial) profits in the U.S. economy may contribute to the results here, they are unlikely to account for these results, given the small size of the foreign sector relative to the domestic economy. In this sense, the argument is exactly analogous to the one presented for U.S. profits earned abroad.

Definition of the Financial Sector

Within the *National Income and Product Accounts,* the *financial sector* corresponds to the following industries: depository institutions, nondepository credit institutions, brokers and dealers in securities and commodities, security and commodity exchanges, and insurance carriers. This represents all industries included in the broader FIRE industry group except insurance agents, real estate, and holding and other investment companies.[1] The "holding and other investment companies" industry is a component of the "other holding and investment companies" group and is not published separately in the Bureau of Economic Analysis's (BEA) industry detail. Thus my approximation to the financial sector is FIRE minus real estate and insurance agents. Because the "holding and other investment companies" industry is small relative to the rest of the financial sector, this is a very close approximation. The only exception to this treatment is the foreign-sector data. The *Balance of Payments* does not provide the same level of industry disaggregation as the *National Income and Product Accounts.* As a result, for U.S. profits earned abroad the financial sector is constructed as FIRE minus real estate; for consistency, the same definition is applied to the foreign tax and foreign-source investment (dividends and interest) income data. Again, this should not affect the results as the "insurance agents" industry is small relative to the size of the financial sector.

Company versus Establishment Basis for Industrial Classification

Industrial classifications may be determined on an "establishment" basis or on a "company" basis. An establishment is an economic unit at a single physical location. A company is composed of one or more establishments owned by the same legal entity, regardless of physical location. Establishments are assigned an industrial classification on the basis of their principle product. While companies may own establishments in many different industries, companies are assigned to an industry on the basis of the activity that generates the largest revenue in all establishments. Thus, where data is reported on a company basis, individual establishments may be misallocated to whichever industry dominates revenues for the entire company. Except for the data used in constructing the portfolio income measure and the data on foreign income taxes, all data used in Chapter 2 is reported on—or approximates (see below)—an establishment basis.

Corporate Profits and Depreciation

There are many well-known pitfalls to working with data on corporate profits; perhaps the most significant of these is that there are powerful incentives to disguise earnings. In this regard, it is important to note that the corporate earnings scandals of the late 1990s concerned profits reported on *financial statements*. While profits reported on financial forms are subject to very loose (so-called pro forma) accounting conventions, this is not the case for the profits reported to the Internal Revenue Service (IRS), which form the basis for the analysis contained in Chapter 2. Most critically, stock options *are* expensed in these data. More generally, it is important to put the methodological difficulties associated with working with profit data in perspective: there are significant advantages to using this data, especially relative to most other social science data gathered by survey techniques. The IRS, which collects the "raw" data used in the National Income and Product Accounts, has nearly universal coverage. The response rate is close to 100 percent—impossible to achieve for most social science surveys. While there *are* biases to reporting profits, these biases are well understood. Finally, there are very substantial penalties for misreporting profits to the IRS—a feature that very few social science surveys can claim.

The objective of the BEA in reporting profit data is to measure revenues earned on the basis of *current* production. In addition to removing dividend income and capital gains from the IRS source data, this concept also requires the BEA to adjust IRS data for sources of income that approximate a capital-gain-like windfall, such as profits that result from the effect of inflation on sales from inventories. Consistent with BEA practice, all profit data in Chapter 2 are reported with the inventory valuation adjustment. I do *not* report data with the capital consumption adjustment, however. Because it is conventional to do so, some further explanation is warranted.

A discussion of how the BEA uses IRS data to estimate corporate profits will clarify the relevant issues. In calculating its measure of profits, the BEA first takes IRS profits, adds IRS depreciation allowances back in (as I did in constructing corporate cash flow), and then subtracts its own measure of depreciation from the resulting total. The difference between IRS depreciation allowances and BEA estimates of depreciation is referred to as the "capital consumption adjustment." While profits are commonly reported with the capital consumption adjustment, there are problems with using this adjustment when comparing financial and nonfinancial profits. The IRS reports depreciation allowances on a company basis, whereas the BEA depreciation estimates are constructed using establishment data. Thus, if some financial sector depreciation is misallocated to the nonfinancial sector for the company-based IRS depreciation figure, but correctly allocated to the financial sector for the establishment-based BEA depreciation figure, then the capital consumption adjustment becomes large for nonfinancial firms and small or even negative for financial firms, distorting profit estimates accordingly.[2] Thus, because of the problem of nonfinancial ownership of financial firms, company and establishment data should not be combined when comparing financial and nonfinancial profits.

Foreign-Source Portfolio Income

To construct a portfolio income series that includes foreign-source income, I use data on foreign-source dividends paid to U.S. nonfinancial corporations in the *Corporation Income Tax Statistics*. In addition, information on interest earned by U.S. corporations on foreign investments is available in the *Foreign Tax Credit* data. Unfortunately, information on foreign-source capital gains is published only sporadically in the *Foreign Tax Credit* data; thus, in order to construct a consistent time series, these data are not included here. Inspection of the data in years for which capital gains are reported separately suggests that they are not a large component of foreign-source portfolio income and hence their exclusion should not seriously compromise these results. Profits and depreciation allowances earned abroad by U.S. nonfinancial corporations are similarly added into the denominator of the portfolio income measure. As was done with the domestic measure, foreign-source interest income is subtracted from U.S. profits earned abroad to ensure that the denominator reflects solely nonfinancial sources of income. Finally, because U.S.

profits earned abroad are reported in the *Balance of Payments* data after foreign income and withholding taxes, these taxes are added back into the measure in order to put U.S. profits earned abroad on a pre-tax basis.

The principle challenge for extending the analysis of portfolio income to incorporate foreign-source portfolio income is data availability. Data on dividends paid to U.S. corporations by foreign corporations contained in the IRS *Corporation Income Tax Statistics* are available for the full time series as the domestic portfolio income measure. Data on interest income earned abroad, foreign taxes paid, and depreciation deductions claimed against foreign taxes by U.S. corporations are published in the IRS *Foreign Tax Credit* data for the following years: 1964–1966, 1968, 1972, 1974, 1976, 1978, 1980, 1982, 1984, 1986, 1990, and 1992–1999. Finally, data on U.S. profits earned abroad from the *Balance of Payments* are only available at the proper level of industry disaggregation for the period from 1977 to the present. The intersection of these three data sets makes it possible to construct a time series incorporating the following years: 1978, 1980, 1982, 1984, 1986, 1990, and 1992–1999.

U.S. Profits Earned Abroad

The concept of profits in the *Balance of Payments* data differs somewhat from that used in the *National Income and Product Accounts*. In the *Balance of Payments,* profits are approximated by "direct investment income," which includes both earnings (profits) and net interest. Net interest refers to U.S. parent earnings on loans to foreign affiliates, net of any interest payments on loans from foreign affiliates. Although the BEA does not publish profit data by industry without the net interest figure, net interest is a very small component of direct investment income and thus can be safely ignored.

Direct investment income is prorated by ownership share, regardless of whether U.S. earnings abroad are actually repatriated. For example, imagine a U.S. parent that holds a 60 percent share in a foreign enterprise. If the affiliate reports $100 million in profits, then a sum of $60 million is considered to be U.S. profits earned abroad.

Data availability at the proper level of disaggregation is an issue in constructing the time series for U.S. profits earned abroad used in Chapter 2. For 1950–1965, "finance and insurance" is not reported separately in the *Balance of Payments,* but is included with the category "other industries." For the series from 1966 to 1976, "finance and insurance" is broken out as a separate industry, but the "depository institutions" in-dustry is included in the "other industries" category. Only for the period beginning in 1977 do the data allow an approximation to the definition of the financial sector used in the rest of the Chapter 2. Thus, for the analysis of global profit data, I confine myself to the disaggregated data available for the period beginning in 1977. In more recent years, the analysis is constrained by the foreign tax data (see below), available only through 1999.

Foreign Taxes Paid by U.S. Corporations

Industry-level data on U.S. profits earned abroad are reported after for-eign income and withholding taxes (but before U.S. taxes). Thus, to put these data on the same pre-tax basis as the domestic profit data, these foreign taxes must be added back into profits. Between 1977 and 1999, the IRS published data on *foreign income taxes paid* by U.S. companies for the following years: 1978, 1980, 1982, 1984, 1986, 1988, 1990, 1991, 1992, 1993, 1994, 1995, 1996, 1997, 1998, and 1999. For years in which data are not available, I use *foreign tax credit claimed,* as reported in the *Corporation Income Tax Returns.* The two measures are not equivalent: firms do not necessarily claim all of the credit for which they are eligible (their available credit may exceed the U.S. profits they are offsetting), certain deductions are allowed, and firms are also allowed to "carry over" unused credit from one year to the next (Ward 2000). Inspection of the data for years in which both measures are published, however, indicates that the foreign tax credit is a close proxy for actual taxes paid in most years.

As noted, the data on U.S. profits earned abroad (corrected for the payment of foreign taxes) are incorporated into measures of both "global" portfolio income and "global" financial and nonfinancial profits.[3] In the latter case, the treatment of foreign taxes involves special compli-cations. The data on taxes paid by U.S. firms to foreign governments as-sign industrial classification by industry of parent; the data on U.S. prof-its earned abroad are reported by industry of affiliate.[4] Thus, when these two series are merged, there is some risk that part of the foreign taxes paid will be misallocated across industries. In particular, to the extent that nonfinancial U.S. parents own financial affiliates abroad, financial profits will be understated once taxes are added back into profits.[5] In the analysis presented in Chapter 2, I set aside this problem, reporting U.S. profits earned abroad *before* foreign income and withholding taxes (i.e., foreign taxes are added back into profits), which in any case represents a conservative estimate. An examination of the data reveals that reporting U.S. profits earned abroad *after* foreign income taxes makes little differ- ence for the basic story told in the Chapter 2, other than indicating slightly higher overall levels of financialization in the offshore activities of U.S. corporations.[6]

Notes

1. Introduction

1. I present the relevant empirical evidence for this claim in Chapter 2 of this book. See also Sassen (2001) for a similar observation about the dominance of financial services in the expansion of the service sector in recent decades. Gerald Davis's (2009) recent book *Managed by the Markets* also interprets post-industrialism as reflecting the growing dominance of finance in the economy.

2. Bell (1973: 3) distinguished between "predictions" and "forecasts," although I have used these terms interchangeably here.

3. This is admittedly something of a simplification of Bell's (1973) construct of post-industrialism, which referred to the rise of the service sector only in its *economic* dimension. Bell's formulation also included cultural and political dimensions (or "axial principles").

4. Notably, theorists of every ideological persuasion espoused the view that the state was becoming entangled in a number of insurmountable problems, although the precise nature of these problems was defined somewhat differently. In addition to Bell (1976), see Brittan (1976), Habermas (1973), Huntington (1975), Janowitz (1976), King (1975), O'Connor (1973), Offe (1974, 1976), and Wolfe (1977), among many others.

5. See Vogel (1996) for an especially illuminating interpretation of Polanyi's thesis in the context of the deregulation of financial services and telecommunications in Britain and Japan.

6. I use the term "neoliberalism" sparingly in this book, instead referring directly to "the turn to the market" or "the rise of the market" wherever possible. This avoids some of the confusion that exists around the idea of liberalism, especially as the concept has come to be used in the U.S. context. In addition, this usage marks what is central about neoliberalism—its reliance on "market-like" rule—while avoiding the tendency in much of the literature to define the term

by referring to a laundry list of policies (e.g., monetarism, free trade, deregulation, etc.), without clearly specifying what integrates these various elements into a unified regime. See Somers (2008: 74) for a related discussion.

7. Just as Copernicus demonstrated that the earth revolves around the sun rather than the sun revolving around the earth, so observers of the contemporary economy have learned that corporations revolve around financial markets rather than the other way around (Davis 2009: 5).

8. Data on financial profits in the U.S. economy are from the Bureau of Economic Analysis *Gross Product Originating* Series. I examine the growth of profits in the financial sector more systematically in Chapter 2. While the data analysis presented in that chapter ends in 2001, reports in the business press suggest that financial sector profits continued to dominate nonfinancial profits at least through the beginning of the mortgage market crisis in the summer of 2007 (see, for example, "The Profits Puzzle," *The Economist,* September 15, 2007, 91). The financial crisis has likely now reversed this trend, but whether this represents the end of financialization or merely a temporary setback for the financial sector is difficult to know with certainty.

9. "Alternative Lenders Buoy the Economy, but also Pose Risk," *Wall Street Journal,* June 10, 2002, A1.

10. For some readers, counterpoising "finance" and "production" in this manner will invoke Marxist theory, which treats only those activities that directly produce surplus value as "productive" and all other activities as "unproductive." These connotations are unintended. I view the question of whether specific financial activities are productive of economic value or purely wasteful as an empirical matter, not one that can be settled a priori. Notwithstanding these difficulties, I use this terminology throughout the book, reflecting the fact that the alternatives are equally problematic. Economists often contrast the "financial" and "real" economies, for example, but this has the unfortunate implication that finance is "unreal." More neutral language would simply describe "financial" and "nonfinancial" activities, but because I discuss the financialization of nonfinancial firms at some length (see especially Chapter 2), this language quickly becomes cumbersome.

11. See Evans (2003), Shiller (2000), and Shleifer (2000) for useful surveys of this voluminous literature.

12. Minsky's (1982, 1986) analysis does provide some discussion of specific historical conditions that account for growing financial turbulence in the period since the 1970s. For Minsky, the financial turmoil of the post-1970s period reflects the tendency of "Big Government" to act increasingly aggressively in order to forestall financial crises, a stance that paradoxically encourages speculative behavior.

13. A related, and broader, issue in this literature is the classic question of who controls the modern corporation. This issue is an important one, but takes us somewhat afield from questions concerning the growing importance of financial activities in the economy. For this reason I set it aside here, but interested readers should consult Mizruchi (1996, 2004) for comprehensive reviews of this issue.

14. This is the Panglossian view of "agency theory," a neoclassical perspective that suggests that the institutions of shareholder capitalism effectively align the interests of owners (principals) and managers (agents) by appropriately monitoring or incentivizing the behavior of managers (Fama and Jensen 1983; Jensen and Meckling 1976). Sociologists would concur with agency theorists that shareholder value has implications for management behavior, but they would reject the claim that the institutions of shareholder capitalism produce outcomes that are optimal for the economy or that the existence of these institutions could be fully explained by such optimality, if it existed. See Fligstein and Choo (2005) for an outline of the sociological critique of agency theory.

15. The dramatic rise of institutional investors reflected a number of developments. Perhaps most importantly, advances in information technology and the end of fixed commissions in 1975 significantly lowered transaction costs on trading, encouraging a much higher volume of trade. In addition, in 1974 Congress liberalized restrictions that had prevented life insurance companies and pension funds from investing in equities, opening the market to a flood of institutional money (Lazonick and O'Sullivan 2000). The share of public stock held by institutional investors increased from less than 10 percent in 1950 to account for almost 50 percent of outstanding shares in 2000 (Crotty 2005).

16. Gerald Davis has offered a similar critique of this literature from an "inside" perspective; see especially Davis and Stout (1992) and Davis and Thompson (1994).

17. Proponents of these theoretical traditions may object to being grouped together in this fashion. My intention here is not to paper over the significant differences between Marxist and world-systems perspectives, but rather to acknowledge that these approaches share a lineage in radical social thought and therefore hold certain assumptions in common relative to the other approaches considered here.

18. This is not to suggest that this process occurs smoothly. Rather, each hegemonic transition is associated with growing turbulence in the world system, which may take a variety of forms—intensified interstate rivalries, social conflict, economic volatility, and so on (see Arrighi and Silver 1999).

19. Arrighi was self-aware regarding the analytical trade-offs involved in this approach. In researching *The Long Twentieth Century,* Arrighi (1994: Preface) initially planned a close study of the crisis of the 1970s, but ultimately concluded that a longer temporal horizon and wider geographical scale would yield more insights than staying closer to the ground of any particular historical case. In general, the strategy of this research is to range broadly over a vast terrain in search of recurrent patterns, leaving the precise mechanisms somewhat underspecified (cf. Pollin 1996).

20. My account privileges broad macro-economic policies rather than the narrower regulatory changes given primacy in the shareholder value literature for a number of reasons. First, macro-economic policies are likely to be especially far-reaching in their effects, changing the environment for financial and

nonfinancial firms alike. Second, these policies are likely to be especially durable. Notably, the takeover market spurred by lax anti-trust enforcement was very much a product of the early to mid-1980s and ground to a halt when firms adopted "poison pill" defenses and states instituted anti-takeover protections at the end of the decade (Davis 2009; Stearns and Allan 1996). In contrast, the changes wrought by lax credit and interest rate volatility are structural features of a deregulated economic environment (Kaufman 1986) and hence have shaped the turn to finance from the early 1980s to the present day, as I explain more fully in Chapter 2.

21. Testimony of George Hatsopoulos, president of the American Business Conference, *The High Cost of Capital*, Joint Economic Committee, April 28, 1983, 874.

22. The reasons for the slowdown in economic growth in advanced industrial economies in the post-1970s period are the subject of a vast literature. This important issue is outside the scope of my analysis, but interested readers should refer to Armstrong, Glyn, and Harrison (1991) and Brenner (2006) for two influential (and opposing) views of the problem.

23. The social crisis in the late 1960s and 1970s was, of course, much broader than the set of issues to which I refer here, involving opposition to the war in Vietnam and the civil rights movement as well as broad disaffection from mainstream social and political institutions. I use the term narrowly to refer to social conflict over issues of economic justice.

24. Inflation, of course, not only reflected distributional conflict but was also associated with the oil price shocks of 1973 and 1979. But while the oil price hikes are sometimes treated as exogenous shocks to the U.S. economy, oil producers were responding to a depreciating U.S. dollar. The depreciating dollar was itself a result of the deteriorating U.S. balance of payments position and hence of the inability of U.S. society to live within its means— the macro-level consequence of Bell's (1976) unconstrained political marketplace.

25. In O'Connor's (1973) terminology, the socialization of production existed in tension with the private accumulation of profits.

26. As Block (1981) observes, the existence of a fiscal crisis does not necessarily imply that the expansion of state expenditures itself undermines future growth. In particular, fiscal crisis may simply be a consequence of slow growth that is occurring for other reasons. However, most formulations make the assumption that the increase in state expenditures is itself dysfunctional, placing an additional strain on economies already experiencing a slowdown. In this sense, fiscal crisis can be considered as both cause *and* consequence of slow growth.

27. Habermas (1973) offered another view, suggesting that culture would become disassociated from other realms of social life, a detached sphere where individuals who had been disenfranchised politically and economically could find a place for self-expression while avoiding any disruption to the market.

28. Bell borrowed the phrase from Rudolf Goldsheid, a German sociologist writing in the early twentieth century.

29. The Marxist theorist Claus Offe (1974, 1984) represented a partial exception in suggesting in some of his writing that the turn to the market would allow the state to resolve, temporarily and incompletely, some of the political difficulties it encountered in the late 1960s and 1970s. However, Offe (1984: 288) was unequivocal about the final result of such strategies: "Welfare state capitalist societies simply cannot be remodeled into something resembling pure market societies." On the other end of the ideological spectrum, free market conservatives not only predicted but actively promoted the turn to the market (see Blyth 2002 for an excellent account of the rise of free market ideas). But it is important to remember that this was very much a fringe view even as late as the 1970s. Instead, the mainstream position within economics was associated with Kenneth Arrow's formulation of welfare economics, premised on the notion that markets cannot aggregate individual preferences to derive a social cost function. Brick (2007: 170) draws the following implication: "A bold reading of Arrow's argument would suggest, then, that the satisfaction of social needs required a kind of decision making that went *beyond economics*, requiring choices that rested on *social* values of what is good and just for a community."

2. What Is Financialization?

1. See Orhangazi (2008) for a useful review of the emerging literature on financialization.
2. Data on financial sector profits are calculated from the Bureau of Economic Analysis *Gross Product Originating* Series.
3. This figure is consistent with those reported by a range of firms with captive finance units (see Henry 2005).
4. See Appendix C for a full discussion of these data sources. Systematic attempts to examine the evidence that would support the claim that the U.S. economy has undergone a process of financialization in recent years are still relatively rare in the literature, but interested readers should compare the results here with those reported by Brenner (2002), Crotty (2005), Dumenil and Levy (2004), Epstein and Jayadev (2005), Orhangazi (2008), and Stockhammer (2004).
5. In 2001, the Bureau of Economic Analysis (BEA) changed the manner in which it groups industries, with implications for how the financial sector is defined. Unfortunately, the BEA has not rereleased historical data to reflect these new industry classifications, and thus any series involving a distinction between financial and nonfinancial sectors will have a break in continuity in 2001. These data limitations are not insurmountable, however, and Tomaskovic-Devey and Lin (n.d.) have done preliminary analyses extending some of the results reported here through 2008. In this sense, the substantive argument is the more important for ending my analyses in 2001. The dynamics of the real estate boom and bust rest on somewhat different political and economic foundations than those that underpinned the regime I describe from the 1970s through the end of the 1990s expansion and therefore merit separate investigation.

6. Two important omissions from the analysis should be noted. First, I do not include the public sector as a component of the total economy. I omit the government sector because, while public data is available for employment and contribution to GDP growth, there is no concept analogous to profits with which to gauge the "accumulation" occurring in the public sector. However, this is unlikely to affect the results offered here because government involvement in the economy shows essentially no trend when the entire postwar period is considered. That is, between 1950 and the mid-1970s, the government's contribution to employment and GDP growth trends upward, but then sharply reverses course between the mid-1970s and 2001, ending the period at approximately the same level as in 1950. Second, for related reasons, self-employment is also excluded from consideration here and throughout the chapter. There is no way (short of making ad hoc assumptions) to distill a profit concept from proprietary income, which does not distinguish between profits and compensation. Were it possible to include self-employed workers in the analysis, this would likely increase the share of services in the economy, because the self-employed disproportionately work in services. However, the difference is not likely to be significant, as self-employed workers represent a relatively small share of the total economy.

7. In the following discussion, I use the term "employment" to refer to only the sectoral—and not the occupational—dimension of employment. While occupational data are also occasionally used to assess shifts in the structure of the economy, I do not replicate these analyses here. Occupation is a property that attaches to discrete jobs, whereas employment, GDP, and profit data are typically disaggregated by industry. Thus an examination of the shifting composition of occupations is not strictly comparable to changing patterns of profitability because these measures involve different units of analysis.

8. FIRE is the industry group comprising finance, insurance, and real estate. For the moment, I follow convention and report FIRE as an industry group rather than disaggregating finance and real estate. In the more detailed empirical analysis later in the chapter, I exclude real estate as a component of the financial sector of the economy. Which practice is more appropriate is a complex matter—real estate markets share many characteristics of financial markets, including their speculative nature. At the boundary, the distinction between "financial" and "nonfinancial" sectors of the economy is ambiguous. In the present context, my purpose is to ensure comparability between my analysis and the other work characterizing broad shifts in the structure of the economy. In subsequent sections, where I am more concerned with precision, my purpose is to construct a conservative estimate of financialization.

9. To avoid confusion, here and throughout I refer to the broader category of industries that make up the service sector (public utilities, transport, communications, wholesale, retail, FIRE, and services) as *the service sector,* while referring to the narrower industry simply as *services.*

10. In practice there is a small discrepancy between the measure constructed on the basis of output and the measure constructed on the basis of income (U.S. Department of Commerce 2002).

11. Here and throughout the chapter, profits are reported before taxes and dividends are paid.

12. The point of this exercise is not to suggest that one or another of these perspectives on economic change is more "true" than the other. How one characterizes the nature of long-term structural shifts in the economy—and what data are taken to represent the evidence for these shifts—depends critically on one's theoretical purpose. Both "post-industrialism" and "financialization" represent *analytical constructs,* not claims about the underlying nature of reality in some absolute sense.

13. As I noted in Chapter 1, the contrast here between financial and "productive" sources of income is not intended to suggest that financial activities are necessarily *unproductive* in terms of their creation of economic value. I use "productive" here to refer to *nonfinancial* activities, rather than to invoke the Marxist distinction between activities that produce surplus and those that do not.

14. Typically, accountants report cash flow net of dividends and income taxes (i.e., cash flow=retained earnings+depreciation allowances). Because I am primarily interested in the generation of profit rather than its distribution, I report cash flow before taxes and dividends have been paid.

15. One important adjustment made to the profit data in constructing the measure of corporate cash flow should be noted. While interest income is treated as a component of corporate profits in the *National Income and Product Accounts,* I remove interest income from the profit concept used here so that the denominator of the reported ratio exclusively reflects *nonfinancial* sources of income. The BEA removes dividends and capital gains in calculating the profit concept used in the *National Income and Product Accounts* (see U.S. Department of Commerce 2002), so it is only interest income that requires this adjustment.

16. The argument here closely follows Fred Block's (1990) unpublished investigation of depreciation and national income accounting.

17. There is, of course, the possibility that larger depreciation allowances are not simply a reflection of tax changes, but also reflect an actual shortening of service lives, especially as computer equipment and software have become a more significant component of investment expenditures. Unfortunately, this represents an empirical problem that is not particularly tractable with the available data. To the extent that larger depreciation allowances *are* justified by a real shortening of service lives, the reported measure is a conservative estimate of financialization (because adding depreciation allowances into the denominator results in a smaller value for the overall ratio, especially in recent decades).

18. Even augmented by depreciation allowances, corporate cash flow is still a *net-of-cost* measure: wages, salaries, the cost of materials used in production, and so on, have been subtracted from revenues in computing cash flow. For this reason, portfolio income and corporate cash flow are not strictly comparable data series, and the portfolio income figure should not be interpreted as literally representing the "share" of nonfinancial firms' revenues generated

by financial investments. Nevertheless, corporate cash flow provides a meaningful metric against which we can gauge the growth of portfolio income. In this sense, the measure computed here is similar to a measure often used to describe the financialization of the household sector, the ratio of the value of financial assets to disposable income. The numerator represents a (potential) revenue stream, whereas the denominator is on a net basis, but a comparison of the two still tells us in some meaningful way how "large" a quantity the value of financial assets represents.

19. This phenomenon is well documented with respect to the auto industry (see Froud et al. 2002; cf. Hakim 2004).

20. Higher interest rates also affected the other side of firms' balance sheets, as firms faced significantly higher interest payments on borrowed funds. For this reason, Dumenil and Levy (2004) construct a measure of financialization that nets out assets and liabilities in considering the financial position of firms. While there are good reasons for constructing the measure this way, I have chosen not to follow this practice because it moves away from what we intuitively understand by financialization. That is, on Dumenil and Levy's measure, assets and liabilities *cancel each other out*, such that an economy in which firms both earn income on financial investments *and* are heavily indebted would appear less financialized than an economy in which firms do not have significant financial investments but also carry less debt. In this sense, if the objective is to provide an indicator of the real financial position of firms, then Dumenil and Levy's measure is the more appropriate one. But if the objective is to provide a measure of financialization, netting out assets and liabilities is a problematic procedure. By the same token, it should be remembered that the measure of portfolio income presented here is *not* intended as a reflection of the financial viability of firms because income generated by financial investments has been offset by the increased debt of the nonfinancial sector.

21. Goodwill is the amount paid over the book value of a firm's assets in an acquisition, representing the value of the firm's brand and other intangible sources of value. In this sense, it is a stretch to consider goodwill a financial asset.

22. In the earlier discussion, I used FIRE as a comparison group to manufacturing and services because this is the manner in which industry comparisons are conventionally reported. Here I report profits of the financial sector rather than the broader FIRE industry group. The difference between the two is that FIRE includes real estate whereas the financial sector does not, making the latter estimate the more conservative one.

23. This point holds even when foreign-source dividends are considered. Foreign-source dividends maintain—*but do not increase*—their share of total portfolio income over the period.

24. Dividends received by corporations are removed from profit data by the BEA because they do not reflect income from current production. Similarly, dividends paid by corporations do not affect this analysis because I report profits prior to any distributions.

25. See Appendix C for complete details on the construction of this measure.
26. In the wake of the recent financial crisis, much commentary has assumed that the role of credit expansion in fueling asset price bubbles is a relatively new phenomenon. While it is true that the pace of credit expansion accelerated dramatically after 2001, credit has in fact been growing significantly faster than GDP in the U.S. economy since the early 1980s (see Figure 13).
27. This dynamic was clearly in play in the recent housing boom: the fact that mortgage borrowers could purchase a house with a minimal down payment drove up the value of house prices, validating the original loans and encouraging lending with even slimmer margins. The housing crash demonstrated that the process also works in reverse: with higher down payments required, many fewer people could afford to buy homes, depressing asset prices and therefore constricting the availability of credit for further lending (see Geanakoplos 2009). The important point is that, up or down, these processes are *procyclical,* with changes in credit availability and asset prices setting in motion self-reinforcing boom and bust cycles.
28. Tobin (1997: 302–303) notes that at the level of the economy as a whole, no such "diversion" of investment from productive to financial assets is possible: "No goods and services are consumed, no productive resources are 'diverted,' no net saving or dissaving, occurs when A pays B in exchange for financial assets." In other words, financial asset purchases transfer liquidity from one agent to another, they do not use resources—except in the narrow sense that managing financial transactions requires some investment of human energy and talent (but little physical capital). Of course, one might wonder whether this diversion of human resources is really so trivial—and in another context Tobin (1984) himself decries the inefficiency and waste that a "paper economy" generates. But as a technical matter, Tobin's observation is correct: financial asset transactions do not in themselves use resources at the aggregate level. As a result, we cannot conclude that more financial investment necessarily means less productive investment because, as Pollin (1997: 23) explains, "a dollar spent on a financial transaction does not in any way prevent that same dollar from being spent by its recipient on a dollar of productive investment." Of course, how exactly the dollar is finally spent depends a great deal on the institutional structure of the financial system and its articulation to the broader economy (Grabel 1997). In this regard, the restructuring of the economy described by theorists of shareholder value (see Chapter 1), as well as the empirical observation that increased financial investment has been associated with a decline in productive investment in the U.S. economy in recent decades, does not give much cause for optimism. In addition, Tobin's stricture does not apply to individual firms—here financial investment *can* divert resources from productive investment. See Stockhammer (2004) and Orhangazi (2008) for careful econometric work examining the relationship between financial investment and productive investment in the Organisation for Economic Co-operation and Development (OECD) economies and the U.S. economy at the aggregate level and firm level, respectively.

29. While it is standard in economic models on the determinants of investment to assume that the cost of capital drives investment decisions, more recent work has cast some doubt on the strength of this relationship (e.g., Chirinko 1993; Fazarri 1994). There is little doubt that higher interest rates negatively affect long-term investment, but these researchers suggest that this effect may operate more by depressing sales or by encouraging lender caution rather than by increasing the cost of capital per se. It is not critical for my analysis which of these channels is most important. In any case, there is ample evidence from the business press that, at least during the late 1970s and early 1980s, extreme volatility in interest rates was wreaking havoc on investment decisions and corporate planning. See Poterba and Summers (1995) for suggestive evidence from a survey of business executives conducted in 1990 regarding investment decisions.

30. Malcolm Hopkins, "Keeping Our Capital Intensive Industries Competitive," inserted material in *The Future of Financial Markets*, U.S. House Committee on Energy and Commerce, April 14, 1983, 108–114.

31. "Wringing More Profits from Corporate Cash," *Business Week*, May 12, 1986, 85.

32. "Cash Management," *Business Week*, March 13, 1978, 62.

33. "A Way for U.S. Companies to Make 'Free Money,'" *Business Week*, October 29, 1984, 58.

34. "Cash Management," 62.

35. Ibid.

36. "Wringing More Profits," 85.

37. "Inflation Gives Him More Clout with Management," *Business Week*, August 15, 1977, 84; "Cash Management," 62.

38. Short-term interest rates peaked at 20 percent in January of 1981.

39. "Cash Managers Grow Wary," *Business Week*, April 7, 1980, 88.

40. "Far from Recovery in Capital Spending," *Business Week*, July 12, 1982, 21.

41. Testimony of Malcolm Hopkins, chief financial officer of St. Regis Paper Company, *The Future of Financial Markets*, U.S. House Committee on Energy and Commerce, April 14, 1983, 97.

42. Other factors considered by the commission were declining productivity, rising real wages, and a deteriorating trade balance.

43. *Global Competition: The New Reality, Report of the President's Commission on Industrial Competitiveness* (Washington, DC: Government Printing Office, 1983), 12. Data analyzed by the commission showed that while the decline in the rate of return on manufacturing investment was a long-standing problem dating from at least the late 1960s, the rate of return on financial assets only began to exceed the return on manufacturing investment in 1980, when interest rates turned sharply up.

44. "Why Business Isn't Ready to Join the Cheering on Wall Street," *Business Week*, December 16, 1985, 31.

45. Testimony of George Hatsopoulos, president of the American Business Conference, *The High Cost of Capital*, Joint Economic Committee, April 28, 1983, 4.

46. "Why Business Isn't Ready," 31.
47. Another strategy that allowed nonfinancial firms a measure of protection from volatile interest rates was acquisition of captive finance units. Particularly for capital-intensive firms, ownership of captive finance companies allowed nonfinancial parents to reduce dependence on external capital markets and often provided an alternative source of profits for firms in declining manufacturing industries. See the testimony of Malcolm Hopkins, chief financial officer of St. Regis Paper Company, *The Future of Financial Markets,* U.S. House Committee on Energy and Commerce, April 14, 1983, 94–100.
48. "The Economy: Uncertainty Isn't about to Go Away," *Business Week,* February 22, 1988, 52.
49. "Wringing More Profits," 85.
50. Real interest rates were at historically high levels throughout the 1980s. In the 1990s, real interest rates declined relative to their 1980s peaks, but remained high relative to earlier postwar decades. Of course, in more recent years interest rates have been at historically low rather than high levels, suggesting that volatility rather than absolute level is the defining characteristic of interest rates in a deregulated, financialized environment.
51. A parallel process is the role of exchange rate volatility feeding the growth of the "casino economy" by creating demand for derivative products that hedge against exchange rate risk (Strange 1986).

3. The Social Politics of U.S. Financial Deregulation

1. This last provision of the Banking Act of 1933 consisted of four separate sections that prohibited commercial bank involvement in securities underwriting either directly or through affiliates, banned investment banks from taking deposits, and outlawed shared directorships between commercial banks and investment banks.
2. When a bank "underwrites" a security, it agrees to buy any unsold portion of an issue after it has been offered for sale to the public. Typically, an underwriter also assumes responsibility for marketing the issue (Carosso 1970).
3. The former case was represented by the network of savings and loan associations (or "thrifts"), which emerged as fully autonomous from commercial banks for the first time as a result of the creation of the Federal Home Loan Bank Board in 1932 (Krus 1994). The situation of commercial banking and investment banking was more typical of the latter case. Commercial banks and investment banks existed as separate institutions in the 1920s and earlier decades, but in practice their functions were mixed through the heavy reliance of commercial banks on underwriting activity conducted through securities affiliates (Carosso 1970).
4. Thrifts were not formally subject to Regulation Q ceilings before 1966 (see below), although the thrift industry regulator, the Federal Home Loan Bank Board, imposed "unofficial" ceilings on thrifts during this period.
5. Two mechanisms were important in contracting the capital available for mortgage lending: (1) the flow of funds out of depository institutions, especially

thrifts, who were specialists in mortgage lending; and (2) the shift away from mortgage loans by non-thrift lenders, including commercial banks, who reallocated capital to shorter-term investments in a period of rising market interest rates.

6. Letter from Vivian T. Cates to Representative Wright Patman, September 14, 1973 (reprinted in U.S. House of Representatives Committee on Banking and Currency, *The Credit Crunch and Reform of Financial Institutions, Part II,* September 17, 18, 19, and 20, 1973, 1094; emphasis added).

7. In this respect, housing functioned as an "automatic stabilizer" in the macroeconomy. The classic "automatic stabilizer" in macro-economic management involves the tendency of tax revenues to rise or fall as economic activity expands or contracts, offsetting the overall direction of the economy.

8. See, for example, hearings conducted on the *Report of the Commission on Credit and Money* before the Joint Economic Committee, August 14–18, 1961.

9. Testimony of Henry Fowler, Secretary of the Treasury, *To Eliminate Unsound Competition for Savings and Time Deposits,* U.S. House Committee on Banking and Currency, May 19, 1966, 132.

10. Testimony of John E. Horne, Chairman, Federal Home Loan Bank Board, *To Eliminate Unsound Competition for Savings and Time Deposits,* U.S. House Committee on Banking and Currency, May 11, 1966, 70.

11. Statement of William Proxmire, U.S. senator, *Mortgage Credit,* U.S. Senate Committee on Banking and Currency, June 12, 1967, 57.

12. Testimony of Norman Strunk, Executive Vice President, United States Savings and Loan League, *The Credit Crunch and Reform of Financial Institutions,* U.S. House Committee on Banking and Currency, September 10, 1973, 101.

13. See Greider (1987) for a very perceptive account of the inflation of the 1970s.

14. The term "money center bank" is used to describe large banks that have a significant wholesale business, servicing other banks and large corporations. Citibank and J. P. Morgan Chase are prominent examples.

15. Testimony of Carl E. Bahmeier, Executive Director of California State Bankers Association, *Grassroots Hearings on Economic Problems,* U.S. House Committee on Banking and Currency, December 1, 1969, 198–199.

16. Statement of Representative Leonor K. Sullivan, *Emergency Home Financing,* U.S. House Committee on Banking and Currency, February 2, 1970, 38.

17. "Banks in a Bind: Bankers Are Struggling to Hold on to $4 Billion of Maturing Deposits," *Wall Street Journal,* September 13, 1966.

18. Testimony of Warren L. Smith, economist, *High Interest Rates,* U.S. Senate Committee on Banking and Currency, April 1, 1969, 153.

19. Testimony of Clarence Liller, Chairman, Mortgage Finance Committee of the American Bankers Association, *Mortgage Credit,* U.S. Senate Committee on Banking and Currency, June 28, 1967, 169.

20. "The Money Is Heading to Lusher Pastures," *Business Week,* May 28, 1966, 147–148.

21. See *Interest Rates and Mortgage Credit,* U.S. Senate Committee on Banking and Currency, August 4, 1966.
22. Testimony of Tom R. Scott, Chairman of Legislative Committee, U.S. Savings and Loan League, *The Credit Crunch and Reform of Financial Institutions,* U.S. House Committee on Banking and Currency, September 10, 1973, 58.
23. Testimony of Sam Yorty, Mayor, City of Los Angeles, *Grassroots Hearings on Economic Problems,* U.S. House Committee on Banking and Currency, December 1, 1969, 126–129.
24. Testimony of John V. Lindsay, Mayor, City of New York, *Emergency Home Financing,* U.S. House Committee on Banking and Currency, February 2, 1970, 21–25.
25. Testimony of Joseph Alioto, Mayor, City of San Francisco, and President, U.S. Conference of Mayors, *The Growing Threat of a Domestic Financial Crisis,* August 7, 1974, 2.
26. Statement of Chairman Wright Patman, *Emergency Home Financing,* U.S. House Committee on Banking and Currency, February 3, 1970, 89.
27. GNMA (or "Ginnie Mae") was formed from the Federal National Mortgage Association (FNMA, or "Fannie Mae"), which had been created in 1938 to finance mortgage purchases during the depths of the Depression. FNMA was privatized in 1968, while GNMA remained a public corporation. In 1970, the private Federal Home Loan Mortgage Corporation (or "Freddie Mac") was created to provide competition to Fannie Mae.
28. Testimony of Kenneth Wright, Chief Economist, Life Insurance Association of America, *Emergency Home Financing,* U.S. House Committee on Banking and Currency, February 3, 1970, 87.
29. Statement of Representative Chalmers Wylie, *Emergency Home Financing,* U.S. House Committee on Banking and Currency, February 3, 1970, 105–106.
30. Testimony of Lester C. Thurow, economist, *Emergency Home Financing,* U.S. House Committee on Banking and Currency, February 3, 1970, 106.
31. "Congress Tries to Strongarm the Fed," *Business Week,* February 24, 1975, 23.
32. *Interest Rates and Mortgage Credit,* U.S. Senate Committee on Banking and Currency, August 4, 1966.
33. Statement of Senator William Proxmire, *Purchase of Treasury Securities and Interest on Savings Deposits,* U.S. Senate Committee on Banking and Currency, April 3, 1968, 1–2.
34. Testimony of William McChesney Martin, Chairman, Federal Reserve Board, *Deposit Rates and Mortgage Credit,* September 10, 1969, 86–87.
35. *Deposit Rates and Mortgage Credit,* U.S. Senate Committee on Banking and Currency, September 9, 10, 22, 1969.
36. *Selective Credit Policies and Wage-Price Stabilization,* U.S. Senate Committee on Banking, Housing, and Urban Affairs, March 31, April 1, 7, 1971.
37. *An Act to Lower Interest Rates and Allocate Credit,* U.S. House Committee on Banking, Currency, and Housing, February 6, 1975, 203.
38. Even more bizarre, the incriminating document was a letter from the Federal Reserve to bank presidents suggesting that cattle feedlot operators be given priority in credit decisions. See *An Act to Lower Interest Rates and Allocate*

Credit, U.S. House Committee on Banking, Currency, and Housing, February 6, 1975, 274–282.

39. Statement of Chairman Wright Patman, *Emergency Home Financing,* House Committee on Banking and Currency, February 3, 1970, 90.

40. Testimony of Arthur Burns, Chairman, Federal Reserve Board, *Selective Credit Policies and Wage-Price Stabilization,* U.S. Senate Committee on Banking, Housing, and Urban Affairs, March 31, 1971.

41. *Selective Credit Policies and Wage-Price Stabilization,* U.S. Senate Committee on Banking, Housing, and Urban Affairs, March 31, April 1, 7, 1971; *An Act to Lower Interest Rates and Allocate Credit,* U.S. House Committee on Banking, Currency, and Housing, February 4, 5, 6, 1975.

42. Testimony of Arthur Burns, Chairman, Federal Reserve Board, *Selective Credit Policies and Wage-Price Stabilization,* U.S. House Committee on Banking, Housing, and Urban Affairs, March 31, 1971, 23–39.

43. Testimony of William E. Simon, Secretary of the Treasury, *An Act to Lower Interest Rates and Allocate Credit,* U.S. House Committee on Banking, Currency, and Housing, February 4, 1975, 19.

44. Ibid., 18, 20.

45. Ibid., 19

46. Ibid., 20.

47. Penn Central's bankruptcy involved the commercial paper market, which regulators feared would seize up as a result. Regulators removed interest rate ceilings on large-denomination CDs to ensure that firms unable to secure financing in the commercial paper market would be able raise funds by issuing certificates of deposit. The measure was introduced as a temporary response to financial crisis, but as it happened, interest rate ceilings were never reinstated on large-denomination certificates.

48. *The Report of the President's Commission on Financial Structure and Regulation,* U.S. Senate Committee on Banking, Housing, and Urban Affairs, August 1973.

49. Mortgage loans were typically amortized over a period of thirty years. As such, mortgages extended during periods of low interest rates acted as a drag on thrift earnings for years into the future, restricting thrifts' ability to compete with banks for deposits.

50. Testimony of Norman Strunk, Executive Vice President, United States League of Savings and Loan Associations, *Financial Institutions Act—1973,* U.S. Senate Committee on Banking, Housing, and Urban Affairs, May 15, 1973, 380.

51. Testimony of Rex J. Morthland, President, American Bankers Association, *Financial Institutions Act—1973,* U.S. Senate Committee on Banking, Housing, and Urban Affairs, May 14, 1973, 301.

52. Testimony of Embree Easterly, President, Independent Bankers Association, *Financial Institutions Act of 1973,* U.S. Senate Committee on Banking, Housing, and Urban Affairs, May 14, 1973, 348.

53. Testimony of Nathanial Rogg, Executive Vice President, National Association of Homebuilders, *Housing and Financial Reform,* U.S. Senate Committee on Banking, Housing, and Urban Affairs, December 11, 1974, 4.

54. Testimony of Henry B. Schechter, Director of the Department of Urban Affairs, AFL-CIO, U.S. Senate Committee on Banking, Housing, and Urban Affairs, August 6, 1974, 111.

55. Testimony of William E. Simon, Deputy Secretary of the Treasury, *Financial Structure and Regulation,* U.S. Senate Committee on Banking, Housing, and Urban Affairs, November 6, 1973, 23.

56. Testimony of George C. Martin, President, National Association of Homebuilders, *The Credit Crunch and the Reform of Financial Institutions,* U.S. House Committee on Banking and Currency, September 10, 1973, 42.

57. Testimony of Arthur F. Burns, Chairman, Federal Reserve Board, *The Credit Crunch and Reform of Financial Institutions,* U.S. House Committee on Banking and Currency, September 12, 1973, 316.

58. Savings and loan associations were permitted to offer wild-card certificates, as long as they did not exceed 5 percent of total time and savings deposits.

59. Testimony of Frank Willie, Chairman, Federal Deposit Insurance Corporation, *The Credit Crunch and Reform of Financial Institutions,* U.S. House Committee on Banking and Currency, September 13, 1973, 388.

60. Testimony of Edward C. Schmults, Acting Secretary of the Treasury, *Variable Rate Securities and Disintermediation,* U.S. Senate Committee on Banking, Housing, and Urban Affairs, July 24, 1974, 3.

61. The 1970 law that regulated bank holding companies only encompassed multi-bank holding companies, exempting from regulation holding companies owning a *single* bank (even a mammoth one, like National City Bank).

62. Testimony of Edwin B. Brooks, Legislative Committee, U.S. League of Savings and Loan Associations, U.S. Senate Committee on Banking, Housing, and Urban Affairs, July 25, 1974, 206.

63. "The Big Float: Variable Notes for Small Investors Seen as Major Trend—Many Firms to Tap Huge Personal Savings," *Wall Street Journal,* July 5, 1974.

64. Ibid.

65. Testimony of Frank Willie, Chairman, Federal Deposit Insurance Corporation, *Variable Rate Securities and Disintermediation,* U.S. Senate Committee on Banking, Housing, and Urban Affairs, July 24, 1974, 9.

66. In addition, commercial banks had recently adopted the "floating prime," continually adjusting the rate they charged their best loan customers to the market.

67. Testimony of Thomas R. Bomar, Chairman, Federal Home Loan Bank Board, *Variable Rate Securities and Disintermediation,* U.S. Senate Committee on Banking, Housing, and Urban Affairs, July 24, 1974, 11.

68. Testimony of Raymond Edwards, Chairman of the Board, Glendale Federal Savings and Loan, *Variable Rate Mortgage Proposal and Regulation Q,* U.S. House Committee on Banking, Currency, and Housing, April 8, 1975, 51. See also testimony of Lloyd Bowles, Chairman of Legislative Committee, U.S. League of Savings Associations, *Now Accounts, Federal Reserve Membership, and Related Issues,* U.S. Senate Committee on Banking, Housing, and Urban Affairs, June 21, 1977, 241.

69. Testimony of Rex J. Morthland, President, American Bankers Association, *Financial Institutions Act of 1975*, U.S. Senate Committee on Banking, Housing, and Urban Affairs, May 14, 1975, 245.

70. Testimony of Nathanial Rogg, Executive Vice President, National Association of Homebuilders, *Housing and Financial Reform*, U.S. Senate Committee on Banking, Housing, and Urban Affairs, December 11, 1974, 5–6.

71. Testimony of Geno Baroni, President, National Center for Urban Ethnic Affairs, *Variable Rate Mortgage Proposal and Regulation Q*, U.S. House Committee on Banking, Currency, and Housing, April 9, 1975, 213.

72. Dean Cannon Jr., Executive Vice President, California Savings and Loan League, *Variable Rate Mortgage Proposal and Regulation Q*, U.S. House Committee on Banking, Currency, and Housing, April 8, 1975, 96.

73. Technically, there is an important distinction between a variable rate mortgage and a mortgage with an escalator clause: the variable rate mortgage is tied to a market index and adjusts *automatically*, whereas the escalator clause is exercised at the discretion of the lending institution. The seemingly arbitrary nature of the escalator clause may in part explain why these mortgages provoked such strong reactions from homeowners.

74. "Prudential Drops Escalation Clause—Homeowners Group to Disband, Directors to Seek Legislation," *Los Angeles Times*, October 7, 1966, SG8.

75. Council on Urban Life, *The Escalator Clause: Raising Mortgage Rates in Wisconsin*, March 1974, Papers of Dennis J. Conta: Box 1, Folder 14, 1969–1979. Milwaukee Manuscript Collection, Wisconsin Historical Society.

76. "Protestors Pack State Capitol Rotunda," *Stevens Point Daily Journal*, March 19, 1974, 7.

77. Council on Urban Life, *The Escalator Clause*.

78. "Protestors at State Capitol Urge De-escalation of Mortgages," *Racine Journal Times*, March 14, 1974, 5A.

79. Council on Urban Life, *The Escalator Clause*.

80. See *Variable Rate Mortgage Proposal and Regulation Q*, U.S. House Committee on Banking, Currency, and Housing, April 8, 9, 10, 1975; and *Variable Rate Mortgages*, U.S. Senate Committee on Banking, Housing, and Urban Affairs, April 14, 15, 16, 17, 1075.

81. The FINE study recommended requiring that one-third of the directors of financial corporations have no affiliation to the financial industry and that the terms of members of the Federal Reserve Board be shortened to allow more effective congressional oversight of the central bank. These measures were eventually dropped from the legislation introduced in the House, which retained the basic formula of the rejected *Financial Institutions Act*. The major change from the earlier legislation was that rather than retaining (somewhat liberalized) asset composition requirements as the main means of assuring financing for housing, the FINE study dispensed with these requirements and instead offered incentives to lenders that dedicated a certain proportion of their capital to mortgage finance. See *Financial Institutions and the Nation's Economy (FINE) "Discussion Principles,"* U.S. House Committee on Bank-

ing, Currency, and Housing, December 2, 3, 4, 5, 8, 9, 10, 11, 12, 16, 17, 18, 1975; January 20, 21, 22, 27, 28, 29, 1976.

82. Savings and loan associations favored the bill because it retained the differential; commercial banks opposed the legislation for the same reason (even while making it possible for banks to receive the differential if they specialized in mortgage finance). Organized labor and homebuilders found the provisions in the bill designed to assure adequate funds to housing inadequate. Consumer groups supported the financial reform bill for its allowance for the payment of interest on checking accounts and its repeal of interest rate ceilings, although they wanted implementation of both of these provisions accelerated. See *Financial Reform Act of 1976*, U.S. House Committee on Banking, Currency, and Housing, March 4, 9, 11, 16, 1976.

83. Testimony of William E. Simon, Deputy Secretary of the Treasury, *Financial Structure and Regulation*, U.S. Senate Committee on Banking, Housing, and Urban Affairs, November 6, 1973, 21.

84. See U.S. Senate Committee on Banking, Housing, and Urban Affairs, *Money Market Mutual Funds*, January 24, 30, 1980.

85. Letter from Dorothy L. Licthy to Senator William Proxmire, March 10, 1976 (reprinted in *Money Market Mutual Funds*, U.S. Senate Committee on Banking, Housing, and Urban Affairs, January 24, 30, 1980, 312; emphasis added).

86. Testimony of Robert H. McKinney, Chairman, Federal Home Loan Bank Board, *Interest Rate Regulation on Small Savings Accounts*, U.S. House Committee on Government Operations, March 22, 1979, 118.

87. Testimony of Irvine H. Sprague, Chairman, Federal Deposit Insurance Corporation, *Proposed Small Saver Deposit Instruments*, U.S. House Committee on Banking, Finance, and Urban Affairs, May 7, 1979, 67.

88. *Class Action Petition to Index Maximum Rates to Inflation, and/or to Provide Consumer Warnings to Depositors*, filed on behalf of the Gray Panthers, California Legislative Council for Older Americans, and the Campaign for Economic Democracy, October 19, 1978.

89. Testimony of Robert Gnaizda, attorney, Public Advocates, Inc. (representing the Gray Panthers, the Campaign for Economic Democracy, and the California Legislative Council for Older Americans), *Interest Rate Regulation on Small Savings Accounts*, House Government Operations Committee, March 20, 1979, 10.

90. *Class Action Petition to Index Maximum Rates to Inflation, and/or to Provide Consumer Warnings to Depositors*, filed on behalf of the Gray Panthers, California Legislative Council for Older Americans, and the Campaign for Economic Democracy, October 19, 1978.

91. Memo to Esther Peterson from Curt Jernigan, Regulation Q Task Force, February 26, 1979, Esther Peterson Papers, Schlesinger Library, Folder #1865.

92. Testimony of Robert Gnaizda, attorney, Public Advocates, Inc. (representing the Gray Panthers, the Campaign for Economic Democracy, and the California Legislative Council for Older Americans), *Depository Institutions Deregulation Act of 1979*, U.S. Senate Committee on Banking, Housing, and Urban Affairs, June 27, 1979, 4.

93. Testimony of Robert H. McKinney, Chairman, Federal Home Loan Bank Board, *Equity for the Small Saver,* U.S. Senate Committee on Banking, Housing, and Urban Affairs, April 11, 1979, 37; testimony of Henry B. Schechter, Director of Department of Urban Affairs, AFL-CIO, *The Consumer Checking Account Equity Act of 1979,* U.S. House Committee on Banking, Finance, and Urban Affairs, June 12, 1979, 408.

94. "Carter Bids to Lift Bank-Interest Curb—Strong Opposition Is Expected to Consumer Deposit Proposal," *New York Times,* May 23, 1979, A1.

95. The court ruling also encompassed other "check like" instruments, including share drafts issued by credit unions, and remote transfer services which allowed depositors to shift money from savings to checking accounts instantaneously. See *Depository Institutions Deregulation Act of 1979,* Part 1, U.S. Senate Committee on Banking, Housing, and Urban Affairs, June 21, 1979.

96. Interest rate decontrol was the most significant aspect of this mammoth piece of legislation, but the Depository Institutions Deregulation and Monetary Control Act (DIDMCA) also gave thrifts greater flexibility in lending and investment activities, expanded membership in the Federal Reserve System, and authorized negotiable order of withdrawal accounts and automatic transfers between savings and checking accounts. Authorization of the variable rate mortgages was *not* included in the legislation, but regulators took advantage of the imminent repeal of interest rate ceilings in order to liberalize restrictions on variable rate mortgages in the months leading up to the passage of DIDMCA.

97. This situation reflects the difference in maturity between the two sides of the lender's balance sheet. *Liabilities*—demand deposits and time deposits used as loan capital—immediately reflect short-term fluctuations in interest rates. In contrast, *assets*—outstanding loans, typically for mortgages and consumer durables—are only adjusted to reflect market rates of interest periodically. Thus, in a period of rising interest rates, the costs associated with attracting and retaining deposit money increase more quickly than earnings on loan portfolios, catching lenders in an earnings squeeze that discourages new lending.

98. Interview with Roger Kubarych, HVB Americas, Inc., New York City, July 9, 2002.

99. Felix Beck, Mortgage Bankers Association, *Adjustable Rate Mortgages,* U.S. House Committee on Banking, Finance, and Urban Affairs, September 22, 1981, 587.

100. Testimony of Milton Stewart, President, National Small Business Association, U.S. House Committee on Banking and Currency, *Credit Crunch and the Reform of Financial Institutions, Part I,* September 10, 1973, 92.

101. Testimony of Lyle Gramley, Governor, Federal Reserve Board, U.S. House Committee on Banking, Finance, and Urban Affairs, *Present and Future Conditions of Credit Markets: The Impact of Federal Deficits, Part 1,* October 27, 1981, 63.

102. In particular, implementation of the Community Reinvestment Act (CRA), which was passed in 1977, was a focus of credit activism in the 1980s and 1990s. The CRA requires depository institutions to assume an "affirmative obligation" to meet the credit needs of the communities in which they are chartered. One provision of the CRA allows community groups to block a bank merger application until the Federal Reserve certifies the bank's CRA performance as adequate. As a result, increased bank merger activity in the second half of the 1980s provided community activists additional leverage in popular campaigns against financial institutions. See "Neighborhood Challenges to Big Bank Mergers, *National Journal,* July 18, 1987; "Leaning on Banks to Lend to the Poor," *Business Week,* March 2, 1987; "ACORN: Community Activists Challenge Banks," *Southern Banker,* December 1986.

103. Testimony of Congressman Willis Gradison, *Financial Institutions and the Nation's Economy (FINE) "Discussion Principles,"* U.S. House Committee on Banking, Currency, and Housing, December 12, 1975, 1339.

104. Testimony of Stephen S. Gardner, Deputy Secretary of the Treasury, *Financial Institutions and the Nation's Economy (FINE) "Discussion Principles,"* U.S. House Committee on Banking, Currency, and Housing, December 9, 1975, 620.

105. Testimony of Gail Cincotta, Executive Director, National Training and Information Center, *Financial Restructuring: The Road Ahead,* U.S. House Committee on Energy and Commerce, April 5, 1984, 504–505; Testimony of Albert Fishbein, Executive Director, Center for Community Change, *Impact of Bank Reform on Consumers,* U.S. House Committee on Banking, Finance, and Urban Affairs, April 10, 1991, 353.

106. Testimony of Glenn Nishimura, Legislative Representative, Consumer Federation of America, *Competitive Equity in the Financial Services Industry, Part 1,* U.S. Senate Committee on Banking, Housing, and Urban Affairs, February 29, 1984, 1099.

107. Testimony of Elena Hanggi, President, ACORN, *Impact of Bank Reform Proposals on Consumers,* U.S. House Committee on Banking, Finance, and Urban Affairs, April 10, 1991, p. 40; Testimony of Michael Waldman, Director, Public Citizen, *Restructuring the Banking Industry, Part I,* U.S. House Committee on Banking, Finance, and Urban Affairs, April 18, 1991, 67.

108. Historians of the consumer movement make it clear that this narrowing of the political agenda of the consumer movement was not unique to the experience of financial deregulation, nor to the restricted time period examined here. See the outstanding works by Lizabeth Cohen (2003) and Meg Jacobs (2005). For an illuminating view of the consumer movement's role in deregulation politics by a sociologist, see Monica Prasad's (2006) *The Politics of Free Markets.*

109. The mechanism linking financial deregulation to inflation is that easy access to credit allows demand to be transmitted to the market without restraint, freeing individuals competing for goods and services to bid up prices.

4. The Reagan Administration Discovers the Global Economy

1. In describing the transition to from a low to a high interest rate regime in the early 1980s, I refer to *real* interest rates. Nominal interest rates were high in the 1970s, but real rates of interest were actually negative during this decade. The real rate of interest refers to the nominal rate minus the rate of inflation, and is the more relevant measure for understanding the actual impact of the interest rate on economic behavior.

2. The precise mechanism here is the "hurdle rate" that capitalists face in considering any given investment; see the discussion in Chapter 2.

3. More accurately, inflation was not so much avoided as *transferred* from the nonfinancial economy to financial markets. Until recently, central bankers did not consider asset price inflation a problem; in the context of the financial crisis that began in the summer of 2007, this is changing.

4. In addition to the system of fixed exchange rates maintained under the Bretton Woods system, the existence of regulatory controls restricting the free movement of capital internationally represented another constraint on the size of deficits countries could run in this period. Capital controls were liberalized gradually and in a piecemeal fashion, with the United States leading the way in 1974, the United Kingdom following suit in 1979 and 1980, and the rest of the Organisation for Economic Co-operation and Development liberalizing in the later part of the 1980s (see Abdelal 2007 for an excellent account). As we will see below, the liberalization of global capital markets was necessary for deficit financing to emerge as a solution to the fiscal crisis confronted by Reagan administration policymakers.

5. Helleiner (1994: 148) leaves open the question of the intentionality of policymakers in reconstructing global finance.

6. Under the gold standard, a country importing more goods than it exported would have to export gold to cover the resulting deficit in its current account. This would effectively reduce the money supply in the country, contracting the economy and slowing demand. The resulting fall in domestic consumption would reduce imports, eventually restoring the country's external position to balance. Although the automaticity of the classic gold standard is somewhat idealized in the literature, the mechanism described nevertheless provides a rough approximation of how the system functioned in practice (Eichengreen 1996). Incidentally, a similar mechanism was presumed to underlie the operation of floating exchange rates, which explains why this reform of the international monetary system was so popular among champions of laissez-faire economics such as Milton Friedman. The notion was that under floating rates, much like a gold standard system, countries experiencing a current account deficit would have to supply their currency on world markets to pay for the excess of imports over exports. This would cause the currency in question to depreciate in value (because its supply had increased relative to demand), raising the cost of imports and lowering the cost of exports relative to other currencies. This shift in the relative valuation of imports and exports would cause the first to fall and the second to rise, automatically returning

the country to balance in its external account. What Friedman and others missed is the fact that capital flows take place not only to service trade under a floating rate regime, but also for *speculative* purposes. The implication is that changes in currency valuations may occur for reasons that have little to do with underlying trade positions and may therefore fail to bring about the appropriate adjustment in imports and exports. For excellent expositions of the underlying issues, see Blecker (1999), Eatwell and Taylor (2000), and Felix (2005).

7. In theory, currencies were adjustable under Bretton Woods (hence the term "adjustable peg"), although in practice a devaluation tended to be a traumatic event for a country and as such was strenuously avoided. Decisions to devalue the pound sterling first in 1949 and again in 1967, for example, were experienced as cataclysmic events, as was the 10-percent devaluation of the dollar in 1971 (Helleiner 1994).

8. See D'Arista (2003) for an ambitious proposal to reform the international monetary system along the lines initially proposed by Keynes.

9. Gowan (1999: x) is explicit that he is inferring backward from the ultimate results of Nixon's policy. He notes, "The method is to read back from actual policy outputs to hypotheses about policy goals." Unfortunately, this strategy of analysis tends to dramatically overstate the coherence of policy actions (cf. Panitch 2000).

10. To be sure, the eminent international economist Charles Kindleberger had become associated with the notion that U.S. deficits did not necessarily signal decline because the U.S. economy had a "comparative advantage" in financial intermediation (see Despres, Kindelberger, and Salant 1966). As such, it was appropriate that the U.S. economy play "banker to the world," drawing in short-term capital flows from abroad and reexporting this capital in the form of longer-term foreign direct investment (in the process, generating a deficit on the current account). But while this idea circulated in academic circles in the mid-1960s, it did not become embedded in the Nixon administration in the same manner that, for example, supply-side ideas would later come to permeate Reagan's economic cabinet.

11. In O'Connor's (1973) formulation, the latter type of spending performed a legitimation function as it allowed the state to conceal its role supporting private capital accumulation (see also Habermas 1973). In this sense, the two roles were inherently contradictory: to the extent that the state successfully supported accumulation, it acquired a legitimation deficit, and to the extent that it achieved legitimation, it acquired an accumulation deficit. Fiscal crisis and legitimation crisis were organically linked (see Chapter 1).

12. See especially the work of Robert Collins (1996, 2000) on the economic crisis of 1968.

13. See Brenner (2002, 2006) for an account of the profits crisis that emphasizes the former aspect, and see Glyn et al. (1990) for an account focusing on the latter. I agree with Crotty (1999) that these two explanations for the fall in profits are not mutually exclusive (in the way that Brenner, in particular, suggests).

14. The obstacles to raising taxes in this period were more political than economic, as Johnson deferred imposing a tax surcharge to avoid eroding support for an unpopular war (Collins 1996).

15. In accounts of the 1970s, price hikes by the Organization of the Petroleum Exporting Countries are typically treated as exogenous shocks to the U.S. economy. Given that the oil producers were responding to the steady erosion of their earnings caused by the depreciation of the dollar in the wake of Vietnam-era budget deficits, the "exogenous" nature of these shocks is subject to question.

16. Early in his term, Carter introduced a weak stimulus package in the form of a tax rebate, but he withdrew it before Congress could consider it. See Schulman (1998) for an analysis of the relationship of the Carter presidency to supply-side economics.

17. Some of the most ardent supply-siders, such as Paul Craig Roberts, later denied that they had ever endorsed the idea, embodied in the famous Laffer Curve, that the tax cuts would be revenue-neutral (or even revenue-enhancing). But as Martin Feldstein (1994: 25) notes, the supply-siders—Roberts included—left behind a substantial paper trail, making subsequent attempts to distance themselves from Laffer appear somewhat disingenuous.

18. Lawrence Kudlow and Beryl Sprinkel, "Financial Warnings," April 28, 1981, Cabinet Councils, Box 12, Ronald Reagan Presidential Library; Jerry Jordan, "Economic Summary," October 6, 1981, Cabinet Councils, Box 16, Ronald Reagan Presidential Library; L. Kudlow, "Financial and Economic Outlook," January 21, 1982, Cabinet Councils, Box 19, Ronald Reagan Presidential Library; L. Kudlow, "Financial Markets Update," August 6, 1982, Cabinet Councils, Box 26, Ronald Reagan Presidential Library.

19. "Recovery Shrugs off the Deficit," *Business Week,* June 6, 1983, 24–26.

20. As Murphy (1997: 95) explains, "Until the 1980s, Japanese households had effectively no option for financing major expenditures except for savings. Credit cards, installment plan financing for consumer durables, and other forms of consumer credit all were stymied in order to encourage savings at every point."

21. Private Saving+Budget Surplus–Domestic Investment=Exports–Imports. This formula became the basis of the famous debate over the "twin deficits"— that is, the notion that the trade deficit was caused by the budget deficit.

22. Murray Weidenbaum, "The United States and the International Economy," September 16, 1981, Cabinet Councils, Box 13, Ronald Reagan Presidential Library; emphasis added.

23. Niskanen came under intense political pressure after making the speech as he was interpreted as being dismissive of the deficit: "Murray Weidenbaum, the Chair of the CEA, disassociated himself from my remark, and three Republican Senators called for my immediate resignation" (interview with William Niskanen, Washington, D.C., July 18, 2002).

24. William Niskanen, "Characteristics of the Current Recovery," October 5, 1984, Cabinet Councils, Restricted Materials, Box 31, Ronald Reagan Presidential Library.

25. Interview with William Niskanen.
26. "Monetarism" refers to the theory that the rate of growth in the money supply is the sole determinant of real economic outcomes (see M. Friedman 1968). According to monetarist doctrine, the role of the central bank should be confined to controlling the money supply rather than attempting to directly stimulate growth or create employment. Although in theory monetarism prescribes only a constant rate of growth of the money supply (neither stimulating nor contracting the economy), in practice monetarist policies tend to be quite restrictive, as was the case during the Volcker years (see Chapter 5).
27. Interest rates declined in nominal terms following the monetarist experiment, but because inflation fell off even more sharply, *real* interest rates remained at unprecedented levels through the 1980s. The real interest rate is the nominal rate minus the rate of inflation.
28. As explained in the previous chapter, without interest rate ceilings rationing borrowers out of the market, *all* could seek access to credit, with the result that interest rates in the economy were bid sharply higher.
29. During a period of rising prices (i.e., inflation), money loses value: it takes more of a given unit of currency to purchase the same quantity of any commodity. As inflation proceeds, then, the real value of debt is eroded as the dollars used to retire debt are worth less than the dollars in which the debt was originally accumulated. For this reason, inflation tends to ease the fiscal burden of indebted governments. Of course, no central bank knowingly creates inflation to burn off government debt; rather, as Greider (1987: 560) notes, monetization is a much more "gradual and ambiguous" process.
30. Greider borrowed the phrase from populist House Democrat Wright Patman, who had used it to refer to Lyndon Johnson's economic policy.
31. Interview with Beryl Sprinkel, Chicago, Illinois, August 16, 2002. See also Beryl Sprinkel, "Financial Strategy for Reducing Inflation and Interest Rates," October 6, 1982, Cabinet Councils, Restricted Materials: Box 23, Ronald Reagan Presidential Library.
32. Interview with Jane D'Arista, Hadlyme, Connecticut, July 16, 2002.
33. Ibid.
34. Data is from the *1989 Economic Report of the President*. The size of the federal budget deficit in these years was $208 billion in 1983, $185 billion in 1984, $212 billion in 1985, and $221 billion in 1986. Thus the share of the federal budget deficit financed by foreign capital ranged from slightly under half in 1983 to *all* of the budget deficit in 1986.
35. There was still, to be sure, political pressure on Reagan to "do something" about the deficit; he very grudgingly acceded to tax increases in 1982 and 1984. The tax increases were relatively small in the face of the gaping hole in the federal budget, however (Poterba 1994).
36. Suppose that an American firm needs to sell its widget for $10 to realize a profit. Further suppose that the yen is trading ¥150 to $1. This means that the American widget sells in Tokyo for ¥1,500. Now suppose that the dollar appreciates so that, under the new exchange rate, one dollar is worth ¥300.

The widget now sells for ¥3,000 in Tokyo. Assuming that local producers' costs are unchanged, they are in a position to undersell the American producer, whose price has doubled. The example may seem extreme, but these values are in line with the magnitude of the change in the dollar/yen exchange rate over the 1980s.

37. Paul Krugman, "Is the Yen Undervalued?" September 30, 1982, Martin S. Feldstein, Files: Box 1, Ronald Reagan Presidential Library.

38. Paul Krugman, "Caterpillar Tractor's Yen Study: An Evaluation," October 25, 1982, Martin S. Feldstein, Files: Box 1, Ronald Reagan Presidential Library.

39. Consistent with its strong free market orientation, the Treasury Department had declared an official policy of "non-intervention" in the foreign exchange market as of May 1981.

40. Bergsten described the origins of the yen/dollar agreement: "George Shultz realized that the U.S.–Japan relationship was headed for a crack-up over this. And so he took control of it . . . and tried to set up this yen-dollar talk as a procedure to defang some of the trade protectionism in favor of moving the exchange rate. But [the State Department] turned it over to Treasury to run it. Treasury hijacked it, given the ideological orientation of the Treasury against any intervention in the exchange markets . . . what they did then was [to direct negotiations] toward the liberalization of the financial markets. That was not the purpose at all of the original exercise, it was to get the exchange rate to correct. But once they gave it to Treasury, that objective was aborted, and Treasury went off in this direction of liberalization of Japanese financial markets, which had nothing to do with the issue that had motivated it" (interview with C. Fred Bergsten, Washington, D.C., July 19, 2002).

41. Interview with Jeffrey Frankel, Cambridge, Massachusetts, July 12, 2002.

42. In a November 10, 1983, interview published in the *Washington Post,* for example, Regan remarked, "They won't share [their] savings with anyone else. Any Japanese company can come over here and borrow in our markets and take our savings; we cannot go over to their markets with impunity and borrow whatever we want over there, so what we're saying is, open up your capital markets and learn to share. *And in that way you will help to strengthen your yen and our dollar won't be nearly as strong*" (quoted in Frankel 1984: 27). This analysis by the treasury secretary is remarkable in two respects. First, it was arguably the United States, with its growing dependence on foreign capital, that needed to learn to "share." Second, Regan demonstrates a rather weak understanding of economics by asserting that increased outflows (i.e., borrowing) from Japan would strengthen the yen. A correct analysis is that if U.S. residents are borrowing from Japan, then Japanese residents are purchasing U.S. assets, increasing the demand for—and hence the value of—the dollar.

43. "Minutes of the Cabinet Council of Economic Affairs," October 27, 1982, Cabinet Councils, Restricted Materials: Box 23, Ronald Reagan Presidential Library.

44. It is entirely plausible that Donald Regan was confused about the true effect of Japanese capital market liberalization on the direction of capital flows, as

Frankel (1994) suggests. In spite of his Wall Street background, Regan's grasp of economics was tenuous at best. However, it is not plausible, given both archival materials and an interview with Sprinkel conducted by the author, that Beryl Sprinkel was similarly confused, although even he may have believed that in the long run Japanese capital market liberalization would strengthen the yen.

45. Interview with C. Fred Bergsten.

46. Interview with Jeffrey Frankel.

47. "Minutes of the Cabinet Council of Economic Affairs," April 12, 1983, Cabinet Councils, Restricted Materials: Box 26, Ronald Reagan Presidential Library.

48. Interview with Jeffrey Frankel.

49. The Treasury Department also stressed the "safe haven" view: that capital was flowing to the United States because U.S. markets offered investors a refuge from political and economic turmoil elsewhere in the world. Similar arguments resurfaced in the 1990s, when they were somewhat more plausible. See Frankel (1988) for an attempt to adjudicate between the various explanations offered for the capital inflows into the United States in the 1980s.

50. This is not to say that the business community missed the significance of the budget deficit, more generally. On the contrary, business leaders were nearly unanimous in their calls to reduce the deficit, even if it meant foregoing some part of the tax cut they had received (Destler and Henning 1989).

51. CEA member William Niskanen noted that the Department of Commerce and the Department of Agriculture did not share this viewpoint, but with regard to economic affairs, it was the opinion of the Treasury Department, the OMB, and the State Department that carried the greatest weight with the administration. To the extent that the Commerce Department and Agriculture Department gained any influence in the matter, it was by channeling the protectionist sentiment growing in the Congress, especially in Reagan's second term (Interview with William Niskanen).

52. The term "Feldstein Doctrine" was coined by Fred Bergsten.

53. Although the strong dollar displaced the export sector, resulting in a large trade deficit, the associated capital inflows at the same time protected interest rate-sensitive sectors from what would be (even) higher interest rates in the absence of the inflows. Thus Feldstein argued that the net effect of capital inflows on national income was negligible.

54. Martin Feldstein, "Is the Dollar Overvalued?" April 8, 1983, Cabinet Councils, Restricted Materials: Box 26, Ronald Reagan Presidential Library; Council of Economic Advisers, "The U.S. Trade Deficit: Causes, Prospects, and Consequences," October 4, 1983, Cabinet Councils: Box 42, Ronald Reagan Presidential Library.

55. Treasury Department, "Causes and Consequences of U.S. Deficits on Trade and Current Account," October 4, 1983, Cabinet Councils: Box 42, Ronald Reagan Presidential Library.

56. William Poole, "Interest Rates, Stock Prices, and Monetary Policy," June 19, 1984, Cabinet Councils: Box 52, Ronald Reagan Presidential Library.

57. J. Gregory Ballentine, "International Capital Flows," October 26, 1984, Cabinet Councils, Restricted Materials: Box 31, Ronald Reagan Presidential Library; Sidney Jones, "Report of the Working Group on International Trade on the Probability of Large Merchandise and Current Account Deficits Continuing for Several Years," December 14, 1984, Cabinet Councils: Box 55, Ronald Reagan Presidential Library; Roger Porter, "Minutes of Cabinet Council on Economic Affairs," January 22, 1985, Cabinet Councils, Restricted Materials: Box 31, Ronald Reagan Presidential Library. Volcker's comments—and their effects on the financial markets—are reported in *Business Week* (February 20, 1984; March 5, 1984; March 19, 1984; October 15, 1984).

58. See Destler and Henning (1989) for the former view and Frankel (1994) for the latter.

59. "Why The Big Apple Shines in the World's Markets," *Business Week,* July 23, 1984, 101.

60. "Why the Treasury's Plan to Sell Debt Overseas May Not Fly," *Business Week,* October 22, 1984, 129.

61. "The Markets Bet against Henry Kaufman," *Business Week,* February 11, 1985, 88.

62. At the time the memo was written, Beryl Sprinkel had moved from the Treasury Department to chair the CEA. Donald Regan, who had been Treasury Secretary during the first Reagan administration, switched places with James Baker to become Chief of Staff in January 1985.

63. The specific proposal under consideration involved a resurrection of the gold standard, a perennial favorite of supply-siders in the Reagan administration.

64. Beryl Sprinkel, "Lehrman's Paper 'Protectionism or Monetary Reform: The Case for a Modernized Bretton Woods,'" October 21, 1985, Beryl Sprinkel Files: Box 2, Ronald Reagan Presidential Library; emphasis added.

65. The latter point has given rise to the common perception that foreign capital inflows have contributed to lower interest rates generally. This is correct in a narrow sense, but the problem with this proposition is that it assumes all else is equal. Without access to unlimited supplies of foreign capital, the Reagan administration would have arguably been forced to live within its means, reducing pressure on capital markets and likely contributing to a *lower,* not higher, interest rate environment (D'Arista interview).

66. See, for example, the testimony of Malcolm T. Hopkins, Chief Financial Officer, St. Regis Paper Company, *The Future of Financial Markets,* U.S. House Committee on Energy and Commerce, April 14, 1983, 94–114.

67. In the wake of the current financial crisis, there is an emerging understanding that inflation in asset prices is as threatening to economic stability as inflation in the price of goods. Needless to say, this is a very belated realization (see Chapter 5).

68. Indeed, this "system" appeared so self-sustaining that some observers dubbed it a successor regime to Bretton Woods (Dooley, Folkerts-Landau, and Garber 2003). In the wake of the current financial crisis, the extent to which "Bretton Woods II" was dependent on the continuing ability of the U.S. economy to serve as a market for foreign producers has become clear. Now

that the U.S. economy is unable to play this role, higher interest rates relative to the rest of the world will once again be a necessary inducement to finance the U.S. deficit, as was the case in the 1980s (and to a lesser extent, the 1990s as well).

5. The Making of U.S. Monetary Policy

1. Federal Reserve policymakers are not elected, of course, but faced these pressures indirectly, as congressional representatives charged with oversight of monetary policy *are* elected and are generally eager to find a scapegoat for poor economic performance.
2. The following discussion draws on Clouse (1994), Edwards (1997), Feinman (1993), Goodfriend and Whelpley (1987), and Meulendyke (1998).
3. Ensuring that economic growth occurs in a sustainable fashion is a relatively new concern for monetary policy. The Federal Reserve has served in this role only since the 1960s. In earlier periods, other functions, such as containing financial crises, were more central to the conduct of monetary policy.
4. Interest rates that directly influence economic behavior include rates on mortgages and auto loans, in the case of consumer expenditures, and rates in the corporate bond market, in the case of business investment.
5. Interview with Alan Blinder, Princeton, New Jersey, July 8, 2002.
6. More accurately, all types of depository institutions—including commercial banks, savings banks, thrift institutions, and credit unions—are subject to reserve requirements (Feinman 1993: 570). For simplicity, in this chapter I refer only to banks, but this is shorthand for all depository institutions.
7. In addition, banks are wary of excessive reliance on the discount window because overuse may invite increased supervision by bank regulators.
8. As will be discussed below, this association weakened in the 1980s, with important consequences for policymakers (Meulendyke 1998).
9. In recent decades, attrition in the Federal Reserve's membership has been a serious problem as banks have increasingly opted out of the system by chartering themselves as national banks or adopting other types of charters not subject to the regulation of the Federal Reserve. Lowering reserve requirements is one response to this problem, as is a more recent rule change that for the first time allows the Federal Reserve to pay interest on reserves held against deposits. The main issue here is that as the total amount of capital held in reserve in the U.S. banking system declines, there is less and less of a fulcrum against which the levers of monetary policy can work, potentially eroding the effectiveness of policy. While a full treatment of this problem is beyond the scope of this chapter, see D'Arista (2002) for an illuminating discussion of this issue.
10. Banks do not earn any interest on reserves and so have an incentive to loan any amount held in excess of reserve requirements plus any additional amount needed for clearing purposes.
11. This position rests on a venerable academic literature. The seminal work here is Kydland and Prescott's (1977) argument that central bankers deliberately

create inflation to "trick" economic agents—who mistake rising prices for increased demand—into producing more output. While the notion that central bankers purposely engineer inflation strains belief in the contemporary context (Blinder 1998), the underlying idea that policy moves must be unanticipated to be effective remains an influential one in the central banking literature. See Cuckierman and Melzer (1986) for an important statement of this more general view.

12. Interview with Charles Schultze, Washington, D.C., July 24, 2002.
13. FOMC transcripts, February 2–3, 1981, 31.
14. Interview with Charles Schultze.
15. The FOMC is the policymaking arm of the Federal Reserve System. It consists of the seven governors of the Federal Reserve Board who are permanent members, four rotating presidents of the twelve regional Federal Reserve Banks, and the President of the Federal Reserve Bank of New York, who is considered a permanent member.
16. FOMC transcripts, October 6, 1979, 4–28.
17. Ibid., 8.
18. In the following narrative, all references to "governor" refer to the governors of the Federal Reserve Board. Similarly, with the exception of references to Presidents Reagan or Carter, "president" refers to one of the presidents of the regional Federal Reserve Banks.
19. FOMC transcripts, October 6, 1979, 19.
20. The reasons for the miscalculation reflected the ongoing structural shift in the economy associated with the process of financial deregulation discussed in Chapter 3. As noted, without quantitative restraints on the expansion of credit, such as provided by interest rate ceilings, policymakers would have to rely entirely on the price of credit to restrain the economy. Individuals turned out to be much less responsive than expected to the price of credit in guiding their investment and consumption decisions, with the result that much higher interest rates were required to restrain the economy than policymakers had anticipated (see Kaufman 1986).
21. FOMC transcripts, February 2–3, 1981, 1.
22. FOMC transcripts, September 18, 1979, 13; see also FOMC transcripts, October 4, 1979—Memorandum.
23. Greider (1987) provides a useful account of the episode.
24. FOMC transcripts, April 22, 1980, 10–22.
25. FOMC transcripts, September 16, 1980, 24.
26. Ibid.
27. FOMC transcripts, October 21, 1980, 16.
28. I owe the thermostat metaphor to Alan Blinder (1998).
29. FOMC transcripts, February 2–3, 1981, 3. Throughout the transcripts, there are numerous references to the "political cover" provided by money supply targeting. See, for example, FOMC transcripts, June 30–July 1, 1982, 56; FOMC transcripts, December 20–21, 1982, 35; FOMC transcripts, February 8–9, 1983, 21–32; FOMC transcripts, March 28–29, 1983, 42–43;

FOMC transcripts, December 16–17, 1985, 9; FOMC transcripts, December 15–16, 1989, 20.

30. Monetarists were well represented in the congressional banking committees and among President Reagan's economic advisers and hence were unlikely to broadly oppose the policy, even if they objected to aspects of its implementation. Indeed, the fact that there was already a constituency for the policy in Congress had been part of Volcker's gambit in adopting money supply targeting. See FOMC transcripts, October 6, 1979, 8.

31. The most serious of these was the Mexican debt default in August 1982, but the resolve of the committee was also tested by the failure of a series of domestic financial institutions, including Drysdale Securities in May 1982 and the Penn Square Bank in July 1982. See transcripts from that year of FOMC meetings and conference calls held on May 18, May 20, June 30–July 1, and August 24.

32. Interview with Stephen Axilrod, Lyme, Connecticut, July 15, 2002.

33. FOMC transcripts, June 30–July 1, 1982, 44–58; FOMC transcripts, August 24, 1982, 44–45.

34. FOMC transcripts, June 30–July 1, 1982, 89.

35. FOMC transcripts, July 12–13, 1982, 55.

36. FOMC transcripts, February 8–9, 1983, 89.

37. FOMC transcripts, March 26–27, 1984, 70–71.

38. M2 is defined as M1 plus time deposits and money market mutual funds; M3 consists of M2 plus large denomination financial instruments, such as "jumbo" certificates of deposit.

39. FOMC transcripts, June 30–July 1, 1982, 56.

40. FOMC transcripts, March 28–29, 1983, 42.

41. FOMC transcripts, March 28–29, 1983, 42–43; FOMC transcripts, August 22–23, 1983, 22–24; FOMC transcripts, March 26, 1985, 33; FOMC transcripts, May 19, 1987, 44; FOMC transcripts, July 7, 1987, 6–14.

42. FOMC transcripts, March 31, 1987, 42.

43. FOMC transcripts, November 22, 1988, Appendix—Kohn Statement.

44. FOMC transcripts, March 28, 1988, Appendix—Kohn Statement.

45. FOMC transcripts, July 7, 1987, 14.

46. FOMC transcripts, March 28, 1988, 12.

47. FOMC transcripts, December 13–14, 1988, 9.

48. FOMC transcripts, August 21, 1984, 33.

49. Ibid., 25.

50. FOMC transcripts, December 13–14, 1988, 9.

51. FOMC transcripts, November 3, 1987, Appendix—Kohn Statement.

52. FOMC transcripts, December 15–16, 1987, 2–16.

53. FOMC transcripts, August 16, 1988, 36.

54. FOMC transcripts, March 29, 1988, Appendix—Kohn Statement.

55. FOMC transcripts, July 7, 1987, 6.

56. FOMC transcripts, December 13–14, 1988, Appendix—Kohn Statement.

57. FOMC transcripts, March 29, 1988, Appendix—Kohn Statement.

58. Ibid., 30.
59. FOMC transcripts, November 14, 1989, Appendix—Sternlight Statement.
60. FOMC transcripts, December 15–16, 1987, Appendix—Kohn Statement.
61. FOMC transcripts, December 18–19, 1989, 91.
62. More broadly, the rational expectations "revolution" in macro-economics provides the intellectual context for discussions of credibility. The central tenet of rational expectations theory is that economic actors factor expectations about future policy actions into their behavior today. See Lucas (1972), Muth (1961), and Sargent and Wallace (1975) for seminal contributions to this literature.
63. FOMC transcripts, December 18–19, 1989, Appendix—Stockman, Silfman, and Hooper Statement; FOMC transcripts, July 2–3, 1990, Appendix—Prell Statement.
64. FOMC transcripts, September 7, 1990—Conference Call; FOMC transcripts, October 30, 1991—Conference Call; FOMC transcripts, June 30–July 1, 1992, 42; FOMC transcripts, November 16, 1993, 69; FOMC transcripts, December 21, 1993, 20, 32–33.
65. FOMC transcripts, December 21, 1993, 37.
66. FOMC transcripts, December 18–19, 1989, 43.
67. FOMC transcripts, November 17, 1992, Appendix—Kohn Statement.
68. FOMC transcripts, October 15, 1993—Conference Call.
69. In an earlier era, taping of the meetings—then used to prepare what were called "Memoranda of Discussion," elaborate summaries of what transpired in meetings closer in purpose to verbatim transcripts than to what are now released as minutes—had been public knowledge, but the practice of retaining these tapes was apparently discontinued by Chairman Arthur Burns when the Freedom of Information Act was passed in the mid-1970s. During this period, the chairman and top staff were aware of the tapes, even if committee members were not. Stephen Axilrod, secretary of the FOMC for many years, noted: "We did not stop keeping the tapes of the meetings. We had the tapes all the way back. I asked every incoming Chairman after I became Secretary—I asked Paul [Volcker], and I asked [G. William] Miller—'You want to destroy the tapes?' 'I'm not going to destroy these tapes'" (Interview with Stephen Axilrod).
70. FOMC transcripts, October 5, 1993—Conference Call; FOMC transcripts, October 15, 1993—Conference Call; FOMC transcripts, October 22, 1993—Conference Call.
71. FOMC transcripts, December 14, 1992—Conference Call.
72. FOMC transcripts, July 6–7, 1993, 78.
73. FOMC transcripts, November 16, 1993, 1–63.
74. FOMC transcripts, July 6–7, 1993, 83.
75. FOMC transcripts, November 17, 1992, 54–60.
76. FOMC transcripts, December 21, 1993, 26.
77. FOMC transcripts, August 17, 1993, 34.
78. FOMC transcripts, July 6–7, 1993, 78.
79. The full Directive, with the statement of the policy "bias," was *not* released.

80. FOMC transcripts, February 3–4, 1994, 30.
81. FOMC transcripts, February 2–3, 1993, 69.
82. FOMC transcripts, November 17, 1992, 58.
83. FOMC transcripts, February 3–4, 1994, 33.
84. The text of the statement read: "Chairman Greenspan announced today that the Federal Open Market Committee decided to increase slightly the degree of pressure on reserve positions. The action is expected to be consistent with a small increase in money market rates. The decision was taken to move toward a less accommodative stance in monetary policy in order to sustain and enhance the economic expansion. Chairman Greenspan decided to announce the action immediately so as to avoid any misunderstanding of the Committee's purposes, given the fact that this is the first firming of reserve conditions by the Committee since early 1989." FOMC transcripts, February 3–4, 1994, 59.
85. FOMC transcripts, February 28, 1994—Conference Call.
86. FOMC transcripts, March 22, 1994, Appendix—Kohn Statement.
87. FOMC transcripts, August 20, 1991, Appendix—Lindsey Statement; emphasis added.
88. FOMC transcripts, July 1–2, 1997, 78–81.
89. FOMC transcripts, June 29–30, 1999, 92.
90. FOMC transcripts, March 22, 1994, 43–44.
91. Between 1983 and 2000, the Federal Reserve made policy adjustments between meetings on ninety-eight occasions. Of these intermeeting moves, ninety-six occurred before the change in disclosure policy in 1994. Between 1994 and 2000, the Federal Reserve made intermeeting policy adjustments on *two* occasions (Thornton and Wheelock 2000: 8). In more recent years, the terrorist attacks of September 2001 and the financial turmoil of 2007–2009 have provided the only occasions for intermeeting moves in the federal funds rate target.
92. FOMC transcripts, August 16, 1994, Appendix—Kohn Statement; FOMC transcripts, August 16, 1994, 32–34; FOMC transcripts, January 31–February 1, 1995, 6; FOMC transcripts, August 20, 1996, Appendix—Kohn Statement; FOMC transcripts, August 20, 1996, 40; FOMC transcripts, March 25, 1997, Appendix—Kohn Statement; FOMC transcripts, November 17, 1998, 93, 99.
93. See Taylor (2001) for a clean economic model explaining this phenomenon. Essentially, the intuition is the following: if a bank expects that the Federal Reserve will lower its target for the federal funds rate *tomorrow*, it will delay purchases of federal funds *today* in anticipation of the lower rate. This has the effect of immediately reducing the demand for federal funds and depressing the rate (i.e., before the Trading Desk has actually conducted any open market operations) (Meulendyke 1998: 180).
94. The phenomenon soon became the focus of a flurry of academic research, much of it written by economists associated with the Federal Reserve and published in the journals of the regional Federal Reserve Banks. For representative works in this voluminous literature, see Blinder et al. (2001); Broaddus

(2001); Freedman (2002); B. Friedman (2002); Guthrie and Wright (2000); Kohn and Sack (2003); Lange, Sack, and Whitesell (2001); Poole and Rasche (2000); Poole, Rasche, and Thornton (2002); Sellon (2002); and Woodford (2002).

95. FOMC transcripts, January 30–31, 1996, Appendix—Kohn Statement; emphasis added.

96. FOMC transcripts, July 5–6, 1995, Appendix—Simpson Statement.

97. Ibid., 8.

98. Ibid., 11.

99. FOMC transcripts, May 21, 1996, 16.

100. The *only* adjustments in policy during this period were two easing moves in 1998 in response to the East Asian financial crisis. The fact that interest rates were left basically unchanged even during a period of significant global financial turmoil is particularly remarkable.

101. FOMC transcripts, November 12, 1997, 54; FOMC transcripts, December 16, 1997, 29–30.

102. FOMC transcripts, November 12, 1997, 54.

103. Ibid., 76.

104. FOMC transcripts, June 30–July 1, 1998, Appendix—Kohn Statement.

105. FOMC transcripts, March 31, 1998, 87.

106. FOMC Transcripts, June 29–30, 1999, 10–11.

107. Ibid., 89.

108. Interview with Donald Kohn, Washington, D.C., July 18, 2002; interview with Janet Yellen, Berkeley, California, June 1, 2002.

109. FOMC Transcripts, June 29–30, 1999, 89.

110. FOMC Transcripts, November 16, 1999, 70.

111. FOMC Transcripts, January 29–30, 2002, 120.

112. FOMC transcripts, December 13–14, 1988, 9.

113. FOMC transcripts, August 16, 1988, Appendix—Kohn Statement; ibid., 33–37; FOMC transcripts, February 7–8, 1989, Appendix—Kohn Statement; FOMC transcripts, December 13–14, 1988, 13.

114. "Transparency and Central Banking," speech by Roger W. Ferguson, April 19, 2001, Washington, D.C.

115. FOMC transcripts, November 16, 1999, 62–73; FOMC transcripts, December 21, 1999, 59–80.

116. Janet Yellen, former member of President Clinton's Council of Economic Advisers, discussed Rubin's position at length (interview with Janet Yellen, June 1, 2002). According to Douglas Cliggott, an analyst for J. P. Morgan Chase, this view was widely shared on Wall Street during the 1990s (interview with Douglas Cliggott, New York City, July 11, 2002).

117. FOMC Transcripts, March 22, 1994, 44.

118. It seems plausible that the market reaction to the 1994 tightening move convinced policymakers that similar moves would be risky—committee members evinced growing concern about the possibility of "cracking" the market as the 1990s boom extended. In addition, the Greenspan doctrine reflected an influential new body of academic work—most closely associ-

ated with then Princeton economist Ben Bernanke—that argued that speculative bubbles could not be identified preemptively but only after the fact (Bernanke and Gertler 1999). Bernanke received a hearing for his ideas before an enthralled Chairman Greenspan at the 1999 annual Jackson Hole meeting of Federal Reserve policymakers (Cassidy 2008). Bernanke was subsequently appointed to the Federal Reserve Board of Governors, eventually assuming the chairmanship when Greenspan retired in 2006.

119. This is not to suggest that policymakers were in a position to set policy completely autonomously from markets in previous periods. The implementation of policy always involved discerning information by observing developments in markets, and this process was a somewhat convoluted one under any policy regime. The point here is simply that it became *more so* under the regime of transparency, as Greenspan observed when he complained, "We are losing our ability to understand what the markets are telling us" (FOMC transcripts, June 29–30, 1999, 89). Greenspan's worry was a constant theme in the FOMC transcripts in the late 1990s.

120. FOMC transcripts, August 21, 2001, 77.

121. Ibid.

6. Conclusion

1. Bell gave special attention to the availability of time as the paradigmatic form of scarcity in post-industrial society. Developing a similar line of reasoning, Fred Hirsch (1976) argued for the continuing existence of what he termed "social scarcity" even as material abundance grew. Social scarcity was based on the increasing salience of "positional goods"—goods with a value based on their exclusive character—in determining social status. Where such positional goods are concerned, Hirsch (1976: 176) noted, distributional tensions would persist even in the context of growing prosperity. Of course, as Hirsch wrote these words, growth was faltering rather than surging ahead, but his point that distributional conflict was not dependent on declining prosperity is valid, nonetheless.

2. Of course, these are not mutually exclusive: a new social compact defining social priorities would necessarily reflect processes of contestation. We should be wary of the suggestion that there is an underlying or latent consensus in American society that merely needs to be revealed in order to provide a political framework for distributional justice. Bell's discussion *can* be read as implying an underlying consensus, although in my view this reading of his work is not necessary.

3. Hay (2007) uses the term "non-governmental public" to refer to quasi-public entities that are not formally incorporated into the decision-making apparatus of the government. Corporations that have taken on responsibilities formerly assumed by government represent a key example. Note that while the transfer of governmental responsibilities to corporations is typically referred to as "privatization," this usage reflects a very different sense of "private" than the relegation of some question to the domestic sphere

(the sense in which I use the term "private" below). For helpful clarification on these issues, see Weintraub (1997).

4. Philosopher Michael Sandel (1996) sees more similarity than difference in Keynesian and neoliberal economic management, as both take a step away from earlier republican traditions that involved the state in morally preparing citizens to participate in public life. Keynesian managers eschewed such moral questions for the more antiseptic pursuit of aggregate growth, consistent with the liberal tradition that viewed all such attempts by the state to shape the character of citizens with suspicion.

5. This is not to suggest that redistribution has not occurred under financialization, as the post-1970s period has witnessed a dramatic increase in income and wealth inequality in the U.S. economy. It is merely to suggest that issues of distribution have not been politicized in recent years, and they remain relatively absent from public discourse.

Appendix A

1. The Bank of Japan is, to my knowledge, the only other central bank to release verbatim transcripts of its meetings. These transcripts are released with a ten-year lag, whereas the Federal Reserve releases its transcripts with a five-year lag.

Appendix C

1. In 2001 the Bureau of Economic Analysis (BEA) changed the manner in which it groups industries, replacing the Standard Industrial Code (SIC) with the North American Industrial Classification System (NAICS). These classificatory systems use different definitions of "financial" and "nonfinancial" sectors. This discussion reflects industry groups prior to that change.

2. The problem persists even when IRS depreciation allowances are converted to an establishment basis in the BEA's *Gross Product Originating* series. This is likely the case because the conversion is based on an employment matrix, rather than capital stock. I am indebted to Shelby Herman of the BEA for suggesting this possibility.

3. My use of the term "global" here departs from conventional usages. I use the term to refer to activities in the territorial United States and to the worldwide activities of U.S. corporations. I do *not* refer to economic activity undertaken by firms of any nationality, anywhere in the world.

4. The industry of parent classification should correspond closely to domestic statistics compiled on a company basis. The industry of affiliate classification approximates data reported on an establishment basis. In compiling the profits earned abroad data, the BEA only consolidates foreign-affiliate operations "if they are in the same country and in the same three-digit industry or if they are integral parts of the same business operation" (Mataloni 1995: 51).

5. Financial parents might also own nonfinancial foreign affiliates, of course. This is less common, however, so it is reasonably safe to assume that the bias in the data is in the direction indicated.

6. Technically, this problem was also present in the portfolio income measure, which similarly used two different data sources to merge data on foreign taxes paid and profits earned abroad. Because the portfolio income measure only refers to nonfinancial firms, however, the problem can be safely ignored. The issue of foreign taxes becomes somewhat more vexing in the sectoral analysis, where determining the boundary between financial and nonfinancial industries is central to interpreting what these data indicate about patterns of economic change.

References

Abdelal, Rawi. 2007. *Capital Rules: The Construction of Global Finance*. Cambridge, MA: Harvard University Press.

Adrian, Tobias, and Hyun Shin Shin. 2009. "Liquidity and Leverage." Staff Report No. 328. New York: Federal Reserve Bank of New York.

Armstrong, Philip, Andrew Glyn, and John Harrison. 1991. *Capitalism since 1945*. New York: Blackwell.

Arrighi, Giovanni. 1994. *The Long Twentieth Century: Money, Power, and the Origins of Our Times*. New York: Verso.

———. 2007. *Adam Smith in Beijing: Lineages of the Twenty-First Century*. New York: Verso.

Arrighi, Giovanni, and Jason Moore. 2001. "Capitalist Development in World Historical Perspective." Pp. 56–75 in *Phases of Capitalist Development: Booms, Crises, and Globalization*, edited by R. Albritton, M. Itoh, R. Westra, and A. Zuege. London: Macmillan.

Arrighi, Giovanni, and Beverly Silver. 1999. *Chaos and Governance in the Modern World System*. Minneapolis: University of Minnesota Press.

Axilrod, Stephen. 2000. "The Role of Interest Rates in Federal Reserve Policymaking: Discussion." Pp. 70–75 in *The Evolution of Monetary Policy and the Federal Reserve System over the Past Thirty Years: A Conference in Honor of Frank E. Morris*, edited by R. W. Kopcke and L. E. Browne. Boston: Federal Reserve Bank of Boston.

Bank for International Settlements. 2001. *Annual Report*. Basle, Switzerland: Bank for International Settlements.

Barro, Robert, and David Gordon. 1983a. "A Positive Theory of Monetary Policy in a Natural Rate Model." *Journal of Political Economy* 91:589–610.

———. 1983b. "Rules, Discretion, and Reputation in a Model of Monetary Policy." *Journal of Monetary Economics* 12:101–121.

Bell, Daniel. 1967. "The Year 2000—The Trajectory of an Idea." Pp. 1–13 in *Toward the Year 2000: Work in Progress*, edited by D. Bell. Boston: Houghton Mifflin.

———. 1973. *The Coming of Post-Industrial Society: A Venture in Social Forecasting*. New York: Basic Books.

———. 1976. *The Cultural Contradictions of Capitalism*. New York: Basic Books.

Bellamy Foster, John, and Fred Magdoff. 2009. *The Great Financial Crisis: Causes and Consequences*. New York: Monthly Review Press.

Bernanke, Ben, and Mark Gertler. 1999. "Monetary Policy and Asset Price Volatility." Pp. 77–128 in *New Challenges for Monetary Policy*. Jackson Hole, WY: Federal Reserve Bank of Kansas City.

Blecker, Robert. 1999. *Taming Global Finance: A Better Architecture for Growth and Equity*. Washington, DC: Economic Policy Institute.

Blinder, Alan. 1997. "Is Government Too Political?" *Foreign Affairs* 76: 115–126.

———. 1998. *Central Banking in Theory and Practice*. Cambridge, MA: MIT Press.

———. 2004. *The Quiet Revolution: Central Banking Goes Modern*. New Haven, CT: Yale University Press.

———. 2005. "What Have We Learned since October 1979?" *Federal Reserve Bank of St. Louis Review* 87:283–286.

Blinder, Alan, Charles Goodhart, Philipp Hildebrand, David Lipton, and Charles Wyplosz. 2001. *How Do Central Banks Talk?* Geneva: International Center for Monetary and Banking Studies.

Block, Fred. 1977. *The Origins of International Economic Disorder: A Study of United States International Monetary Policy from World War II to the Present*. Berkeley: University of California Press.

———. 1981. "The Fiscal Crisis of the Capitalist State." *Annual Review of Sociology* 7:1–27.

———. 1987. *Revising State Theory: Essays on Politics and Postindustrialism*. Philadelphia: Temple University Press.

———. 1990. *Postindustrial Possibilities: A Critique of Economic Discourse*. Berkeley: University of California Press.

Bluestone, Barry, and Bennett Harrison. 1982. *The Deindustrialization of America: Plant Closings, Community Abandonment, and the Dismantling of Basic Industries*. New York: Basic Books.

Blyth, Mark. 2002. *Great Transformations: Economic Ideas and Institutional Change in the Twentieth Century*. Cambridge: Cambridge University Press.

Boies, John, and Harland Prechel. 2002. "Capital Dependence, Business Political Behavior, and Change to the Multilayered Subsidiary Form." *Social Problems* 49:301–326.

Borrio, Claudio. 1997. "The Implementation of Monetary Policy in Industrial Countries: A Survey." Bank for International Settlements Working Papers No. 47. Basle, Switzerland: Bank for International Settlements.

Borrio, Claudio, and Philip Lowe. 2002. "Asset Prices, Financial and Monetary Stability: Exploring the Nexus." Bank for International Settlements Working Papers No. 114. Basle, Switzerland: Bank for International Settlements.

Braudel, Fernand. 1982. *Civilization and Capitalism, 15th–18th Century*, vol. 2: *The Wheels of Commerce*. Translated by S. Reynolds. Berkeley: University of California Press.

Brenner, Robert. 2002. *The Boom and the Bubble: The U.S. in the World Economy*. London: Verso.

———. 2006. *The Economics of Global Turbulence*. London: Verso.

Brick, Howard. 2007. *Transcending Capitalism: Visions of a New Society in Modern American Thought*. Ithaca, NY: Cornell University Press.

Brittan, Samuel. 1976. "The Economic Contradictions of Democracy." Pp. 96–137 in *Why Is Britain Becoming Harder to Govern?* edited by A. King. London: British Broadcasting Corporation.

Broaddus, J. Alfred, Jr. 2001. "Transparency in the Practice of Monetary Policy." *Economic Quarterly* 87:1–9.

Bryan, Dick, and Michael Rafferty. 2006. *Capitalism with Derivatives: A Political Economy of Financial Derivatives, Capital and Class*. New York: Palgrave Macmillan.

Burnham, Peter. 1999. "The Politics of Economic Management." *New Political Economy* 4:37–54.

———. 2001. "New Labour and the Politics of Depoliticisation." *British Journal of Politics and International Relations* 3:127–149.

———. 2006. "Depoliticisation: A Comment on Buller and Flinders." *British Journal of Politics and International Relations* 8:303–306.

Calleo, David. 1982. *The Imperious Economy*. Cambridge, MA: Harvard University Press.

Campbell, John, and Ove Pedersen. 2001. "Introduction." Pp. 1–23 in *The Rise of Neoliberalism and Institutional Analysis*, edited by J. L. Campbell and O. K. Pedersen. Princeton, NJ: Princeton University Press.

Carosso, Vincent. 1970. *Investment Banking in America*. Cambridge, MA: Harvard University Press.

Carruthers, Bruce, Terrence Halliday, and Sarah Babb. 2001. "Institutionalizing Markets, or the Market for Institutions? Central Banks, Bankruptcy Law, and the Globalization of Financial Markets." Pp. 94–126 in *The Rise of Neoliberalism and Institutional Analysis*, edited by J. L. Campbell and O. K. Pedersen. Princeton, NJ: Princeton University Press.

Cassidy, John. 2008. "Anatomy of a Meltdown: Ben Bernanke and the Financial Crisis." *The New Yorker*, December 1: 48–63.

Castells, Manuel. 1996. *The Information Age: Economy, Society, and Culture*, vol. 1: *The Rise of the Network Society*. New York: Blackwell Publishers.

Chernow, Ron. 1990. *The House of Morgan: An American Banking Dynasty and the Rise of Modern Finance*. New York: Simon & Schuster.

Chirinko, Robert. 1993. "Business Fixed Investment Spending: Modeling Strategies, Empirical Results, and Policy Implications." *Journal of Economic Literature* 31:1875–1911.

Chorev, Nitsan. 2007. *Remaking U.S. Trade Policy: From Protectionism to Globalization.* Ithaca, NY: Cornell University Press.

———. 2009. "The Judicial Transformation of the State: The Case of U.S. Trade Policy, 1974–2004." *Law and Policy* 31:31–68.

Clark, Colin. 1940. *The Conditions of Economic Progress.* London: Macmillan.

Clemens, Elisabeth. 2005. "The Power of Ideas? The Possibility of a Myth of Shareholder Value." *Political Power and Social Theory* 17:207–212.

Cleveland, Harold van, and Thomas Huertas. 1985. *Citibank, 1812–1970.* Cambridge, MA: Harvard University Press.

Clouse, James. 1994. "Recent Developments in Discount Window Policy." *Federal Reserve Bulletin* 80:965–977.

Cohen, Benjamin. 1977. *Organizing the World's Money: The Political Economy of International Monetary Relations.* New York: Basic Books.

Cohen, Lizabeth. 2003. *A Consumer's Republic: The Politics of Mass Consumption in Postwar America.* New York: Vintage Books.

Collins, Robert. 1996. "The Economic Crisis of 1968 and the Waning of the 'American Century.'" *American Historical Review* 101:396–422.

———. 2000. *More: The Politics of Economic Growth in Postwar America.* Oxford: Oxford University Press.

Cooper, George. 2008. *The Origin of Financial Crises: Central Banks, Credit Bubbles, and the Efficient Market Fallacy.* New York: Vintage Books.

Covert, James, and Gary McWilliams. 2006. "At Sears, Investing—Not Retail—Drive Profit." *Wall Street Journal,* November 17, C1.

Crotty, James. 1999. "Review of Robert Brenner's *Turbulence in the World Economy.*" *Challenge* 42:108–130.

———. 2005. "The Neoliberal Paradox: The Impact of Destructive Product Market Competition and 'Modern' Financial Markets on Nonfinancial Corporation Performance in the Neoliberal Era." Pp. 77–110 in *Financialization and the World Economy,* edited by G. A. Epstein. Northampton, MA: Edward Elgar.

Crouch, Colin. 1978. "Inflation and the Political Organization of Economic Interests." Pp. 217–239 in *The Political Economy of Inflation,* edited by F. Hirsch and J. H. Goldthorpe. Cambridge, MA: Harvard University Press.

Crozier, Michael, Samuel P. Huntington, and Joji Watanuki. 1975. *The Crisis of Democracy.* New York: New York University Press.

Cukierman, Alex. 1992. *Central Bank Strategy, Credibility, and Independence.* Cambridge, MA: MIT Press.

Cukierman, Alex, and Allan Meltzer. 1986. "A Theory of Ambiguity, Credibility, and Inflation under Discretion and Asymmetric Information." *Econometrica* 54:1099–1128.

D'Arista, Jane. 2002. "Rebuilding the Transmission Belt for Monetary Policy." Report in the Financial Markets and Society Series. Philomont, VA: Financial Markets Center.

———. 2003. "Reforming the Privatized International Monetary and Financial Architecture." Pp. 721–750 in *Handbook of International Banking,* edited by A. W. Mullineaux and V. Murinde. Northampton, MA: Edward Elgar.

Davis, Gerald. 2009. *Managed by the Markets*. New York: Oxford University Press.

Davis, Gerald, Kristina Diekmann, and Catherine Tinsley. 1994. "The Decline and Fall of the Conglomerate Firm in the 1980s: A Study in the Deinstitutionalization of an Organizational Form." *American Sociological Review* 59:547–570.

Davis, Gerald, and Susan Stout. 1992. "Organization Theory and the Market for Corporate Control: A Dynamic Analysis Characteristics of Large Takeover Targets." *Administrative Science Quarterly* 37:605–633.

Davis, Gerald, and Tracy Thompson. 1994. "A Social Movement Perspective on Corporate Control." *Administrative Science Quarterly* 39:141–173.

Despres, Emil, Charles Kindelberger, and Walter S. Salant. 1966. "The Dollar and World Liquidity: A Minority View." *The Economist*, February 5, 218.

Destler, I. M., and C. Randall Henning. 1989. *Dollar Politics: Exchange Rate Policymaking in the United States*. Washington, DC: Institute for International Economics.

Dobbin, Frank, and Dirk Zorn. 2005. "Corporate Malfeasance and the Myth of Shareholder Value." *Political Power and Social Theory* 17:179–198.

Dooley, Michael, David Folkerts-Landau, and Peter Garber. 2003. "An Essay on the Revived Bretton Woods System." Working Paper 9971. Cambridge, MA: National Bureau of Economic Research.

Dumenil, Gerard, and Dominique Levy. 2004. *Capital Resurgent: Roots of the Neoliberal Revolution*. Cambridge, MA: Harvard University Press.

Eatwell, John, and Lance Taylor. 2000. *Global Finance at Risk: The Case for International Regulation*. New York: The New Press.

Edwards, Cheryl. 1997. "Open Market Operations in the 1990s." *Federal Reserve Bulletin* 83:859–874.

Eichengreen, Barry. 1996. *Globalizing Capital: A History of the International Monetary System*. Princeton, NJ: Princeton University Press.

Eisinger, Jesse. 2004. "Ahead of the Tape." *Wall Street Journal*, February 9, C1.

Epstein, Gerald, and Arjun Jayadev. 2005. "The Determinants of Rentier Incomes in OECD Countries: Monetary Policy, Financial Liberalization, and Labor Solidarity." Pp. 46–74 in *Financialization and the World Economy*, edited by G. Epstein. Northampton, MA: Edward Elgar.

Espeland, Wendy Nelson, and Paul Hirsch. 1990. "Ownership Changes, Accounting Practice, and the Redefinition of the Corporation." *Accounting, Organizations, and Society* 15:77–96.

Evans, Lawrance. 2003. *Why the Bubble Burst: U.S. Stock Market Performance since 1982*. Northampton, MA: Edward Elgar.

Fama, Eugene, and Michael Jensen. 1983. "Separation of Ownership and Control." *Journal of Law and Economics* 26:301–325.

Fazarri, Steven. 1994. "Monetary Policy, Financial Structure, and Investment." Pp. 35–63 in *Transforming the U.S. Financial System*, edited by G. A. Dymski, G. Epstein, and R. Pollin. Armonk, NY: M. E. Sharpe.

Feinman, Joshua. 1993. "Reserve Requirements: History, Current Practice, and Potential Reform." *Federal Reserve Bulletin* 79:569–589.

Feldstein, Martin. 1994. "American Economic Policy in the 1980s: A Personal View." Pp. 1–79 in *American Economic Policy in the 1980s*, edited by M. Feldstein. Chicago: National Bureau of Economic Research.

Felix, David. 2005. "Why International Capital Mobility Should be Curbed, and How It Could Be Done." Pp. 384–408 in *Financialization and the World Economy*, edited by G. A. Epstein. Northampton, MA: Edward Elgar.

Ferguson, Thomas. 1990. "Industrial Conflict and the Coming of the New Deal: The Triumph of Multinational Liberalism in American." Pp. 3–31 in *The Rise and Fall of the New Deal Order, 1930–1980*, edited by G. Gerstle and S. Fraser. Princeton, NJ: Princeton University Press.

Fligstein, Neil. 1990. *The Transformation of Corporate Control*. Cambridge, MA: Harvard University Press.

———. 2001. *The Architecture of Markets: An Economic Sociology of Twenty-First-Century Capitalist Societies*. Princeton, NJ: Princeton University Press.

———. 2005. "The End of (Shareholder Value) Ideology?" *Political Power and Social Theory* 17:223–228.

Fligstein, Neil, and Jennifer Choo. 2005. "Law and Corporate Governance." *Annual Review of Law and Social Science* 1:61–84.

Fligstein, Neil, and Taekjin Shin. 2007. "Shareholder Value and the Transformation of the U.S. Economy, 1984–2000." *Sociological Forum* 22:399–424.

Flinders, Matthew, and Jim Buller. 2006. "Depoliticization: Principles, Tactics, and Tools." *British Politics* 1:1–26.

Frankel, Jeffrey. 1984. *The Yen/Dollar Agreement: Liberalizing Japanese Capital Markets*. Washington, DC: Institute for International Economics.

———. 1988. "International Capital Flows and Domestic Economic Policies." Pp. 559–627 in *The United States in the World Economy*, edited by M. Feldstein. Chicago: National Bureau of Economic Research.

———. 1994. "The Making of Exchange Rate Policy in the 1980s." Pp. 293–341 in *American Economic Policy in the 1980s*, edited by M. Feldstein. Chicago: National Bureau of Economic Research.

Freedman, Charles. 2002. "The Value of Transparency in Conducting Monetary Policy." *Federal Reserve Bank of St. Louis Review* 84:155–160.

Friedman, Benjamin. 2002. "The Use and Meaning of Words in Central Banking: Inflation Targeting, Credibility, and Transparency." Working Paper 8972. Cambridge, MA: National Bureau of Economic Research.

Friedman, Milton. 1968. "The Role of Monetary Policy." *American Economic Review* 58:1–17.

Frobel, Folker, Jurgen Heinrichs, and Otto Kreye. 1980. *The New International Division of Labor: Structural Unemployment in Industrialised Countries and Industrialisation in Developing Countries*. Translated by P. Burgess. Cambridge: Cambridge University Press.

Froud, Julie, Colin Haslam, Sukhdev Johal, and Karel Williams. 2000. "Shareholder Value and Financialization: Consultancy Promises, Management Moves." *Economy and Society* 29:80–110.

————. 2002. "Cars after Financialisation: A Case Study in Financial Under-Performance, Constraints, and Consequences." *Competition and Change* 6:13–41.

Froud, Julie, Sukhdev Johal, Adam Leaver, and Karel Williams. 2006. *Financialization and Strategy: Narrative and Numbers*. London: Routledge.

Gao, Bai. 2009. "The Dollar Standard and the Global Production System: The Institutional Origins of the Global Financial Crisis." Paper presented at the annual meeting of the American Sociological Association, San Francisco, August 8–11.

Geanakoplos, John. 2009. "Solving the Present Crisis and Managing the Leverage Cycle." Paper presented at a Tobin Project conference on "Ferment in the Face of Crisis." White Oak, FL, April 24–26.

Gilpin, Robert. 1987. *The Political Economy of International Relations*. Princeton, NJ: Princeton University Press.

Glyn, Andrew, Alan Hughes, Alain Lipetz, and Ajit Singh. 1990. "The Rise and Fall of the Golden Age." Pp. 39–125 in *The Golden Age of Capitalism*, edited by S. Marglin and J. Schor. Oxford: Oxford University Press.

Goldthorpe, John. 1978. "The Current Inflation: Towards a Sociological Account." Pp. 186–214 in *The Political Economy of Inflation*, edited by F. Hirsch and J. H. Goldthorpe. Cambridge, MA: Harvard University Press.

————. 1987. "Problems of Political Economy after the Postwar Period." Pp. 363–407 in *Changing Boundaries of the Political: Essays on the Evolving Balance between State and Society, Public and Private in Europe*, edited by C. S. Maier. New York: Cambridge University Press.

Goodfriend, Marvin. 1986. "Monetary Mystique: Secrecy and Central Banking." *Journal of Monetary Economics* 17:63–92.

————. 1991. "Interest Rates and the Conduct of Monetary Policy." *Carnegie-Rochester Conference Series on Public Policy* 34:7–30.

————. 2005. "The Monetary Policy Debate since October 1979: Lessons for Theory and Practice." *Federal Reserve Bank of St. Louis Review* 87:243–262.

Goodfriend, Marvin, and William Whelpley. 1987. "Federal Funds: Instrument of Federal Reserve Policy." Pp. 289–302 in *Contemporary Developments in Financial Institutions and Markets*, edited by T. Havrilesky and R. Schweitzer. Arlington Heights, IL: Harlan Davidson.

Goodhart, Charles. 2000. "Can Central Banking Survive the IT Revolution?" *International Finance* 3:189–209.

Gough, Ian. 1981. "State Expenditures in Advanced Capitalism." *New Left Review* 92:53–92.

Gowa, Joanne. 1983. *Closing the Gold Window: Domestic Politics and the End of Bretton Woods*. Ithaca, NY: Cornell University Press.

Gowan, Peter. 1999. *The Global Gamble: Washington's Faustian Bid for World Dominance*. London: Verso.

————. 2001. "Explaining the American Boom: The Roles of Globalisation and United States Global Power." *New Political Economy* 6:359–374.

Grabel, Ilene. 1997. "Saving, Investment, and Financial Efficiency: A Comparative Examination of National Financial Complexes." Pp. 251–298 in *The*

Macroeconomics of Saving, Finance, and Investment, edited by R. Pollin. Ann Arbor: University of Michigan Press.

Greider, William. 1987. *Secrets of the Temple: How the Federal Reserve Runs the Country.* New York: Simon and Schuster.

Guthrie, Graeme, and Julian Wright. 2000. "Open Mouth Operations." *Journal of Monetary Economics* 46:489–516.

Habermas, Jürgen. 1973. *Legitimation Crisis.* Translated by T. McCarthy. Boston: Beacon Press.

Hakim, Danny. 2004. "Detroit Profits Most from Loans, Not Cars." *New York Times,* July 22, C1.

Harvey, David. 1999. *The Limits to Capital.* London: Verso.

———. 2003. *The New Imperialism.* New York: Oxford University Press.

Hawley, James. 1984. "Protecting Capital from Itself: U.S. Attempts to Regulate the Eurocurrency System." *International Organization* 38:131–165.

Hay, Colin. 2007. *Why We Hate Politics.* Cambridge, UK: Polity Press.

Helleiner, Eric. 1994. *States and the Reemergence of Global Finance: From Bretton Woods to the 1990s.* Ithaca, NY: Cornell University Press.

Henry, David. 2005. "Corporate America's New Achilles Heel: Overreliance on Profits from Finance Units May Be Setting Up Companies for a Fall." *Business Week,* March 28, 32–34.

Hilferding, Rudolf. 1981. *Finance Capital: A Study in the Latest Phase of Capitalist Development.* London: Routledge and Kegan Paul.

Hirsch, Fred. 1976. *Social Limits to Growth.* Cambridge, MA: Harvard University Press.

———. 1978. "The Ideological Underlay of Inflation." Pp. 263–284 in *The Political Economy of Inflation,* edited by F. Hirsch and J. H. Goldthorpe. Cambridge, MA: Harvard University Press.

Hirsch, Fred, and John Goldthorpe, eds. 1978. *The Political Economy of Inflation.* Cambridge, MA: Harvard University Press.

Hirschman, Albert. 1980. "The Social and Political Matrix of Inflation: Elaborations on the Latin American Experience." Pp. 177–207 in *Essays in Trespassing: Economics to Politics and Beyond.* Cambridge: Cambridge University Press.

Hirst, Paul, and Grahame Thompson. 1999. *Globalization in Question.* Cambridge: Polity Press.

Hobson, John. 1971. *Imperialism: A Study.* Ann Arbor: University of Michigan Press.

Hudson, Michael. 2003. *Superimperialism: The Origin and Fundamentals of U.S. World Dominance.* London: Pluto Press.

Huntington, Samuel P. 1975. "The United States." Pp. 59–118 in *The Crisis of Democracy,* edited by M. Crozier, S. P. Huntington, and J. Watanuki. New York: New York University Press.

Hutton, Will. 1995. *The State We're In.* London: Random House.

Jacobs, Meg. 2005. *Pocketbook Politics: Economic Citizenship in Twentieth-Century America.* Princeton, NJ: Princeton University Press.

Janowitz, Morris. 1976. *Social Control of the Welfare State.* New York: Elsevier.

Jensen, Michael, and William Meckling. 1976. "Theory of the Firm: Managerial Behavior, Agency Cost, and Ownership Structure." *Journal of Financial Economics* 11:5–50.

Kaufman, Henry. 1986. *Interest Rates, Markets, and the New Financial World.* New York: Times Books.

Keynes, John Maynard. 1963. *Essays in Persuasion.* New York: W. W. Norton & Company.

Kindleberger, Charles P. 1978. *Manias, Panics, and Crashes: A History of Financial Crises.* New York: John Wiley and Sons.

King, Anthony. 1975. "Overload: Problems of Governing in the 1970s." *Political Studies* 23:284–296.

Kirshner, Jonathan. 2001. "The Political Economy of Low Inflation." *Journal of Economic Surveys* 15:41–70.

Knodell, Jane. 1994. "Financial Institutions and Contemporary Economic Performance." Pp. 114–160 in *Understanding American Economic Decline,* edited by M. A. Bernstein and D. E. Adler. Cambridge: Cambridge University Press.

Kohn, Donald, and Brian Sack. 2003. "Central Bank Talk: Does it Matter and Why?" Washington, DC: Board of Governors of the Federal Reserve System.

Konings, Martijn. 2008. "The Institutional Foundations of U.S. Structural Power in International Finance: From the Re-emergence of Global Finance to the Monetarist Turn." *Review of International Political Economy* 15:35–61.

Krus, Jill. 1994. "Saving the Financial System: Financial Reform in the 1930s." PhD dissertation, University of Notre Dame.

Kydland, Finn, and Edward Prescott. 1977. "Rules Rather than Discretion: The Inconsistency of Optimal Plans." *Journal of Political Economy* 85:473–492.

Lange, Joe, Brian Sack, and William Whitesell. 2001. "Anticipations of Monetary Policy in Financial Markets." FEDS paper no. 2001-24. Washington, DC: Federal Reserve Board.

Lazonick, William, and Mary O'Sullivan. 2000. "Maximizing Shareholder Value: A New Ideology for Corporate Governance." *Economy and Society* 29: 13–35.

Lenin, Vladimir. 1939. *Imperialism, the Highest Stage of Capitalism: A Popular Outline.* New York: International Publishers.

Leyshon, Andrew, and Nigel Thrift. 2007. "The Capitalisation of Almost Everything: The Future of Economy and Finance." *Theory, Culture, and Society* 24:79–115..

Lindsay, Robert. 1963. "Negotiable Time Certificates of Deposit." *Federal Reserve Bulletin* 49:458–468.

Lucas, Robert. 1972. "Expectations and the Neutrality of Money." *Journal of Economic Theory* 4:103–124.

Magdoff, Harry, and Paul M. Sweezy. 1987. *Stagnation and the Financial Explosion.* New York: Monthly Review Press.

Mataloni, Raymond. 1995. "A Guide to BEA Statistics on U.S. Multinational Companies." *Survey of Current Business* 75:38–55.

Merton, Robert. 1959. "Notes on Problem-Finding in Sociology." Pp. ix–xxxiv in *Sociology Today: Problems and Prospects,* edited by R. Merton, L. Broom, and L. S. Cottrell. New York: Basic Books.

Meulendyke, Anne-Marie. 1998. *U.S. Monetary Policy and Financial Markets.* New York: Federal Reserve Bank of New York.

Miller, Arthur. 1974. "Political Issues in Trust in Government." *American Political Science Review* 68:951–972.

Minsky, Hyman. 1975. *John Maynard Keynes.* New York: Columbia University Press.

———. 1982. *Can "It" Happen Again? Essays on Instability and Finance.* Armonk, NY: M. E. Sharpe.

———. 1986. *Stabilizing an Unstable Economy.* New Haven, CT: Yale University Press.

Mizruchi, Mark. 1996. "What Do Interlocks Do? An Analysis, Critique, and Assessment of Research on Interlocking Directorates." *Annual Review of Sociology* 22:271–298.

———. 2004. "Berle and Means Revisited: The Governance and Power of Large U.S. Corporations." *Theory and Society* 33:519–617.

Mizruchi, Mark, and Howard Kimeldorf. 2005. "The Historical Context of Shareholder Value Capitalism." *Political Power and Social Theory* 17: 213–221.

Murphy, R. Taggart. 1997. *The Weight of the Yen.* New York: W. W. Norton.

———. 2006. "East Asia's Dollars." *New Left Review* 40:39–64.

———. 2008. "Asia and the Meltdown of American Finance." *Economic and Political Weekly* 43:15–21.

Muth, John. 1961. "Rational Expectations and the Theory of Price Movements." *Econometrica* 29:315–335.

Niskanen, William. 1988. *Reaganomics: An Insider's Account of the Policies and the People.* Oxford: Oxford University Press.

Nocera, Joseph. 1994. *A Piece of the Action: How the Middle Class Joined the Money Class.* New York: Simon & Schuster.

O'Connor, James. 1973. *The Fiscal Crisis of the State.* New York: St. Martin's Press.

Offe, Claus. 1974. "Structural Problems of the Capitalist State." Pp. 31–54 in *German Political Studies,* vol. 1, edited by K. von Beyme. London: Sage.

———. 1976. "Crises of Crisis Management: Elements of a Political Crisis Theory." *International Journal of Politics* 6:29–67.

———. 1984. *Contradictions of the Welfare State.* Cambridge, MA: MIT Press.

Orhangazi, Ozgur. 2008. *Financialization and the U.S. Economy.* Northampton, MA: Edward Elgar.

Panitch, Leo. 2000. "The New Imperial State." *New Left Review* 2:5–20.

Pauly, Louis W. 1995. "Capital Mobility, State Autonomy, and Political Legitimacy." *Journal of International Affairs* 48:369–388.

Phillips, Kevin. 1994. *Arrogant Capital: Washington, Wall Street, and the Frustration of American Politics.* New York: Little, Brown, and Company.

Polanyi, Karl. 2001. *The Great Transformation: The Political and Economic Origins of Our Times.* Boston: Beacon Press.

Pollin, Robert. 1996. "Contemporary Economic Stagnation in World Historical Perspective." *New Left Review* 219:109–118.

———. 1997. "Introduction." Pp. 1–33 in *The Macroeconomics of Saving, Finance, and Investment,* edited by R. Pollin. Ann Arbor: University of Michigan Press.

Poole, William, and Robert Rasche. 2000. "Perfecting the Market's Knowledge of Monetary Policy." Working Paper 2000-010A. St. Louis: Federal Reserve Bank of St. Louis.

Poole, William, Robert Rasche, and Daniel Thornton. 2002. "Market Anticipations of Monetary Policy Actions." *Federal Reserve Bank of St. Louis Review* 84:65–93.

Poterba, James. 1994. "Federal Budget Policy in the 1980s." Pp. 235–270 in *American Economic Policy in the 1980s,* edited by M. Feldstein. Chicago: National Bureau of Economic Research.

Poterba, James, and Lawrence Summers. 1995. "A CEO Survey of U.S. Companies' Time Horizons and Hurdle Rates." *Sloan Management Review* 37:43–53.

Prasad, Monica. 2006. *The Politics of Free Markets: The Rise of Neoliberal Economic Policymaking in Britain, France, Germany, and the United States.* Chicago: University of Chicago Press.

Rose, Nicolas, and Peter Miller. 1992. "Political Power beyond the State: Problematics of Government." *British Journal of Sociology* 43:173–205.

Sandel, Michael. 1996. *Democracy's Discontent: America in Search of a Public Philosophy.* Cambridge, MA: Harvard University Press.

Sargent, Thomas, and Neil Wallace. 1975. "'Rational' Expectations, the Optimal Monetary Instrument, and the Optimal Money Supply Rule." *Journal of Political Economy* 83:241–254.

Sassen, Saskia. 2001. *The Global City: New York, London, Tokyo.* Princeton, NJ: Princeton University Press.

Schulman, Bruce. 1998. "Slouching toward the Supply Side: Jimmy Carter and the New American Political Economy." Pp. 95–116 in *The Carter Presidency: Policy Choices in the Post–New Deal Era,* edited by G. M. Fink and H. D. Graham. Lawrence: University Press of Kansas.

Sellon, Gordon. 2002. "The Changing U.S. Financial System: Some Implications for the Monetary Transmission Mechanism." *Economic Review,* Federal Reserve Bank of Kansas City (First Quarter):5–35.

Sellon, Gordon, and Deanna VanNahmen. 1988. "The Securitization of Housing Finance." *Economic Review,* Federal Reserve Bank of Kansas City (July/August):3–20.

Shiller, Robert. 2000. *Irrational Exuberance.* Princeton, NJ: Princeton University Press.

———. 2008. *The Subprime Solution: How Today's Financial Crisis Happened, and What to Do about It.* Princeton, NJ: Princeton University Press.

Shleifer, Andrei. 2000. *Inefficient Markets: An Introduction to Behavioral Finance.* New York: Oxford University Press.

Silver, Beverly. 2003. *Forces of Labor: Workers' Movements and Globalization since 1870.* New York: Cambridge University Press.

Sloan, Allan. 1985. "Why Is No One Safe (from Hostile Corporate Takeovers)?" *Forbes,* March 11, 134–140.

Somers, Margaret. 2008. *Genealogies of Citizenship: Markets, Statelessness, and the Right to Have Rights.* New York: Cambridge University Press.

Starr, Paul, and Ellen Immergut. 1987. "Health Care and the Boundaries of Politics." Pp. 221–254 in *Changing the Boundaries of the Political: Essays on the Evolving Balance between State and Society, Public and Private in Europe,* edited by C. S. Maier. New York: Cambridge University Press.

Stearns, Linda Brewster, and Kenneth Allan. 1996. "Economic Behavior in Institutional Environments: The Corporate Merger Wave of the 1980s." *American Sociological Review* 61:699–718.

Steinherr, Alfred. 1998. *Derivatives: The Wild Beast of Finance.* New York: John Wiley and Sons.

Stiglitz, Joseph. 1990. "Symposium on Bubbles." *Journal of Economic Perspectives* 4:13–18.

Stockhammer, Engelbert. 2004. "Financialisation and the Slowdown of Accumulation." *Cambridge Journal of Economics* 28:719–741.

Stockman, David. 1986. *The Triumph of Politics: How the Reagan Revolution Failed.* New York: Harper and Row.

Strange, Susan. 1986. *Casino Capitalism.* New York: Basil Blackwell.

Taylor, John. 2001. "Expectations, Open Market Operations, and Changes in the Federal Funds Rate." *Federal Reserve Bank of St. Louis Review* 83:34–47.

Thornton, Daniel, and David Wheelock. 2000. "A History of the Asymmetric Policy Directive." *Federal Reserve Bank of St. Louis Review* 82:1–16.

Thurow, Lester. 1980. *The Zero-Sum Society: Distribution and the Possibilities for Economic Change.* New York: Basic Books.

Tilly, Charles. 1984. *Big Structures, Large Processes, Huge Comparisons.* New York: Russell Sage.

Tobin, James. 1984. "On the Efficiency of the Financial System." *Lloyd's Bank Review* 153:1–15.

———. 1997. "Comment." Pp. 299–304 in *The Macroeconomics of Saving, Finance, and Investment,* edited by R. Pollin. Ann Arbor: University of Michigan Press.

Tomaskovic-Devey, Donald, and Ken-Hou Lin. n.d. "Economic Rents and the Financialization of the U.S. Economy." Unpublished paper, Sociology Department, University of Massachusetts.

Triffin, Robert. 1961. *Gold and the Dollar Crisis.* New Haven, CT: Yale University Press.

U.S. Department of Commerce. 2002. "Corporate Profits: Profits before Tax, Profits Tax Liability, and Dividends." Washington, DC: Bureau of Economic Analysis.

Useem, Michael. 1996. *Investor Capitalism: How Money Managers Are Changing the Face of Corporate America.* New York: Basic Books.

Vogel, Stephen. 1996. *Freer Markets, More Rules: Regulatory Reform in Advanced Industrial Countries.* Ithaca, NY: Cornell University Press.

Volcker, Paul. 2002. "Monetary Policy Transmission: Past and Future Challenges." *Federal Reserve Bank of New York Economic Policy Review* 8:7–11.

Volcker, Paul, and Toyoo Gyohten. 1992. *Changing Fortunes: The World's Money and the Threat to American Leadership.* New York: Times Books.

Wallich, Henry. 1984. "Recent Techniques of Monetary Policy." *Economic Review,* Federal Reserve Bank of Kansas City (May):21–30.

Walter, Andrew. 1993. *World Power and World Money: The Role of Hegemony and International Monetary Order.* New York: Harvester Wheatsheaf.

Ward, Nicholas. 2000. "Corporate Foreign Tax Credit, 1996: An Industry and Geographic Focus." *Statistics of Income Bulletin* 19:180–235.

Watson, Matthew. 1999. "Rethinking Capital Mobility, Reregulating Financial Markets." *New Political Economy* 4:55–75.

Weaver, R. Kent. 1986. "The Politics of Blame Avoidance." *Journal of Public Policy* 6:371–398.

Weintraub, Jeff. 1997. "The Theory and Politics of the Public/Private Distinction." Pp. 1–42 in *Public and Private in Thought and Practice: Perspectives on a Grand Dichotomy,* edited by J. Weintraub and K. Kumar. Chicago: University of Chicago Press.

Williams, Karel. 2000. "From Shareholder Value to Present-Day Capitalism." *Economy and Society* 29:1–12.

Williamson, John. 1977. *The Failure of World Monetary Reform, 1971–1974.* New York: New York University.

Wojnilower, Albert. 1980. "The Central Role of Credit Crunches in Recent Financial History." *Brookings Papers on Economic Activity* 2:277–339.

———. 1985. "Private Credit Demand, Supply, and Crunches—How Different Are the 1980s?" *American Economic Review* 75:351–356.

Wolfe, Alan. 1977. *Limits of Legitimacy: Political Contradictions of Contemporary Capitalism.* New York: Free Press.

Woodford, Michael. 2002. "Monetary Policy in the Information Economy." Pp. 297–412 in *Economic Policy for the Information Economy.* Jackson, Hole, WY: Federal Reserve Bank of Kansas City.

Zorn, Dirk. 2004. "Here a Chief, There a Chief: The Rise of the CFO in the American Firm." *American Sociological Review* 69:345–364.

Zorn, Dirk, Frank Dobbin, Julian Dierkes, and Man-Shan Kwok. 2004. "Managing Investors: How Financial Markets Reshaped the American Firm." Pp. 269–289 in *The Sociology of Financial Markets,* edited by K. Knorr-Cetina and A. Preda. New York: Oxford University Press.

Index

JOB #:   168033

Author Name: Krippner

Title of Book: Capitalizing on Crisis

ISBN: 9780674050846

Publisher: Harvard Univ. Press

Trim Size: 6.125 x 9.25

Bulk in mm: 14

Capitalizing on Crisis

CAPITALIZING ON CRISIS

The Political Origins of the
Rise of Finance

GRETA R. KRIPPNER

Harvard University Press
Cambridge, Massachusetts, and London, England   2011

Library of Congress Cataloging-in-Publication Data

Krippner, Greta R.
Capitalizing on crisis : the political origins of the rise of finance /
Greta R. Krippner.
p.   cm.
Includes bibliographical references and index.
ISBN 978-0-674-05084-6 (alk. paper)
1. Finance—United States.
2. Financial services industry—United States.
3. United States—Economic conditions—2001–2009.
4. Monetary policy—United States.   I. Title.
HG181.K725   2010
332.0973—dc22   2010004511

For Sandy

Contents

Figures

Acknowledgments

As a historical sociologist, I am especially cognizant that our efforts as scholars are both cumulative and collective. In tracing the financialization of the U.S. economy to a series of political, economic, and social dilemmas confronted by policymakers in the 1970s, I have relied on the writings of an earlier generation of scholars who described those dilemmas—and without whose work the ideas contained in this book would be unthinkable. While the contributions of these scholars to this book were unknowing, my task here is to acknowledge those who made contributions of a more deliberate sort. It is a great pleasure to finally be able to do so.

This work has had the long gestation typical of books that begin as dissertations, and as such I have generated a long list of debts, spanning several stages of my life, shifting constellations of mentors, colleagues, and friends, and three academic institutions. My first debt is to my dissertation advisors, Jane Collins and Erik Wright, who helped me to launch this project at the University of Wisconsin. Jane gave me my initial orientation to sociological research, and her model of following one's questions no matter where they lead was formative. Erik's analytical rigor is famous among his students, and honing my arguments to his objections provided excellent training over the years. Other members of the dissertation committee—Jamie Peck, Mark Suchman, and Stephen Bunker—served their function on the committee admirably. As a fellow traveler exploring a set of related questions about neoliberal states, I found Jamie's various contributions especially welcome. Mark proved that he is perhaps the most intellectually versatile person I know by providing me with a set of written comments following the defense that kept me busy for approximately two years. I would like to think that Stephen Bunker's free spirit (I can still see him leaning back, cowboy boots propped up on his desk) lives in these pages.

Two other remarkable scholars became involved with this project at the dissertation stage and continued to be involved in subsequent years. As I was preparing a prospectus, Giovanni Arrighi generously invited me to come to Baltimore to consult with him on the project. Those initial conversations provided intellectual sustenance that would carry me through first the dissertation and later the writing of this book. Giovanni urged me to think boldly about the questions I was asking and not to be constrained by narrow disciplinary debates. I have endeavored to follow this advice, even when it sometimes led me in a different direction than the one in which Giovanni himself was traveling. Fred Block has the unique distinction of being the one person who read both the prospectus and the final version of the manuscript—and nearly every piece of paper I produced in between those two documents. Over the years, Fred has provided me with perceptive, detailed comments that typically went beyond merely pointing out the problems in various formulations to offer very concrete and tractable solutions. At a more personal level, Fred is one of the most reliable, loyal, and kind people I know, and I'm delighted that what began as a series of exchanges over national income accounting has developed into an enduring friendship.

I began my postgraduate school career as an assistant professor at the University of California, Los Angeles, where a number of my colleagues provided helpful comments on earlier versions of this manuscript, including Bill Roy, Michael Mann, Rogers Brubaker, and Ruth Milkman. I am especially grateful to Ruth, not only for her contributions to the work, but also for being a grounding presence as I negotiated multiple transitions in my life. The University of Michigan, my current intellectual home, has provided a wonderfully conducive environment for finishing this book. I could not imagine a warmer or more embracing intellectual community, and I especially want to thank Mark Mizruchi, Gerald Davis, Margaret Somers, and the participants of Michigan's Economic Sociology Workshop for their perceptive comments on various chapters of this book. Elizabeth Bruch did not read chapters but nevertheless told me at a particularly difficult moment that I had a "wonderful book inside"— words for which I will always be grateful.

Outside of my own institution, many other scholars took time away from their own work to provide comments on mine. Although I have attempted to keep good records, this list will inevitably be incomplete, and

I apologize to anyone who has been omitted. For their comments, spanning many years, I thank Sarah Babb, Dean Baker, Eduardo Canedo, James Crotty, Gerald Epstein, Peter Evans, Neil Fligstein, Robert Pollin, Monica Prasad, and Engelbert Stockhammer. Nitsan Chorev deserves special mention as someone whom I have subjected to multiple drafts and who has dutifully complied with these requests, in the process developing into a key interlocutor and close friend.

Over the course of working on this book, I had the opportunity to present preliminary versions of chapters at invited talks at numerous institutions, including UCLA, the Johns Hopkins University, the University of Michigan, the University of California, Berkeley, Cornell University, Harvard University, York University, the University of British Columbia, Brown University, the Ohio State University, and the New School for Social Research. I am grateful to these audiences for their patience and their interest and for many excellent suggestions.

Funding for research for various components of this work has been provided by the Graduate School at the University of Wisconsin, the National Science Foundation, UCLA's Center for American Politics and Public Policy, and the Rackham Graduate School at the University of Michigan. Some of these funds enabled me to hire three excellent research assistants. Anthony Alvarez and Angela Jamison at UCLA helped me to compile a database of congressional hearings that formed the basis of the analysis in Chapter 3. At Michigan, Dan Hirschman's assistance in navigating the final manuscript revisions can only be described as heroic.

Research is only as good as the material at the researcher's disposition. In this regard, I am grateful to the interview subjects who shared with me their perspective on the events explored in this book: Stephen Axilrod, C. Fred Bergsten, Ron Blackwell, Alan Blinder, Douglass Cliggot, Jeffrey Frankel, Benjamin Friedman, David Huether, Donald Kohn, Roger Kubarych, William Niskanen, Martin Regalia, Alice Rivlin, Charles Schultze, Beryl Sprinkel, Albert Wojnilower, and Janet Yellen. Jane D'Arista not only agreed to be interviewed (and put me up at her lovely Connecticut home while we conducted the interview over the course of two days), but also continued to serve as an informal consultant on the project, sharing her vast knowledge of the workings of the international monetary system. I also benefited from the assistance of the excellent research staff at the Bureau of Economic Analysis and the Federal Reserve Bank of New York, who responded kindly, promptly, and competently to many research queries.

My editor at Harvard University Press, Michael Aronson, has offered excellent guidance through the process of revising this book. I am appreciative of his skills as an editor and his belief in the project from an early stage. I am also grateful to the five anonymous reviewers who provided insightful comments on the manuscript during two rounds of review.

Portions of Chapters 2 and 5 have appeared elsewhere. An early iteration of Chapter 2 was published in the *Socio-Economic Review* 3 (2005): 173–208; a different version of Chapter 5 appeared in *Theory and Society* 36 (2007): 477–513. I am grateful to Oxford University Press and Springer Science+Business Media, respectively, for allowing me to reprint this material.

Finally, I owe a debt of gratitude to my family. My two grandmothers, both formative influences, saw the beginning of this project but not its end. Helen Krippner was the first banker in the family, perhaps providing the original inspiration for my interest in some of the questions explored in this book. More likely, though, Grandmother Krippner's contribution lies elsewhere, as her drive and discipline and relentless pursuit of self-improvement have generally translated well into the academic environment. Luella Brandt was a master storyteller. Her love of narrative has, I believe, made its way into these pages, hopefully stripped of her tendency to embellish. My parents, Ray and Clarice Krippner, encouraged a love of learning but also maintained a healthy skepticism toward academic institutions. This orientation has enabled me to partake of the intellectual excitement of the academic life without getting too caught up (I hope) in its trappings. My sister, Leah Krippner, has distracted from the proceedings with her zany humor—and her wonderful family. Margot Canaday, my twin sister, has been my close intellectual companion for much of this journey. Our shared trajectory through graduate school and into professional academic careers has been a source of deep satisfaction and only occasional (contained) sibling rivalry. To those who wonder whether we feel the same pain, the answer is "no," but we did develop the same revision strategy for our books without discussing it. Finally, I owe a debt of gratitude to Margot's witty and gracious partner, Rachel Spector, who has tolerated not just one but two book projects in her personal life.

My deepest debt is to Sandy Levitsky, my partner, whose contributions to this book are impossible to enumerate. Almost ten years ago, Sandy helped me track down contact information for some of my more elusive interview subjects. A few nights ago, she helped me embed figures in the final manuscript. In the years in between, she has been involved in this project in every way imaginable, from spotting misplaced commas to seeing (before I did) the argument that connected the empirical chapters of the book. Sandy has helped me to strategize every aspect of the research and writing of this book, counseling me through various setbacks and keeping faith alive when I, frankly, had lost it. Everyone who has written a book knows the suffering and the joy in such an endeavor. How much more bearable the suffering and how much greater the joy when it is shared so completely with another person. For this, I dedicate this book to Sandy.